FRANK LLOYD WRIGHT:

DESIGNS FOR AN AMERICAN LANDSCAPE 1922–1932

Frank Lloyd Wright

DESIGNS FOR AN AMERICAN LANDSCAPE 1922–1932

DAVID G. DE LONG
general editor

ANNE WHISTON SPIRN

C. FORD PEATROSS

ROBERT L. SWEENEY

Harry N. Abrams, Inc., Publishers,
in association with the
Canadian Centre for Architecture,
the Library of Congress, and
the Frank Lloyd Wright Foundation

This book accompanies the exhibition *Frank Lloyd Wright: Designs for an American Landscape, 1922–1932*, organized by the Library of Congress, The Frank Lloyd Wright Foundation, and the Centre Canadien d'Architecture/Canadian Centre for Architecture with David G. De Long, guest curator. The exhibition will be shown at the Canadian Centre for Architecture, Montréal, from June 18 to September 22, 1996, and at the Library of Congress, Washington, D.C., during the Fall of 1996.

Exhibition Organizing Committee

Library of Congress
Irene Ursula Burnham, *Director, Interpretive Programs Office;* Tambra Johnson, *Exhibits Coordinator, Interpretive Programs Office;* C. Ford Peatross, *Curator, Center for American Architecture, Design, and Engineering Project*

Canadian Centre for Architecture
Nicholas Olsberg, *Chief Curator;* Gwendolyn Owens, *Assistant Director, Museum Services;* Helen Malkin, *Exhibitions Coordinator*

The Frank Lloyd Foundation
Bruce Brooks Pfeiffer, *Director, Frank Lloyd Wright Archives, Taliesin West*

Advisory Committee

Anthony Alofsin, *University of Texas;* Neil Levine, *Harvard University;* Bruce Brooks Pfeiffer, *Frank Lloyd Wright Archives*

Publication of this catalogue has been supported by a grant from the Graham Foundation for Advanced Studies in the Fine Arts.

For the Canadian Centre for Architecture

Manager, Publications Services:
Christine Dufresne

For Harry N. Abrams, Inc.

Project Director: Margaret L. Kaplan
Editor: Diana Murphy
Designer: Judith Hudson

Library of Congress Cataloguing-in-Publication Data

Spirn, Anne Whiston, 1947–
Frank Lloyd Wright : designs for an American landscape / David G. De Long, editor : Anne Spirn, Ford Peatross.
p.   cm.
Catalogue of an exhibition co-sponsored by the Canadian Centre for Architecture and the Library of Congress.
Includes bibliographical references and index.
ISBN 0–8109–3981–9 (hc)
ISBN 0–8109–2664–4 (pbk)
1. Wright, Frank Lloyd, 1867–1959—Exhibitions. 2. Organic architecture—United States—Exhibitions. I. Peatross, Ford. II. De Long, David Gilson, 1939–   . III. Centre canadien d'architecture. IV. Library of Congess. V. Title.
NA737.W7A4 1996
720' .92–dc20   95–30509

Photograph Credits

Architectural Drawing Collection, University Art Museum, University of California, Santa Barbara: 73; CCA, Montréal, Photography Services: 9, 24, 28, 32, 47, 56, 57, 68, 69, 128, 139, 167, 175, 176; Fisher Fine Arts Library, University of Pennsylvania: 169; Fondation LeCorbusier: 172; Musei Cicivi, Como: 171; Staatsgalerie Stuttgart: 168; State Historical Society of Wisconsin: 147–150, 154–156, 162, 164, 166; The Avery Architectural and Fine Arts Library, Columbia University, New York: 46; The Frank Lloyd Wright Foundation: 6, 8, 10–20, 22, 23, 25–27, 29–31, 35, 37–40, 43–45, 48–50, 52–55, 59–66, 67, 70, 72, 76–78, 80–83, 88, 89, 91, 92, 94–97, 101–111, 113, 115, 119, 121, 125–127, 129–137, 140–146, 151–153, 157–161, 163, 165, 179; The Library of Congress: 1–4, 21, 34, 36, 41, 42, 58, 71, 73, 74, 79, 87, 90, 98, 116–118, 170, 178; The Museum of Modern Art, New York: 33, 174; The U.S. National Park Services: 84, 85, 86; The Wolfsonian, Miami Beach, Florida: 177; UCLA, Los Angeles: 5.

Copyright

·720.92
DEL   2/4/98

CONTENTS

Preface

It has been six years since Ford Peatross, of the Library of Congress, Nicholas Olsberg, of the Canadian Centre for Architecture, and Bruce Brooks Pfeiffer, of The Frank Lloyd Wright Foundation, first met to explore the possibility of a joint project that would examine in depth a critical epoch in Wright's work. Together with David De Long, it was decided to focus on five seminal projects of the 1920s that would demonstrate a unique dialogue between structure and land. The resulting publication constitutes at once a rigorous analysis of a body of work that took a revolutionary view of the relationship between building and landscape; a means of introducing important cultural questions related to the connections among the automobile, the suburb, the resort, and the idea of wilderness; and a demonstration of the power of architecture to involve itself in these wider issues.

Wright is the unavoidable central figure in American architecture, and new assessments of his work are essential to the vitality of architectural culture in North America. By focusing on a crucial idea, and on the questions of process, intention, and context that surround it, we hope to begin a more widespread rethinking of Wright's work, so that the next generation of architects will be better able to appraise his ability to generate new ideas.

One of the happiest results of our collaboration has been the ability to reunite drawings long dispersed among different institutions and hence to dramatically expand their meaning. In sharing ideas among us on the shape and character of the exhibition, we have each benefited from the varied perspectives we bring to the presentation of architectural issues. Ultimately, however, the success of this venture belongs to David De Long, who has pursued his commission as curator and editor with unusual grace and intelligence. Special thanks are also due to George Ranalli, whose work on modeling the five projects has clarified much of their design history; to Anthony Alofsin and Neil Levine, who – with the authors in this catalogue – have helped guide the exhibition at critical points in its development; and to Bruce Brooks Pfeiffer for his early commitment to the project and for his deep involvement in its content and administration.

We are pleased to acknowledge support for this catalogue from the Graham Foundation for Advanced Studies in the Fine Arts, as part of its multi-year grant to the Canadian Centre for Architecture's American Century series.

JAMES BILLINGTON
Librarian of Congress
RICHARD CARNEY
Chief Executive Director, The Frank Lloyd Wright Foundation
PHYLLIS LAMBERT
Director, Canadian Centre for Architecture

Introduction

NICHOLAS OLSBERG

A struggle against nature never appealed to me.
The struggle for and with Nature thrilled me and
inspired my work.

FRANK LLOYD WRIGHT

An Autobiography, Book Six, "Broadacre City"

Five revolutionary projects by Frank Lloyd Wright form the primary subject of this catalogue – the Doheny Ranch development, the Lake Tahoe summer colony, the A. M. Johnson desert compound, the automobile objective for Gordon Strong (all proposed between 1923 and 1925), and the hotel and houses for San Marcos in the Desert (1928–29). None were built. Each represented a different response to the promises inherent in new patterns of leisure and in the automobile, which would service them. Each advanced Wright's new interest in complex angled geometries, in integral ornament, and in highly textured materials. And each proposed singularly bold solutions to the problem of incorporating a human architecture into the wilderness landscapes to which a newly mobile society was drawn. This has always been a problematic body of work. Until now the basic histories of these proposals have resisted accurate reconstruction, and Wright's larger intentions have remained a mystery. Some have seen in them an intrusive and arrogant attempt to redesign the site itself. Others, noting their richly laced textures and intricate forms, their

sense of luxury and grandeur, have seen them as a troubling and retrograde departure from the sort of architectural thinking that had earlier allied Wright with the simplifying premises of the modern movement.

Indeed, Wright had promised, in the last words of the first full introduction to his work, that it would now "grow more truly simple; more expressive with fewer lines, fewer forms; more articulate with less labour; more plastic; more fluent, although more coherent; more organic." But his life and practice in the next, "lost" years were studded with tragedies and travels, discoveries and diversions. As David De Long points out in the central essay in this catalogue, Wright chose, once he returned permanently to the United States in 1922, not to refine and simplify the course and cause of his earlier work, but to reinvent himself – in new territory, for new clients, in projects of greater scale, and with a new agenda dictated by a newly mobile America, whose progressive thinkers were increasingly bound to the idea of regionalism and to an anti-urban Jeffersonian revival. In this peculiarly American context – largely divorced from and increasingly opposed to the maturing currents of European modernism, exploring the landscapes and suburbs of the new West, and turning to non-Western sources for new architectural imagery – Wright used these projects not only to celebrate the car and roadway but also as a crucible in which to redefine his doctrine of modernity. "Plainness," he concluded as he finished San Marcos in the Desert, "is not simplicity. . . . Nine pounds where three are sufficient is obesity. But to eliminate expressive words in speaking or writing – words that *intensify* or vivify meaning – is not simplicity. Nor is similar elimination in architecture."[1]

Analyzing these projects anew, with a wealth of fresh archival sources at hand, De Long and Anne Spirn argue that these prototypes for a new architecture forged from a deep reading of terrain led Wright along a path markedly different from that of his fellow architects; that they generated the fund of ideas and approaches from which his later work, from Fallingwater to the Marin County Civic Center (and most especially the two Taliesins), derived; and that they express both Wright's excitement at the discovery of the American wilderness and the discipline with which he analyzed its forms and processes. In their celebration of new landscapes, new functions, and new forms, these designs amount to Wright's first effort to break wholly new ground and seek that "Democratic Vista" Sullivan had called for – "the undreamed of, a versatility, a virtuosity, a plasticity as yet unknown." Leaving behind his earlier attempts to build in sympathy with the land, Wright invented in them built forms that would indeed "*intensify*," and perhaps complete, the natural structures they were to work within.[2]

Wright himself invited us to see in these projects a reflection upon mankind's relationship to nature, and upon the architect's role in healing the breach between the two. They coincide with the elaboration of an increasingly unsentimental and ambitious theory of organic architecture, and they draw upon an increasingly dynamic, harsh, and complex view of the natural world. In the light of Wright's advancing thinking about nature, the five proposals can be seen as an evolving metaphysical

poem – rooted in the same distinctively American enthusiasms for which Whitman in his time had found one language, and for which Wright in his strove to find another. "Walt Whitman?" asked Wright. "Yes. Of course he knew the truth of what I am saying if ever a man did know it. He said it much better than I can say it but no better than I can build it, thank you."[3]

Wright's intentions cannot thus be fully understood without revisiting his philosophy of nature, especially as it evolved in this experimental decade. There is an essential clarity and materialism to Wright's thought that has long been obscured, both by his own willingness to cloud his thinking in slogans and by critics' determination to place his ideas in too close a line either with his family's supposed transcendental Unitarianism or with an Emersonian idealism that Wright himself sometimes found superficial and "sentimental." Both are important as a point of departure, but not as a rigid frame for his evolving philosophy. He himself put the matter plainly: "I grew up a rationalist. My religion so far as it went was Unitarian. After I became old enough to discriminate between dogmatism and principle, Philosophy came to me gradually and mostly by way of the farm. . . , the mysterious beauties and obvious cruelties of Nature – interlocking interchanges of the universe. . . . And then I became a seeker after Truth of Form."[4]

One could therefore argue that Wright became an architect in order to express a philosophy of nature, rather than using a philosophy of nature to explicate his architecture. The roots of this nature-thought were embedded in his childhood. His mother, Anna, remembered "how closely to nature" she kept her children, "near, near to the heart of God." She found in the Japanese landscape a better sense of "the meaning of life" and believed that "a square yard of vetch will reveal the most profound secrets of our destiny." His sister Maginel recalled "one's mother, father, aunts and uncles...always quoting Emerson." Wright's father's nightly conversations on music focused on the natural law, on an inner rightness or universal harmony that a Bach or Beethoven could uncover. It is not surprising, then, to find Wright talking of nature as the ruling principle of his thought and work from the start. "Go to Nature, thou builder of houses, consider her ways," he wrote in his first lectures. "Learn from Nature her simple truths of form, function, and grace of line.... Nature's things seem to belong where they are put and to grow from their site."[5]

From this premise – that the critical observation of natural forms was the key to all expression in built ones – Wright developed, over the years before 1911, a sequence of hypotheses that lay the groundwork for all his thinking. Among these is the belief that there is "a quality in man's nature that reaches upward to the spiritual sun for expression, as the Life principle in the plant reaches toward the more evident, but less real sun"; that man expresses this aspiration through building, as the plant achieves it through morphology; but that "we have laid upon us an artificiality that...conceals ourselves and...deforms...the fulfilment of the Life principle implanted in us." To rescue himself from the artificiality in which the imagination has been trapped, man must follow the rule of nature by which "form and function are one" and in which "the practical is not one thing and the Beautiful another" to discover an abstract language of forms – a language in sympathy with natural laws but "in no sense naturalistic."[6]

For Wright, it was the burden of the architect to uncover this "highest, most subjective" grammar of forms, "the universal writing of humanity" through which civilization can forge its reconciliation with the natural world. In this extravagant view, Architec-

ture was itself the personification of the infinitely varied natures of men and women in relation to the universe: their morphology, "their only prophecy, the only light." All of Wright's thinking about architecture starts from this heroic transcendentalism, the belief that the architect is granted the gift of "perceiving and portraying the harmony of organic tendencies," the ability to reveal a universal order, to situate man within that order, and thereby to give us "a glimpse of something essentially of the fiber of our own nature."[7]

From 1913 onward we find Wright gradually enlarging this view of nature, intensifying its materialism, deepening its secular tone, and purging sentimentality from the rhetoric in which it is expressed. An important new cluster of ideas emerges. First, "in rebellion against sentimentality in general," Wright proposed a "faith in the surface of things..., the nature of wood, glass and iron – internal nature." It is one of the ironies of his journey through the wilderness projects of the twenties that Wright came to discover a new sense of the spirit within this increasingly materialist view of nature. "We must have the ground firm under our feet, and then ... we find that spirituality, the real spirit, is a growth from within, from earth upward, not from heaven downward."[8]

Second, Wright came to see in the ground something more than the visible forms of plant life that had cultivated his earlier sense of the organic, to recognize in its topographical geometries, and in the light that changed them, a more cosmic and fluid sort of natural order. From this new focus on the very crust of earth, seen as a "titanic battlefield," he derived a new fascination for structure, for Froebel's organic geometries, and for the idea of conflict and elasticity: "All materials lie piled in masses or float as gasses in the landscape of this planet much as the cataclysms of creation left them. . . . They are all externally modified by time as they modify this earth in a ceaseless procession of change. . . . Contrasted with . . . this titanic wreckage – are placid depths and planes of mutable water or the vast depth-plane of the immutable sky hung with evanescent clouds. . . . This is the earthly abode of the buildings man has built. . . . The changes all speak in unison of cosmic law. . . . These cosmic laws are the physical laws of all man-built structures as well as the laws of landscape." This more plastic reading of the natural world led in turn to the idea of a "continuous becoming" and to the redefinition of "organic," a term he now "used not in a biological sense but in the philosophical sense of a living entity."[9]

As these ideas progressed – and as he began to see them expressed in the floating world of Lake Tahoe, the pools at the Death Valley compound, the perpetual spiral of the Strong planetarium, the ephemeral "desert ships" of the Ocatilla camp, or the "dotted lines" of San Marcos in the Desert – Wright reached with difficulty for a written language to clarify them. He developed the notion of inner geometries, concealed within larger forms; he proposed the idea that there may be a discernible "organic pattern of all things . . . the hidden mystery of creation"; and he suggested the overweening concept of architecture as an act of reconciliation among the "warring forces" within nature. Indeed, as his view of nature grew ever larger and more forbidding, so too did his idea of architecture. "It is," he could finally say, "at least the geometric pattern of things, of life, of the human and social world. It is at best that magic framework of reality that we sometimes touch upon when we use the word 'order.'"[10] Wright, in short, now began to equate Architecture with Nature. It is toward such a valiant and comprehensive view of the role of architecture in revealing and contributing to the order of a larger universe that these five projects lead, and it is as an expression of that ambitious sensibility that they should be seen.

Notes

1 Frank Lloyd Wright, "In the Cause of Architecture" (1908), in *Frank Lloyd Wright: Collected Writings*, vol. I, 1894–1930, ed. Bruce Brooks Pfeiffer (New York: Rizzoli in association with The Frank Lloyd Wright Foundation, 1992), 86–100; Frank Lloyd Wright, Preface to *Ausgeführte Bauten und Entwürfe von Frank Lloyd Wright*, in Pfeiffer, *Collected Writings* I, 103–15; Frank Lloyd Wright, "An Autobiography" (1932), in *Frank Lloyd Wright: Collected Writings*, vol. II, 1930–1932, ed. Bruce Brooks Pfeiffer (New York: Rizzoli in association with The Frank Lloyd Wright Foundation, 1992), 204–5.

2 Louis Sullivan, *The Autobiography of an Idea* (New York: Press of the American Institute of Architects, 1924; reprint, New York: Dover Publications, 1956), 283–84.

3 Frank Lloyd Wright, "Ceiling or No Ceiling" (1945), in *Frank Lloyd Wright: Collected Writings*, vol. IV, 1939–1949, ed. Bruce Brooks Pfeiffer (New York: Rizzoli in association with The Frank Lloyd Wright Foundation, 1994), 227–80.

4 Frank Lloyd Wright, "An Autobiography: Book Six, Broadacre City" (1943), in Pfeiffer, *Collected Writings* IV, 242–54. "I know with what suspicion the man is regarded who refers matters of fine art back to Nature" (Wright, "In the Cause of Architecture" [1908]).

5 Anna Lloyd Wright, Scrapbooks and Diaries, The Frank Lloyd Wright Foundation, Scottsdale, Arizona; Maginel W. Barney Scrapbooks, Frank Lloyd Wright Home and Studio, Oak Park, Illinois; Frank Lloyd Wright, "The Architect and the Machine" (1894) and "Architect, Architecture and the Client" (1896), in Pfeiffer, *Collected Writings* I, pp. 20–26 and 27–38, respectively. "Beethoven's music is itself the greatest proof I know of divine harmony alive in the human spirit" (Wright, "An Autobiography: Book Five, Form" [1943], in Pfeiffer, *Collected Writings* IV, 147).

6 Frank Lloyd Wright, "A Philosophy of Fine Art" (1900) and "The Architect" (1900), in Pfeiffer, *Collected Writings* I, 39–44 and 45–53, respectively.

7 Ibid.; Frank Lloyd Wright, "The Art and Craft of the Machine" (1901), in Pfeiffer, *Collected Writings* I, 59–69; Wright, Preface to *Ausgeführte Bauten und Entwürfe von Frank Lloyd Wright*.

8 Wright, "An Autobiography" (1932), in Pfeiffer, *Collected Writings* IV, 160–61; Frank Lloyd Wright, "Nature and Reality," in *Frank Lloyd Wright: His Living Voice*, ed. Bruce Brooks Pfeiffer (Fresno: California State University Press, 1987), 27–28.

9 Frank Lloyd Wright, "Architecture and Modern Life" (1937), in *Frank Lloyd Wright: Collected Writings*, vol. III, 1931–1939, ed. Bruce Brooks Pfeiffer (New York: Rizzoli in association with The Frank Lloyd Wright Foundation, 1993), 216–49; Karl E. Jensen (for F. L. W.) to Mrs. Andrew Porter, May 30, 1934, in Porter Scrapbook, The Frank Lloyd Wright Foundation, Scottsdale, Arizona.

10 Wright, "Architecture and Modern Life."

Designs for an American Landscape, 1922–1932

DAVID G. DE LONG

During the 1920s, as five remarkable projects show, Frank Lloyd Wright developed architectural prototypes of far-reaching consequence. Exploring advanced building technologies and untried geometric patterns, he conceived rural and suburban building complexes that restructured their sites in a manner calculated to heighten the grandeur of each natural setting. Earlier designs had approached their settings more tentatively, with linkages achieved through architectural extensions that ranged widely over the terrain, but that left the sites themselves less changed. Now a new, more persuasive unity between building and site resulted, one in which roads and other movement systems were so skillfully integrated that results of unequaled scale and majesty were achieved.

Paralleling these achievements in the 1920s, Wright began to question the nature of the American city and to predict with uncanny accuracy its gradual dissolution. For him the answer lay not in the rejection of the suburb, but in its acceptance. His designs offer compelling prototypes for that suburb – coherent architectural ensembles that unified their settings while enhancing natural attributes, that celebrated order without sacrificing a sense of expansive freedom. He envisioned nothing less than a new landscape, shaped in response to American ideals as he interpreted them.

Wright's increasingly rigorous manipulation of the terrain reflected an Emersonian belief in nature, one in which a culmination of natural process was human genius. Art derived from nature embodied such genius and expressed underlying truths. Emerson had written, "What is a man but nature's finer success in self-explication?"[1] and elsewhere, "The beauty of nature re-forms itself in the mind, and not for barren contemplation, but for a new creation"; continuing, "A work of art is an abstract or epitome of the world. It is the result or expression of nature, in miniature. . . . Thus in art does Nature work through the will of a man filled with the beauty of her first works."[2] The land itself offered a tangible source for this art: "The land is the appointed remedy for whatever is false and fantastic in our culture. The continent we inhabit is to be physic and food for our mind, as well as our body; The land, with its tranquilizing, sanative influences, is to repair the errors of a scholastic and traditional education, and bring us into just relations with men and things."[3] Yet if the ideal of nature were to be served, such corporeality demanded more, for "the presence of a higher, namely, of the spiritual element is essential to its perfection."[4] William Cronon has clarified these aspects of Wright's philosophy: "For romantics like Emerson and Wright, nature's value was primarily spiritual. Indeed, nature

acquired its meaning for them only in relation to the human soul and divine spirit of which the soul was a manifestation. . . . The multitudes of natural forms were only so much dead matter until touched by spirit, and so it was the role of human beings — especially artists — to breathe life into matter by relating it to the whole of creation and thereby giving it spiritual meaning."[5]

From this position, Wright came to shape the land as a parent shapes a child — not to suppress inherent qualities, but to reveal and enhance them. Only through such intervention could the image of nature approach perfection. Similarly, buildings were not meant to imitate nature, but to signal human presence through sympathetic alliance; as Wright wrote in 1925, "Any building should arise from its site as an expressive feature of that site and not appear to have descended upon it — or seem to be a 'deciduous' feature of it."[6] It was no matter of passive acceptance; as Wright proclaimed, "Architecture is the triumph of Human Imagination over materials, methods, and men, to put man into possession of his own Earth. . . . Architecture is man's great sense of himself embodied in a world of his own making."[7]

Doheny Ranch Development

After long periods of travel, Wright returned to the United States in August 1922. He had been deeply involved with the building of the Imperial Hotel in Tokyo beginning in 1917, and before that, from October 1909 to October 1910 and again from January to April 1911, he had been living in Europe. Even the years between 1911 and 1917 had been unsettled, for a brief period of tranquility at Taliesin was interrupted by a prolonged trip to Japan in 1913, violently disrupted by personal tragedy in 1914, and further eroded by the relentless publicity of a destructive nature that followed.

Except for the prospect of ongoing work for Aline Barnsdall, a problematic client who had proved difficult to please, Wright found himself in 1922 with practically no commissions. As he wrote to Louis Sullivan, "I am extremely hard up — and not a job in sight."[8] Yet his Unitarian background, in its closeness to Transcendentalist thought, supported a period of reevaluation and change that he seemed to seek with enthusiasm. He had come to regard his earlier work — however successful — as a closed chapter, and he sought intelligent criticism that would engender change of a fundamental sort. Beginning these considerations by 1914, he had written, "For every thousand men nature enables to stand adversity, she, perhaps, makes one man capable of surviving success. . . . reaction is essential to progress. . . . Some time ago this work reached the stage where it sorely needed honest enemies if it was to survive. . . . The manner of any work (and all work of any quality has its manner) may be for the time being a strength, but finally is a weakness."[9] In 1922, he accepted such honest reaction from no less a figure than H. P. Berlage, and acknowledged limitations of his recent work in Japan: "Yes — you are right. I have been romancing — engaged upon a great Oriental Symphony — when my own people should have kept me at home. . . . I wish to thank you simply and sincerely for your able minded and generous criticism of my work. Good criticism is itself creative and needed by my country more than anything else — we have not enough of the critical spirit."[10]

Not long after returning from Japan, Wright decided to settle in Los Angeles. "Have pitched in here to locate," he wrote to Sullivan, and for a time he clearly sought to reestablish his practice there.[11] It was a logical choice. Through Barnsdall, he had developed local contacts of some significance.[12] The city of Los Angeles itself was in the early years of

meteoric development; between 1920 and 1930
its population almost tripled, from around five hundred thousand to nearly 1.5 million; in 1923 alone,
more than sixty thousand permits for new buildings
were issued.[13] In December 1923, the director of
the City Planning Commission wrote, "Municipal
territorial expansion is rapidly filling out the metropolitan mosaic; where, in Los Angeles alone, twenty
subdivisions are added on an average each week
to the municipal mosaic; where during 1922 a new
residence was completed every 26 minutes of
the working day" (fig. 1).[14] Those drawn to the city
by its salubrious climate were likely to benefit from
a robust economy stimulated by the area's oil
industry and by readily available capital for local
investment.[15]

The rise of the automobile further stimulated
the economy as it seemed also to stimulate Wright.
In 1924, it was reported that Los Angeles had more
cars per capita (one for every two and nine-tenths
persons) than any other city in the world.[16] With
the automobile came new building typologies, such
as drive-in markets, making their first appearances
in the area.[17] Funding for streets and highways was
the second largest item of governmental expendi-
ture in the 1920s, and a primary factor in the
nation's economic boom;[18] from this Los Angeles
benefitted, and the future promise of the city must
have seemed great indeed.

The rapid growth of Los Angeles stimulated
planning efforts that Wright would have noted. As
early as 1913, comprehensive parkways were proposed by its Parks Commission; the system was to
include widely dispersed public parks, and to be
related sympathetically to the topography.[19] One of
the first components to be realized was a portion
of the Arroyo-Secco Parkway that included a
much-photographed viaduct, promoted as an image
of progressive development (fig. 2).[20] It seems to

3
Bernheimer House, Hollywood,
California. Photograph ca. 1922. The
Library of Congress, Washington,
D.C., Prints and Photographs Division,
U.S. Geog File, Cal. Hollywood, no.
26620

parallel similar arcuated elements in Wright's Doheny project. Broader city planning efforts were under way in Los Angeles by 1920, and in January 1923, an ambitiously expansive Regional Planning Commission was established, reportedly the first such entity within the United States.[21] By then traffic congestion in Los Angeles was generally acknowledged to be the worst in the country; efforts at alleviation included pioneering designations of through streets and the installation of early traffic signals.[22] Not fully perceived at the time, yet ultimately of broader consequence, was the beginning of suburbanization, for between 1923 and 1931, despite a growing population, it was calculated that the number of people entering downtown Los Angeles actually declined by twenty-four percent, with traffic increases occurring instead in outlying areas.[23]

Wright seemed to sense both the best and the worst of the situation. At one level the unplanned, commercially driven construction dismayed him, as he wrote to Sullivan in April 1923: "The region has been cruelly 'exploited' – and is so still."[24] Addressing a larger audience later in the decade, after his own hopes for gain had come to little, he spoke of Los Angeles as a place "where everything, almost, is speculation and soon or late for sale. . . . here I was looking around me in Los Angeles – disgusted. There they were busy with steam-shovels tearing down the hills to get to the top in order to blot out the top with a house in some 'style,' some aesthetic insanity or other."[25] The 1913 Bernheimer house in Hollywood (designed by Franklin M. Small and Walter Webber), and the spotty development that surrounded it near the sites of Wright's own commissions, seems to illustrate that pattern (fig. 3). Wright was drawn instead to land yet undeveloped: "Nearby that arid, sunlit strand is still unspoiled – to show what a poetic thing it was before this homely invasion. Curious tan-gold foothills rise from the tatooed sand-stretches to join slopes spotted as the leopard-skin, with grease bush. . . . This foreground spreads to distances so vast – human scale is utterly lost as all features recede, turn blue, recede, and become bluer still to merge their blue mountain shapes, snow capped, with the azure of the skies."[26] These very elements of local terrain and vast scale underlie his own proposals for the area, answering his query, "What was missing? Nothing more or less than a distinctly genuine expression of California in terms of modern industry and American life – that was all."[27]

Among the most enticing areas of large, undeveloped plots under single ownership was the 411-acre Doheny Ranch, located at the base of the Santa Monica Mountains in what is now Beverly Hills (fig. 4). This long, narrow parcel, roughly one and one-half miles long by one-half mile wide, has the shape of a self-contained realm (fig. 5). Steep, undulating ridges enclose the long east and west boundaries and are linked together by hills across the narrow north edge. From the interior slopes of these ridges, framed views open within across a central, shorter ridge, and to the south, expansive views open out over the city. From the tops of the ridges, more distant views toward the ocean on the west and the San Fernando Valley on the north can be obtained.

The ranch was owned by Edward Laurence Doheny (1856–1935), one of Los Angeles's most wealthy and prominent citizens. His fortune derived from oil that he and his partner, Charles Canfield, had discovered shortly after arriving there in 1892; by 1900, each partner was earning at least $500,000 annually.[28] Doheny, a widower, remarried in 1900 (to Carrie Estelle Betzold of Marshalltown, Iowa), and spent lavishly on a mansion near Adams Boulevard and Figueroa. He assembled the parcels of land comprising the ranch between 1912 and 1913; by then he also owned other ranches, a dwelling in New York City, and a steam yacht. Until his involvement in the Teapot Dome scandal – in August 1924, he was formally charged with bribery in obtaining favorable oil leases from the government, and was cleared only in 1929 – his capabilities must have seemed limitless.

For the Doheny Ranch, Wright proposed a residential development of unparalleled scale. It responded to the expansive qualities of the site, respected local vegetation, and accommodated the automobile in both spatial and architectural terms. It seems likely, though, that Wright's design was prepared not in response to an actual commission, but rather as part of a speculative venture in which he was himself involved, as Robert Sweeney has suggested.[29] Surviving drawings are few in number, and apparently no site plans exist. The only clues to the dates of the project are a property map of the site in the Frank Lloyd Wright Archive – dated February 1923 (fig. 6), and presumably obtained by Wright as he began work – and one early design drawing dated

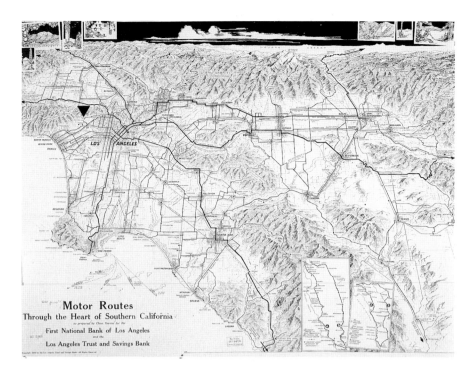

4
Motor Routes Through the Heart of Southern California as Prepared by Chas. Owens for the First National Bank of Los Angeles and the Los Angeles Trust & Savings Bank. 1920. The Library of Congress, Washington, D.C. Black triangle indicates Doheny Ranch site

5
Aerial photograph of the Doheny Ranch site, Beverly Hills, California. 1932. Air Photo Archives, UCLA Department of Geography, Los Angeles

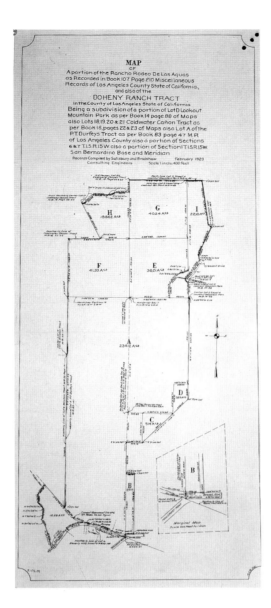

6

Frank Lloyd Wright. *Doheny Ranch,
Beverly Hills, California. Plot survey.*
1923. Line print, 31 × 14 in. The Frank
Lloyd Wright Foundation, 2104.009

March 10, 1923. There are no contracts, nor even
any correspondence, to suggest direct ties between
Wright and Doheny. His confusion about both client
and location – he recalled Doheny as Edward *H.*
rather than *L.* and placed the site in the San Gabriel
rather than the Santa Monica Mountains – further
attest to a lack of any contact with his alleged
client. Instead Wright seems to have allied himself
with a real estate promoter named John B. Van
Winkle (1883–1952), whose business connections
with Doheny may have encouraged their unsolicited
efforts. Given Wright's lack of work, his need to
reestablish his practice, and his understandable desire
to affiliate with wealthy and powerful patrons, it
seems likely that he grew sufficiently impatient as to
seek clients on his own. If so, the project becomes all
the more appealing, for it reflects an idealized vision
uncomplicated by specific, compromising demands.

However initiated, the proposals for the Doheny
Ranch development proclaim a change of direction
in Wright's approach. The project is without exact
parallel in his earlier work, or, indeed, in any work.
Two undated perspectives suggest the totality of his
vision; both appear to depict a view from the east-
ernmost ridge of the site, somewhere along its
southern third, looking across the steep slope of
the intermediate ridge to the higher one beyond. In
the less detailed and presumably earlier of the two
perspectives, the view is taken from a position sufficiently near the bottom of the ridge to show a
ramped roadway leading north up the closer valley
(fig. 7). It is a generalized view; in actuality, the intermediate ridge drops far less to the north (or right)
than is suggested, and glimpses of the ocean shown
far beyond to the west would necessitate a higher
vantage point. In the second perspective, with surviving layout drawings suggesting that it was studied in
greater detail, the topography is more accurately
portrayed and the architectural elements are rendered with sharper detail (fig. 8). The northern slope
of the central ridge corresponds with the site as
seen today, and the higher vantage point (allowing,
with some liberty, a hint of the ocean on the left
horizon) has left the bottom of the valley hidden
within the folds of the hills below.[30]

The fundamental elements of the two Doheny
perspectives differ little. In both, buildings, roadways,
and plantings are conceived as one integrated
totality; it is the vision of the city, or more properly
the suburb, as one structure. Gently sloped roads
step back along the contours of the hills, providing
a unifying pattern of continuous linearity. The roadways themselves are developed in the manner of
viaducts, bridging over smaller valleys on gracefully
arcuated bridges or embanked with richly textured
masonry walls. These walls, elaborated with richer
details, in turn continue to define major planes of
the individual houses with which they are integrated.
Stepped roof-terraces augment the horizontal planes
of the connecting roadways, amplifying an image of
architectural unity at a vast scale. Both roadways
and houses are clustered in ways that structure the
site by selectively shaping and retaining the natural
slopes. The more fragile segments of valleys and
the steepest slopes are left largely untouched, but,
as at Taliesin, joined in the full composition so that
an effect of extraordinary unity results.

7
Frank Lloyd Wright. *Doheny Ranch Development, Beverly Hills, California. Perspective.* 1923. Pencil and colored pencil on tracing paper, 12½ × 28⅞ in. The Frank Lloyd Wright Foundation, 2104.005

8
Frank Lloyd Wright. *Doheny Ranch Development, Beverly Hills, California. Perspective.* 1923. Pencil and colored pencil on tracing paper, 19 × 37 in. Erving and Joyce Wolf Foundation

The perspectives themselves are sufficiently loose as to suggest that nothing other than a general layout was ever conceived, but preliminary designs for three houses provide detailed aspects of another sort. Prototypes that could be adapted to specific locations, they were labeled by Wright "House 'A,'" "House 'B,'" and "House 'C.'" They embody a new spatial typology in Wright's work, related in their interior verticality and terracing to the Thomas P. Hardy house (Racine, Wisconsin, 1905; fig. 9), but now more decisively developed. There is an exaggerated blockiness and mass to the designs, spaces are more formally differentiated, and the play of varied levels is greater. Consistent with Wright's earlier work, each building relates sensitively to its site, yet is more boldly shaped to strengthen an overall composition. Roof terraces – explored with convincing results in Hollyhock House (Los Angeles, 1917–22) – not only contribute to the visual unity of the development, but become more liberally distributed within each house, and angled geometries – new to Wright's work in this period – are incorporated in House 'C.' Underlying the concept was the means of construction that Wright proposed, one new to his work: a system of concrete blocks that he later likened to the expressiveness of woven textiles.

House 'A,' the most conservative of the three prototypes, was apparently conceived for a location just below a major ridge where it would bridge one of the many shallow ravines leading down from the top. A vertically emphasized mass rises at the center of the composition, and walled terraces extend to each side; in the perspective, they continue beyond the border of the drawing, implying limitless continuity (fig. 10). It is an architecture of massive walls, with strongly rendered piers amplifying that mass, and with openings cut through surfaces in a manner that emphasizes thickness and weight. Further emphasizing that weight, unglazed openings in the terraced walls are corbeled, and throughout the design, the joints of the concrete blocks are channeled in a traditional manner.

House 'A' contains two major floors, and the lower (or main) floor features rooms arranged on different levels, adding to the differentiation of its spaces (fig. 11). The house is approached from the left by a roadway paralleling the walled terraces, leading to what Wright labeled a "terrace court." This unusual space, roofed but with unglazed openings, recalls a Tuscan atrium; it leads to a vestibule within the central element of the house. From there, short flights of stairs lead to each adjacent space: to the library overlooking the valley below

9
Frank Lloyd Wright. *Thomas P. Hardy House, Racine, Wisconsin. Perspective.* ca. 1909. Plate 15 in album 1, *Ausgeführte Bauten und Entwürfe von Frank Lloyd Wright* (Berlin: Ernst Wasmuth, 1910). Canadian Centre for Architecture, Montréal

10
Frank Lloyd Wright. *Doheny Ranch
Development, Beverly Hills, California,
House 'A.' Perspective with plan.* 1923.
Pencil and colored pencil on tracing
paper, 16 x 20⅛ in. The Frank Lloyd
Wright Foundation, 2104.004

(toward the bottom of the drawing); to the dining room opening back onto a narrow terrace separating the body of the house from the hill rising behind (toward the top); to a distant walled terrace below and a "studio bedroom" above (toward the right). A formal stairway at the back leads to a roof terrace and living room above. There, on the upper floor, the high-roofed living room at the center defines a cross-axis and links to bedrooms and additional terraces on each side (fig. 12). On the exterior, the single, centrally placed window of the living room, together with the vertical line of its appended fountain, emphasizes a formal verticality (fig. 13).

House 'B' is both more linear and less formal than House 'A,' and the roadway more fully incorporated within the house itself (fig. 14). Its three floors step back to terrace and retain the steep slope behind, and it lacks windows along the back,

so that it could be placed tightly against a hillside. Again the major spaces of the house are contained within a projecting vertical element, and lower walls extend from both sides, acting as bridging elements. On the lower level, these wings contain galleries that look out over the valley below as from a Roman cryptoporticus; at the center is a recreation room (fig. 15). On the intermediate level, the roof of the left gallery is developed as a walled terrace (fig. 16), and over the right gallery, similarly contained with a walled enclosure, is the entrance roadway itself. In the perspective, this roadway is shown extending dramatically away from the house behind a structure of masonry piers that bridge across a steep ravine. At the end of the roadway, adjacent to the house, Wright indicated a circular turntable – not uncommon at the time – where cars could stop and be rotated so as to

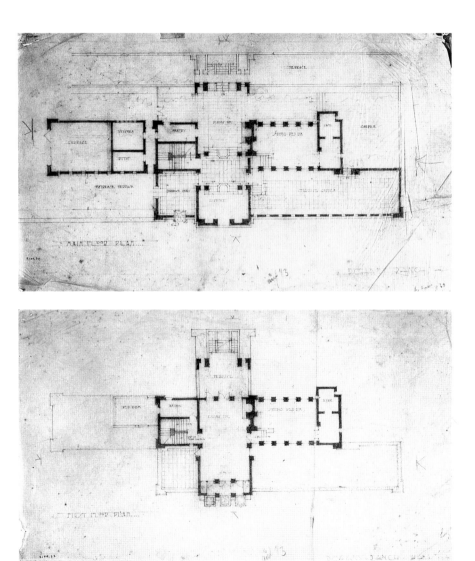

11
Frank Lloyd Wright. *Doheny Ranch Development, Beverly Hills, California, House 'A,' Main Floor. Plan.* 1923. Pencil on tracing paper, 10¾ x 18 in. The Frank Lloyd Wright Foundation, 2104.024

12
Frank Lloyd Wright. *Doheny Ranch Development, Beverly Hills, California, House 'A,' Upper Floor. Plan.* 1923. Pencil on tracing paper, 10⅞ x 18 in. The Frank Lloyd Wright Foundation, 2104.023

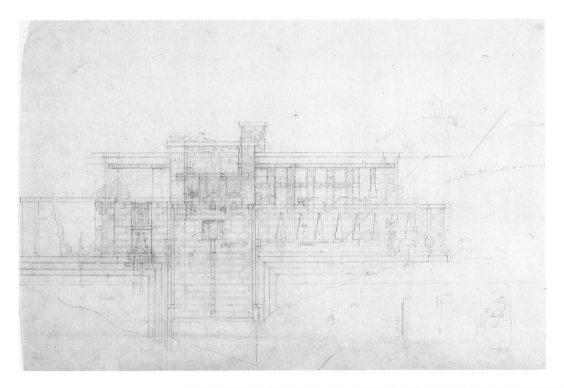

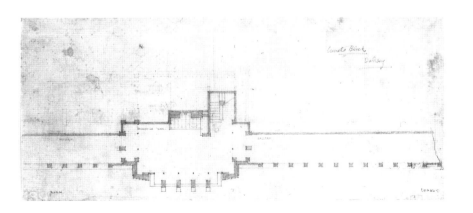

13
Frank Lloyd Wright. *Doheny Ranch Development, Beverly Hills, California, House 'A.' Elevation.* 1923. Pencil on tracing paper, 18 ¼ x 27 ⅜ in. The Frank Lloyd Wright Foundation, 2104.002

14
Frank Lloyd Wright. *Doheny Ranch Development, Beverly Hills, California, House 'B.' Perspective.* 1923. Pencil and colored pencil on tracing paper, 15 ⅝ x 42 ¼ in. The Frank Lloyd Wright Foundation, 2104.007

15
Frank Lloyd Wright. *Doheny Ranch Development, Beverly Hills, California, House 'B,' Lower Floor. Plan.* 1923. Pencil on tracing paper, 8 ⅝ x 18 ⅝ in. The Frank Lloyd Wright Foundation, 2104.020

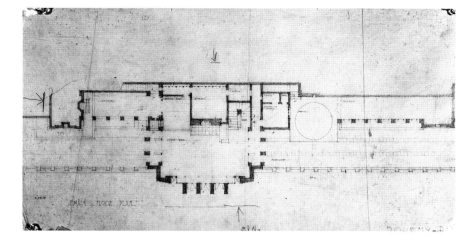

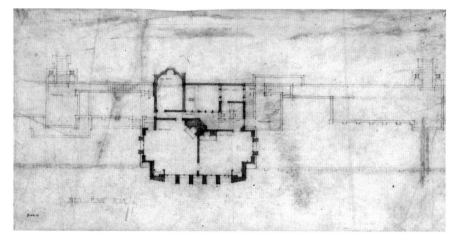

16
Frank Lloyd Wright. *Doheny Ranch Development, Beverly Hills, California, House 'B,' Main Floor. Plan.* 1923. Pencil on tracing paper, 11¼ x 21½ in. The Frank Lloyd Wright Foundation, 2104.019

17
Frank Lloyd Wright. *Doheny Ranch Development, Beverly Hills, California, House 'B,' Upper Floor. Plan.* 1923. Pencil on tracing paper, 11⅛ x 21½ in. The Frank Lloyd Wright Foundation, 2104.017

reverse their direction for the drive out. The living room again occupies the central element, and above, on the third level, are two bedrooms; additional rooms along the back overlook terraces at the sides and an internal court placed over the kitchen (fig. 17).

As shown in the perspective of House 'B,' the complicated joint pattern differs from the conventional pattern of House 'A,' and the resulting interplay of linear elements becomes more abstract. The long, terracing walls of both houses define a clear line of human intervention; below, the land is left in a natural state, and above, a planted garden establishes an intermediate band between the rough terrain and the building. To judge from later projects, such as Taliesin West, the plantings of the terraced gardens would have incorporated additional varieties of local specimens, with plants massed to form a microcosm of the whole. It is, then, a design that subtly shapes the terrain, resulting in a composition that celebrates both the found and the man-made. On the perspective for House 'B,' Wright inscribed, "Doheny hill development; house and garden and garage in connection with roadway, block structure, Los Angeles." On other drawings, as on those for House 'C,' he wrote, "natural bank," "natural slope," and "leave contours undisturbed."

House 'C' indeed continues this pattern, but with a plan that is more compact and more dramatically sited (fig. 18). The house bridges a steep ravine, and it is closely contained, in appearance even compressed, by steep slopes. Because the top level opens in both directions (fig. 19), the house would be suitably placed at the top of a ravine, and by design it seems intended to terminate a valley, as at the north end of the development, where variations of the prototype could be developed as major termini. The boldly projecting terrace, emphasized by angled walls, would persuasively amplify such a situation, as would the inflected planes of the house rising behind. The resulting octagonal shape marks Wright's most compelling use of angled geometries to this time. Never had Wright's work been without angled elements, but in earlier examples they had been confined to bay windows or, at most, individual rooms. Now they configure the entire composition and become a more dominant image of the design.

18
Frank Lloyd Wright. *Doheny Ranch Development, Beverly Hills, California, House 'C.' Perspective with plan.* 1923. Pencil and colored pencil on tracing paper, 17 × 22 ½ in. The Frank Lloyd Wright Foundation, 2104.006

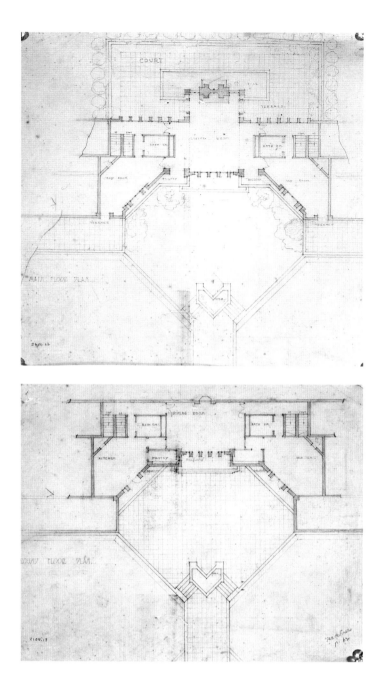

19

Frank Lloyd Wright. *Doheny Ranch
Development, Beverly Hills, California,
House 'C,' Main Floor. Plan.* 1923.
Pencil on tracing paper, 11½ × 12 in.
The Frank Lloyd Wright Foundation,
2104.012

20

Frank Lloyd Wright. *Doheny Ranch
Development, Beverly Hills, California,
House 'C,' Lower Floor. Plan.* 1923.
Pencil on tracing paper, 9¾ × 12⅛ in.
The Frank Lloyd Wright Foundation,
2104.013

The main spaces of the house are symmetrically
arranged on two floors. On the lower floor (fig. 20),
a central dining room is flanked by service spaces
that connect on one side with a bedroom and on
the other with the kitchen. Each of these three
rooms opens to a balcony overlooking the grand
octagonal court below. The upper floor is similarly
arranged, with additional bedrooms flanking the
central living room (see fig. 19). This major space,
shown with a raised ceiling, bridges across the width
of the house to overlook a pool and formal court
behind; the walls of the court could embank a rising
slope if the house were placed below the hill's summit. Neither of the two plans indicates an entrance
or roadway, but these elements are indicated on a
less-finished drawing that has recently come to light
(fig. 21). The house was to be approached from
below, by a roadway that angled in and under the
terrace, pivoting about a central stair within a separate entrance level containing servant rooms and
a garage. As suggested in the rough elevation, the
embanked road would thus become an essential
part of the architectural composition, approaching
along one side of the ravine and continuing out
along the other. A dramatic fountain, planned as part
of the open stairway at the prow of the terrace
and rendered to suggest a waterfall, would have
made the house itself appear as the water's source.
Wright had developed a similarly extended system
of pools at Hollyhock House, and there, too, they
effected special linkage (fig. 22). Here, as indicated
by notes on the drawing in Wright's hand, the cascade joined the "natural bank" and "natural slope"
to the "natural ravine" at their base. Faint lines in the
perspective suggest that the road was once shown,
but later erased.

Within the context of Wright's work, House 'C'
initiates change of a special sort. In part the angles
themselves signal this change, but in this early
manifestation Wright only suggested their ultimate
potential, and the plan is somewhat awkwardly
resolved. More significant is the massing of the
house within its setting, for the site itself seems to
shape the house, and the house, in turn, completes
and enhances its setting through concave connection rather than convex superimposition. Together
with Houses 'A' and 'B,' House 'C' breaks decisively
with Wright's earlier vocabulary, and directions indicated by the Imperial Hotel (design begun, 1913;

21
Frank Lloyd Wright. *Doheny Ranch Development, Beverly Hills, California, House 'C,' Elevation and Plan.* 1923. Graphite and colored pencil on Japanese paper, 27 × 19 ⅝ in. (sheet), 5 ⅜ × 9 ¹³⁄₁₆ in. (overlay). The Library of Congress, Washington, D.C., Gift of Donald D. Walker, 152.69

22
Frank Lloyd Wright. *Hollyhock House (Aline Barnsdall House), Los Angeles. Aerial perspective.* 1917. Pencil and colored pencil on tracing paper, 17 ¾ × 18 ¼ in. The Frank Lloyd Wright Foundation, 1705.002

building completed, 1922) and Hollyhock House are confirmed. In the Doheny scheme, mass is emphasized over volume, interior areas are more differentiated, and ornamental detail is given new prominence. It is almost as if Wright, having established the foundations of modernism some twenty years before, next became the first adherent to seriously question its elements.

In perspectives showing a portion of the entire development, variations of Houses 'A' and 'B' appear in the central band together with other, unspecified houses in the foreground and on the top of the central ridge. Examples of House 'C' – the type best suited to the northern section of the site – do not appear to be represented, unless the person with a parasol in the lower left (see fig. 8) is standing on its upper roof terrace. Altogether some twenty or more houses are shown, and if the same density were continued elsewhere, another twenty would lie unseen within the lower folds of the ridges. The views show approximately one-sixth of the entire 411-acre site, so between 240 and three hundred houses could easily have been accommodated – a reasonable density for the hilly site, and a remarkable commission had it come into being.

In providing for internal diversity within a unified vision, Wright honored his view of American democracy; as he had written, "America, more than any other nation, presents a new architectural proposition. Her ideal is democracy. . . . the whole, to be worthy as a whole, must consist of individual units, great and strong in themselves, not yoked from without in bondage, but united within."[31] Structured roadways became the means of achieving that unity. For Wright, the road itself became a symbol of human freedom; he later wrote, "If you can see the extended highway as the horizontal line of Usonian freedom, there you will see the modern usonian city approaching," and added, "Giant roads, themselves great architecture. . . . They unite and separate – separate and unite the series of diversified units."[32] It was certainly not the first time roads had been incorporated within buildings – by 1910 a book had been published on the subject, as had at least one article (see fig. 169); later, following World War I, Russian architects had explored certain possibilities, and the famous testing track on the roof of Turin's Fiat factory had been completed by 1922 – but surely Wright's proposal was the most persuasive as *architecture*. Its only real rival in this period came later: Le Corbusier's plan for Algiers, which dates from 1930.[33] Yet for Wright the roadways and their automobiles were no mere expedient of planning, nor an attractive symbol of modernity, but rather symbolized the very democracy they served.

Ample precedents for Doheny occur within Wright's own work. His 1895 proposal for the Wolf Lake Amusement Park confirmed an ability to plan large-scale compositions unified according to Beaux-Arts principles of formal axiality. The design is impressive, but conventional in its layout (fig. 23). Acknowledging its conservatism and cognizant of Sullivan's training at the Ecole des Beaux-Arts, Wright later described this design as "characterized to a certain extent by the Sullivanian idiom."[34] By then he had begun to move more independently, and to proclaim his longstanding belief that any building should relate sympathetically to its site: "It should appear to be part of the site and not a foreign element set up boxwise on edge to the utter humiliation of every natural thing in sight."[35] Within the years that followed, as seen in the Avery Coonley house (Riverside, Illinois, 1907), a looser, more original monumentality was achieved. Informally arranged pavilions, extended by terraces, trellised walkways, and a distant garden pavilion, effected an impressive unity with the gently sloped site, yet one that is

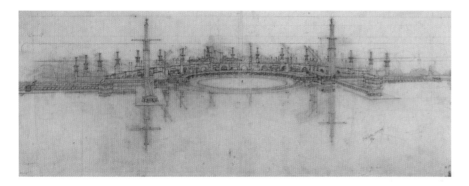

23
Frank Lloyd Wright. *Wolf Lake Amusement Park, near Chicago. Perspective.* 1895. Ink on linen, 24 x 31¾ in. The Frank Lloyd Wright Foundation, 9510.017

essentially passive in nature.[36] The larger Harold
McCormick house (Lake Forest, Illinois, 1907; unbuilt),
rising dramatically above its lakeside setting on
stepped terraces, relates more aggressively to its site,
but apparently Wright did not emphasize this quality
until later, in work done while he was in Europe
preparing plates for the Wasmuth portfolio (fig. 24).[37]

Wright's European stay seems, in fact, to have
stimulated a more decisive approach to large-scale
planning, as Anthony Alofsin has demonstrated.
Reportedly Wright knew of a major city-planning
exhibition held in Berlin and was impressed by
the work of Karl Friedrich Schinkel, especially examples at Potsdam.[38] There he must also have noticed
the extraordinarily vast, cascading terraces of
Sanssouci Park (1744–53, G. W. von Knobelsdorff).
More importantly, he was drawn to a study of
ancient and exotic architecture as a source for new
architecture, and to an appreciation of vernacular
building.[39] Such elements as rusticated masonry
and walled gardens found their way into Hollyhock
House as well as the Doheny development, and
Doheny itself has been compared to Italian hill
towns.[40] Writing of exotic influences in the introduction to the seminal European publication of his
work in 1910, Wright explained, "The appreciation
of beauty on the part of primitive peoples, Mon-
golian, Indian, Arab, Egyptian, Greek, and Goth, was
unerring. Because of this, their work is coming
home to us today in another and truer Renaissance,
to open our eyes that we may cut away the dead
wood and brush aside the accumulated rubbish of
centuries of false education. This Renaissance means
a return to simple conventions in harmony with
nature."[41] In the same publication he emphasized an
appreciation of vernacular architecture:

*The true basis for any serious study of the art of archi-
tecture is in those indigenous structures, the more
humble buildings everywhere, which are to architecture
what folklore is to literature or folksongs are to music,
and with which architects were seldom concerned. . . .
The traits of these structures are national, of the soil;
and, though often slight, their virtue is intimately inter-
related with environment and with the habits of life
of the people. . . . No really Italian building seems ill at
ease in Italy. All are happily content with what ornament and color they carry, as naturally as the rocks
and trees and garden slopes which are one with them.*[42]

24
Frank Lloyd Wright. *Harold McCormick
House, Lake Forest, Illinois. Perspective.*
ca. 1909. Plate 59 in album 2,
*Ausgeführte Bauten und Entwürfe von
Frank Lloyd Wright* (Berlin: Ernst
Wasmuth, 1910). Canadian Centre
for Architecture, Montréal

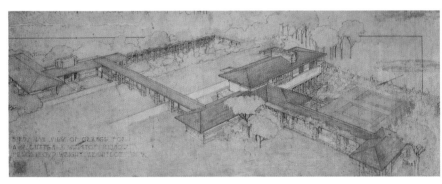

Following his return from Europe in 1911, exotic
influences were largely confined to ornamental
details, as in the A. D. German Warehouse (Richland
Center, Wisconsin, 1915), while broader aspects
of the vernacular took firmer root. Gradually he
came to better appreciate qualities of massiveness
in buildings, to understand how compositional unity
could be achieved informally, and to sense how
that unity could be strengthened through architectural links to specific features of each site. Initially
he worked with his Chicago vocabulary to develop
these large-scale compositions, such as in the
Sherman M. Booth house (Glencoe, Illinois, 1911,
unbuilt; fig. 25). As in the Coonley house, building
elements bridge the driveway, but here the driveway in turn bridges the ravine below, and both
driveway and bridge are fully incorporated within
the long, loosely massed structure. Low stair-towers
that provide access to roof terraces suggest a
continuing fascination with towered Italian buildings
— Wright had included more literal translations in
earlier projects, as the Francisco Terrace apartments
(Chicago, 1895). The A. W. Cutten house (Wheaton,
Illinois, 1911, unbuilt; fig. 26) is less dramatically
sited than Coonley but extends more widely over
its site; the scale of these extensions is new for a
house of this relatively small size, and the driveway,
again treated as a significant element of the design,
features an overlook. In his proposal for the Wood
house (Decatur, Illinois, 1915, unbuilt), water became
a major element of the extended composition,
for the long, low house and its penetrating roadway
partly embank an adjacent lake.

In these same years, larger commissions elicited
more conservative results; perhaps Wright felt
confined by the commercial nature of their programs. Still, his proposal for the Lake Geneva Hotel
(Lake Geneva, Wisconsin, 1912) represents an
advance over his earlier design for the similarly
scaled Horseshoe Inn (Estes Park, Colorado, 1908,
unbuilt) or the larger Como Orchards summer
colony (Darby, Montana, 1912, unbuilt), for the low,
asymmetrical Lake Geneva Hotel is unified more
forcefully with the roadway and lakefront than is
the case in the Horseshoe Inn or Como Orchards
development. Further, Wright's 1913 layout for a
model suburb, though somewhat conventional, suggests early thinking regarding suburban-scaled unities

and the incorporation of the automobile; it featured a large "public garage," had buildings grouped in ways that would "emphasize in an interesting way the street vistas," and had an agreeable density providing "all the charm of variety found in the Gothic colleges of Oxford," as Wright described it.[43]

Most impressive of all in predicting, then paralleling, changing directions of the 1920s was Taliesin, Wright's country estate on which he worked more or less continuously from its inception in 1912 until his death in 1959. Indeed, at the time of his death, he was planning at so vast a scale that it has been described as "the remodelling of the Lloyd-Jones Valley."[44] Early photographs that he took document an intense study of the site (as discussed by Anne Whiston Spirn), and drawings done in conjunction with its first major rebuilding in 1914 show an extraordinarily extended composition of elements that terrace and shape the site. It was in reference to Taliesin that he wrote, "no house should ever be on any hill or on anything. It should be of the hill, belonging to it, so hill and house could live together each the happier for the other"; yet never was the building to be imitative of nature: "Yes, there must be a natural house, not natural as caves and log-cabins were natural but native in spirit and making."[45] In one perspective (fig. 27), the lines between rough and cultivated plantings are clearly delineated as part of the composition, thus emphasizing a working garden as distinct from one less obviously groomed. Sketchy indications of a roadway suggest an interest in design aspects of vehicular movement. He described an elaborate water system with effects not unlike those of Hollyhock House and Doheny, and further explained how Taliesin was structured around courts in a manner that signals another tie with his work of the 1920s: "This modest human programme in terms of rural Wisconsin arranged itself around the hilltop in a series of four varied courts leading one into the other, courts together forming a sort of drive along the hillside flanked by low buildings on one side and by flower gardens against the stone walls that retained the hill-crown on the other."[46] Yet even in so grand a conception as Taliesin of the late teens there is little of Doheny's astonishing sweep. That awaited another beginning, one at least partly inspired by Japan, California, and a renewed study of exotic sources.

Regarding Wright and exotic vocabularies much has been written. A few of these articles are cited below, and most are of interest for proving quite the reverse of what they intend, for it was not the specifics that affected Wright to any significant degree, but instead the underlying principles. That he studied such sources seems certain, but the more he studied the less he relied on obvious visual motifs. Typical in this regard is his tie to Japanese architecture; much was available for his perusal, including the Japanese buildings at the 1893 World's Columbian Exposition in Chicago as well as many published sources.[47] Yet by the time of his first trip to Japan in 1905, he had passed beyond any but the most general of references to specific architectural details. What he seems to have gained more immediately from that trip, from his second trip in 1913, and from long periods of residence there between 1917 and 1922, was a broader appreciation of buildings as they might become part of a larger landscape.

27
Frank Lloyd Wright. *Taliesin II, near Spring Green, Wisconsin. Aerial perspective.* 1914. Ink on paper, 16 × 19 in. The Frank Lloyd Wright Foundation, 1403.002

The purpose of Wright's second visit to Japan was to secure the commission for the Imperial Hotel, and in preparation for this trip he may well have reviewed recent literature. In one such article on Japanese architecture, the prominent American architect Ralph Adams Cram defended domestic examples in a manner paralleling Wright's own support of the Italian vernacular; as Cram wrote, "the castle and domestic architecture are treated as non-existent [by those who have written about Japan].... this is unjust and absurd: it is as though one presumed to judge the architecture of Italy by the works of the High Renaissance."[48] In a second article, Cram wrote of the quality of repose in Japanese architecture, of the beauty of unpainted wood, and of "the exceeding unity and perfection of composition either of single temples or of whole groups," saying, "Nothing could be more subtle and sympathetic than the relationship between the

temples, pagodas and cottages in this country and their natural surroundings. In every line and mass the harmony is complete. The buildings seem to be almost a concentration and perfection of the hills and trees of which they seem to be a part."[49] The temple complex at Nikko had been described in similar terms: "This temple, like all others in Japan, is not a single building, but a collection situated on the terraced slope of a hill, and treated in regard to distribution as a feature of the landscape.... it rises, with tier on tier of crimson lacquer and gold set jewel-like in grooves of giant criptomerias."[50]

Wright visited Nikko at least twice, staying both times in the venerable Kanaya Hotel, within easy walking distance of the temple complex and with dramatic views toward the river and the mountains beyond.[51] His other travels in Japan, and elsewhere in the Orient, are more difficult to document, yet he seems to have gone several times to Kyoto and at least once to Shanghai, where rugs for the Imperial Hotel were being woven.[52] In recalling his impressions of Japan, Wright emphasized the relationship of the buildings to their sites, and he seemed drawn to the image of a unified, cultivated landscape that can still be seen today along the route from Tokyo to Kyoto. In 1917, he wrote that Japanese buildings, "like the rocks and trees, grew in their places. Their gardens were idealized patterns of their landscapes."[53] He later recorded his impression of Japan upon arriving in Yokohama Bay in 1913, partly echoing Cram: "Imagine, if you can, sloping foothills and mountainsides all 'antique' sculpture, carved, century after century, with curving terraces. The cultivated fields rising tier on tier to still higher terraced vegetable fields, green dotted. And extending far above the topmost dotted fields, see the very mountaintops themselves corrugated with regular rows of young pine trees pushing diagonally over... pattern everywhere visible."[54]

As completed, the Imperial Hotel was not radically different from his earlier work, and like the similarly scaled Midway Gardens (Chicago, 1913–14) was formally organized along symmetrical axes, now, however, echoing a Chinese rather than French sense of formal composition.[55] Its rich decorative details successfully mirrored an interpretation of Japanese elements without direct emulation. More deeply reflective of Japan was his incorporation of garden elements (fig. 28); as he wrote, "The

28
View of the Imperial Hotel, Tokyo, by Frank Lloyd Wright. ca. 1923. Fig. 147 in *The Life Work of the American Architect Frank Lloyd Wright* (Stantport, The Netherlands: C. A. Mees, 1925). Canadian Centre for Architecture, Montréal

Imperial Hotel is designed as a system of gardens and sunken gardens and terraced gardens – of balconies that are gardens and loggias that are also gardens – and roofs that are gardens – until the whole arrangement becomes an interpenetration of gardens. Japan is Garden-land."[56] In smaller and less constrained commissions planned for more remote sites in Japan, Wright's plans effected bolder connections. The low, asymmetrical wings of the Odawara Hotel (Nagoya, 1917, partly built; fig. 29) rise from terraces that embank the steep site, and these terraces, not unlike those of the earlier Booth house, are linked by a bridge to a nearby hill.[57] In the Yamamura house, which Wright designed for a site in Ashiya in 1918, the plan is angled in a manner that seems to extend the outcropping of stone at the back of the steep lot.[58] Although the rooms themselves are orthogonal, the verticality of the four-story house, and, more important, its angled

linkage to the hill behind, is premonitory of Doheny's House 'C,' and the canted parapet, which amplifies the departure from a regular layout, looks forward to that of Hollyhock House.[59] One can speculate that Wright's explorations of angled geometries, exploited to effect special relationships with the varied terrains that he was soon to encounter, stems partly from an awareness of their potential awakened while he was in Japan.

While working on his Japanese commissions, Wright was deeply involved in a series of projects for Aline Barnsdall in Los Angeles. The history of these projects is complicated; Wright and Barnsdall had established contact by 1914, and in 1917 he began to design Hollyhock House. During the course of its prolonged construction, between 1919 and 1922, he designed other buildings for her large Olive Hill site, including a theater and related

29
Frank Lloyd Wright. *Odawara Hotel, Nagoya, Japan. Perspective.* 1917. Pencil and colored pencil on tracing paper, 12 x 24¼ in. The Frank Lloyd Wright Foundation, 1706.003

houses as well as a long row of shops along one edge of the property. By early 1920, he had drawn upon the skills of his eldest son, Lloyd, who contributed to the planting design of the complex.[60] Of interest in understanding the Doheny Ranch development is the way in which Wright linked the Barnsdall commissions to his later concrete block houses in Los Angeles (including Doheny), and the similarities of his approach in both Los Angeles and Japan as he sought appropriate interpretation of place. As he wrote in 1923, "I have been, for five years, constructing in a foreign country a romantic epic building, an architect's tribute to a unique nation he has much loved. This structure is not a Japanese building – nor an American building in Tokio. It is simply a free interpretation of the Oriental spirit, once more employing the old handicraft system and native materials to create a rugged, vital, monolithic building that would help Japan create anew the forms for the life that is inevitable to her now." A few lines later, he continued,

The Olive Hill work in Los Angeles is a new type in California, a land of romance – a land that, as yet, has no characteristic building material and no type of building except one carried there by Spanish missionaries in early days. . . . I feel in the silhouette of the Olive Hill house a sense of the breadth and romance of the region and in the type as a whole something adaptable to conditions. This type may be made from the gravel of the decayed granite of the hills easily obtained there and mixed with cement and cast in molds or forms to make a fairly solid mass either used in small units or monolithic in construction, or in combination. This is the beginning of a constructive effort to produce a type that would fully utilize standardization and the repetition of appropriate units.[61]

Later he emphasized his objective of developing a manner of expression appropriate to the region: "Hollyhock House was to be a natural house, naturally built; native to the region of California as the house in the Middle West had been native to the Middle West."[62]

Stimulated by his appreciation of vernacular architecture and by the widely held belief that ancient buildings provided worthy roots, he turned understandably to Pre-Columbian examples as a likely point of departure for an architecture truly native to California. The resulting resemblance of Hollyhock House to Mexican prototypes – especially Pre-Columbian buildings in Palenque, Uxmal, Chichén-Itzá, and Monte Albán – has been much noted.[63] The vocabulary was not new to Wright; he had adapted ornamental details and aspects of massing in earlier designs, for example the A. D. German Warehouse, as previously noted. Hollyhock House reflects a deeper study of Pre-Columbian models, and more fully assimilates general qualities of massing and scale. Of greater consequence in terms of later work are elements that he would develop distinctively in the Doheny project: walled gardens, extensive roof terraces, and an elaborate system of fountains that seemed to emanate from within the building itself (see fig. 22).

Even before Hollyhock House was completed, Wright began to pull away from obvious Pre-Columbian motifs, so that later elements of Olive Hill differ considerably. He soon came to regard Hollyhock House as a special chapter in his career: "I called it a 'California romanza.' This time, frankly, a holiday."[64] By early 1920, as he started to design other elements for the property, he seemed drawn more to the potential of the site itself than to specifics of architectural expression; as he wrote to Aline Barnsdall, "Now, I want to hold on to this hill and make it a beautiful thing."[65] His conceptual view of Olive Hill illustrates this intention (fig. 30). Sketched on stationery from the Wilshire Hotel, it suggested a composition somewhat like the Doheny Ranch development, with building elements used to terrace the hill so that all becomes a single, integrated composition, qualities also emphasized in later perspectives. He further developed the scheme to include an extensive row of shops and apartments along Hollywood Boulevard; with these, it became more conventional, and architectural elements tended to break apart from the larger mass of the hill rising behind (fig. 31).[66] There was little attempt to accommodate the automobile, and none to exploit the architectural potential of roadways. Yet the way was prepared for the Doheny proposal.

There was copious information on Pre-Columbian architecture available to Wright. In addition to the many books and articles that had appeared by 1917, and the many that would follow during the next decade, there were impressive

30

Frank Lloyd Wright. *Olive Hill, Los Angeles. Conceptual sketch.* ca. 1920. Pencil on paper, 6 ⅜ × 10 ⅞ in. The Frank Lloyd Wright Foundation, 1705.001

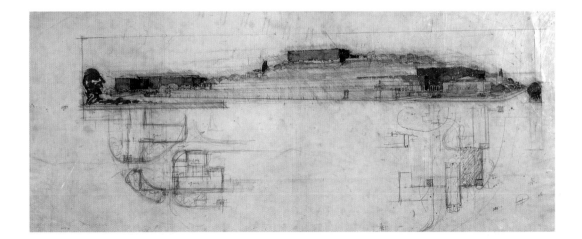

31

Frank Lloyd Wright. *Olive Hill, Los Angeles. Perspective and partial plan.* ca. 1920. Ink with pencil on paper, 21 × 58 in. The Frank Lloyd Wright Foundation, 2005.018

displays of photographs and large plaster casts at both the World's Columbian Exposition of 1893 and the Panama-California Exposition in San Diego, the latter of which Wright reportedly visited with Alfonso Iannelli in January 1915.[67] From these sources, it might be argued, certain details found their way into Wright's ongoing work. The corbeled arches in the much-featured Palace of the Governors at Uxmal, for example, could have inspired the triangular openings in Doheny's House 'A,' and Wright's later development of this motif (in the A. M. Johnson desert compound) would have been encouraged by one illustration's caption, which reported, "The triangular arch is a masterpiece of Architecture."[68]

Such narrow observations help little, however, in understanding Wright's larger objectives. It might as easily be argued that the battered piers of the roadway approaching House 'B' – depicted also in the overall perspectives of the Doheny development – were inspired by the Potala Palace in Lhasa. The first photographs of this Tibetan marvel had been published with much hyperbole during the first decades of the century, and the photograph of the palace that Wright kept above his desk at Taliesin may have been acquired at this time.[69] Yet as his work attests, it was not the details that most captivated Wright, but rather the vast scale of a unified architectural landscape. An illustration of Sayil published in 1920 (fig. 32), remarkably similar to the second Doheny perspective (see fig. 8), illustrates this quality.[70] As Wright reflected late in his career:

Mighty, primitive abstractions of man's nature – ancient arts of the Mayan, the Inca, the Toltec. Those great American abstractions were all earth-architectures: gigantic masses of masonry raised up on great stone-paved terrain, all planned as one mountain, one vast plateau lying there or made into the great mountain ranges themselves; those vast areas of paved earth walled by stone construction. These were human creations, cosmic as sun, moon, and stars! . . . A grandeur arose in the scale of total building never since excelled, seldom equalled.[71]

Except for its historic references, this could be a description of Doheny itself.

Articles linking Pre-Columbian examples in Mexico with Native American architecture would have reinforced Wright's interest. As a unified cultural phenomenon, both could then be valid as a basis for a truly American architecture. One writer proclaimed, "There is an awakening to the place of the native American race in culture history which Americanists are happy to see and encourage," later adding, "In esthetic, ethical, and social efficiency, the Indians surpassed their conquerors."[72] Regarding ties to American Indians, Richard Neutra, who worked briefly in Wright's office, believed widely circulated images of Southwestern pueblo dwellings influenced the design of Doheny.[73] While the flatter and more neutral sites of the pueblos argue against this in the larger sense, their method of construction was not totally unlike Wright's. The appropriateness of pueblo construction to semi-arid conditions had been noted in articles of the period, as had their appearance, "blending in color with the desert from which they are constructed."[74] Indian lore was much in the air at the time; Norman Bel Geddes, who consulted with Wright and Barnsdall on the design of the theater for Olive Hill, was among its many adherents.[75]

Ultimately little came of Wright's plans for the Doheny Ranch. He last mentioned the project as active in October 1923, but seems to have carried it no further than preliminary drawings. The land was eventually sold to an entrepreneur who developed it unimaginatively as the Trousdale Estates, resulting in an all too predictable neighborhood of detached houses that bore a less understanding relationship to their remarkable site. Wright did, however, develop underlying concepts of the Doheny project in a series of commissions for similar sites in the Los Angeles area, and four of these, as completed, demonstrate the applicability of his vision. To be properly understood, these California houses, all of concrete block, should be considered as part of an overall scheme for an idealized development rather than as individual structures; when judged alone they have tended to confound critics, for their extended walls and terraces strike many as overly massive and awkwardly dominant.

Wright himself seems never to have forgotten the larger prospect. For example, his work of the 1920s was published in Europe in a sequence that suggested the block houses as realized components of Doheny; chronological order was largely ignored so that these suburban examples follow the rural prototypes of Tahoe and Nakoma, and the individual block houses seem placed to prove the viability of the larger vision.[76] Given Wright's careful attention to publications on his work, and with his demon-- strated interest in this particular book, he very likely suggested the organization.[77]

The history of the concrete block buildings in the Los Angeles area, and the method of construction that Wright devised, have been fully recorded by Sweeney, so that only a brief summary is needed here.[78] The projects begin with the Alice Millard house, La Miniatura, in Pasadena; it was being designed by early 1923, but Wright was working on the Doheny project, and may have been commissioned late in 1922. Next in sequence came two additional projects for Barnsdall: a second house, in Beverly Hills, which was being designed by April or May 1923, but which remained unbuilt; and the Little Dipper, a community playhouse for the Olive Hill site in Hollywood, which was being designed in August 1923, partly constructed beginning in November, and later converted to a garden structure by R. M. Schindler. The last three commissions were realized, but with nearly unsurmountable problems of construction and cost, as had also beset La Miniatura. All three houses are in Los Angeles. The John Storer house was being designed by August 1923; the Samuel Freeman house, by January or February 1924; and the Charles W. Ennis house, by February 1924. By March of that year Wright seems to have abandoned the idea of establishing a permanent practice in Los Angeles; he had closed his office on Harper Avenue in September 1923, then, between increasingly prolonged trips to Taliesin, resided intermittently in Residence 'B' on Olive Hill, finally giving that up, too.

Fundamental to Wright's approach were the materials and methods by which his designs could be realized. Never, it seems, did he design without reference to these essential elements, though rarely was he bound by their conventional limitations, seeking instead to broaden their potential. His development of concrete blocks into what he called the textile block system illustrates this; the first conceptions of architectural form and the means by which those forms could be realized were intertwined from the beginning, yet his optimistic demands of the actual material made economic realization impossible and any realization difficult.

32

F. H. Ward, photographer. *Building at Sayil, Mexico.* Plate 25, fig. 1 in George Oakley Totten, *Maya Architecture* (Washington, D.C.: The Maya Press, 1926), p. 167. Canadian Centre for Architecture, Montréal. Also published as plate 25.1 in Thomas A. Joyce, *Mexican Archaeology* (London: Philip Lee Warner, 1920)

The textile block system that Wright developed during the 1920s grew out of an early determination to exploit new building techniques as a means of achieving a truly modern architecture. Like many of the pioneering architects of his generation, Wright believed that mechanical processes – akin to prefabrication – would inspire new forms. In his famous 1901 lecture at Hull House, "The Art and Craft of the Machine," he spoke of "multitudes of processes" that were "expectantly awaiting the sympathetic interpretation of the mastermind," and identified the machine – in architecture, analogous to these mechanical processes – as "a marvelous simplifier; the emancipator of the creative mind, and in time the regenerator of the creative conscience." Continuing, he wrote that Americans "must find new forms, new industrial ideals, or stultify both opportunity and form."[79] For Wright, connection between real process and ideal conception was essential; as he later argued, we must use "the machine, which is the real tool, whether we like it or not. . . . to give shape to our ideals."[80]

Wright's experiments with reusable forms in Unity Temple (Oak Park, 1906) reflect a tentative study of process; he seems always to have been frustrated by the elaborate and expensive formwork required for reinforced concrete, and to have sought means of avoiding it. In constructing the Imperial Hotel, he revived – no doubt unknowingly – an ancient Roman technique that made the elimination of formwork possible. As he described in 1923, exterior and interior masonry shells were first erected, and these served both as finish surfaces and as forms for the concrete that would be poured in the space left between, after steel reinforcement (which the Romans had not used) had been positioned therein.[81] By the time of this description he had already proposed the next steps: building those inner and outer masonry shells more cheaply by using concrete block, and making those shells stronger and more flexible by utilizing metal rods placed within channels along the edges of the blocks themselves. The spaces between the inner and outer layers, left hollow, would provide insulation. It was of course to be no ordinary concrete block – what Wright called "the cheapest (and ugliest) thing in the building world" and a "gutter-rat" – but a prefabricated building element transformed through the mechanical process of

reuseable forms into an object of patterned beauty.[82] Floors and ceilings were to be similarly constructed, so that essentially one material would be used throughout. By 1927, following the mixed successes of his Los Angeles buildings, Wright's description of the system was both clear and poetic:

Mechanical steel or aluminum molds are made in which to precast the whole building in a small "unit" of that size. Grooves are provided in the edges of the slab-blocks so a lacing of continuous steel rods may be laid in the vertical and horizontal joints of the block slabs for tensile strength. . . . ultimately we will have another monolith fabricated instead of poured into special wooden molds. . . . A building for the first time in the world may be lightly fabricated, complete, of mono-material – literally woven into a pattern or design as was the oriental rug. . . . we may "weave" an architecture at will – unlimited in quality and quantity except by limitation of imagination.[83]

The use of a single material, which this system made possible, was no mere expedient, but instead, for Wright, the realization of a higher ideal: "The more simple the materials used – the more the building tends toward a mono-material building – the more nearly will 'perfect style' reward an organic plan."[84] He welcomed also its resulting mass, defending it against the light, volumetric enclosure emerging as the expression of modernism in Europe: "rich encrustation of the shells visible as mass, the true mass of the architecture. . . . Genuine 'mass' in this sense will always be modern."[85]

In fact, the ideal was not realized. As Sweeney has documented, none of the Los Angeles commissions made the full use of textile blocks that Wright ultimately envisioned, nor, it seems, did he plan for them to do this. But the gradual progression toward achievement that each succeeding commission demonstrated – ranging from blocks combined with a conventional wood and concrete frame structure in La Miniatura to a more elaborate but still essentially post-and-beam construction system in the Ennis house – shows Wright in pursuit of his dream. And whatever their hidden faults, each design gave at least a small degree of tangibility to the ideal suburban image of the Doheny Ranch project. Similar to the individual units in that project, each of these Los Angeles houses was related to a

RESIDENCE FOR MRS. GEORGE MADISON MILLARD ... FRANK LLOYD WRIGHT ... ARCHITECT ...

33
Frank Lloyd Wright. *La Miniatura (Alice Millard House), Pasadena, California. Perspective.* 1923. Colored pencil and pencil on gampi paper, 20 3/16 × 19 1/16 in. The Museum of Modern Art, New York, Gift of Mr. and Mrs. Walter Hochschild, 240.81

roadway, and when space allowed, these roadways were made an active part of the design, so that vehicular mobility was at least ackowledged. Each structure also embanked or retained the slope of its site through extended walls and terraces, so that an intermediate, clearly bounded area of cultivated garden was created, and this garden area, in turn, linked each building to the surrounding, unchanged terrain. In each successive house he manipulated the blocks themselves with increasing ease, gradually extracting a degree of richness through sensitively located bands of ornament, stepped reveals, and battered profiles, so that effects only suggested in the Doheny drawings were most fully realized in the Ennis house.

Throughout his career, Wright seemed drawn to difficult but dramatic sites, then proved to his satisfaction how those sites could be enhanced and

their hidden qualities revealed. Thus he guided Mrs. Millard away from the conventional site she had originally chosen to a seemingly impractical ravine, designed the house to embank the ravine and form a pool, and gave form to what had appeared formless (fig. 33). "New-born entity where before – emptiness," he wrote, adding, "The whole mass and texture of the home made the eucalyptus trees more beautiful, they in turn made the house walls more so."[86] Radically different in character from his earlier Chicago work and less romantically conceived than Hollyhock House, La Miniatura partly answered Wright's quest for a modern architecture suitable to California, so that he could say, "The humble building gives to architects another simple means to establish an indigenous tradition instead of aping styles from abroad."[87]

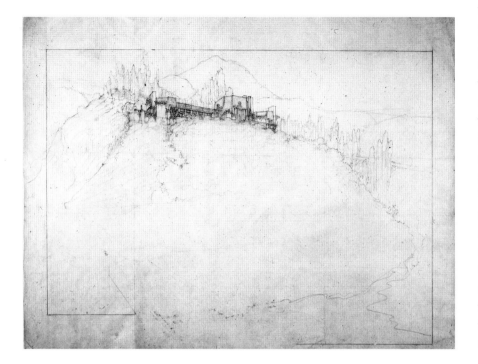

34
Frank Lloyd Wright. *Aline Barnsdall House, Beverly Hills, California. Perspective from below.* 1923. Graphite and colored pencil on Japanese paper, 24 3/16 × 30 7/8 in. The Library of Congress, Washington, D.C., Gift of Donald D. Walker, 152.56

The site Barnsdall selected for her new house in Beverly Hills presented a larger challenge than La Miniatura, and Wright's design remained unbuilt. Writing to Sullivan in March 1923, Wright reported that Barnsdall "has given me a new home to build for her at Beverly — in a beautiful twelve acre mountainside."[88] He positioned the house midway up the mountain, where it would command an extraordinary view of the city below (fig. 34). In a thumbnail sketch at the lower right of a preliminary plan, he recorded the basic form of the house (fig. 35): it would stretch across to ravines on each side, partly enclosing a courtyard behind and linked to the powerful sweep of a roadway that bridged over one ravine then continued along the side of the house, reinforcing its architectural lines (fig. 36). Like this integrated roadway, walled gardens and open loggias that connect wings of the house also parallel aspects of the Doheny project on which Wright was working at the time. Angular elements were incorporated into the design, but were more constrained than in House 'C.' The main living room of the Beverly Hills project, octagonal in shape and with a domed ceiling, projected out toward the major view, and was placed in a way that joined the concave form of the roadway behind with the convex shape of a connected terrace in front. A projecting bay window opposite the roadway echoed the living room's angular shapes. Other drawings show different variations, and suggest the design was left unresolved when, early on, Barnsdall lost interest and abandoned the project.[89]

The community playhouse, called the Little Dipper after its shape, also suffered from Barnsdall's indecision and from her growing perception that Wright was either unable or unwilling to stay within her budget. Like the Coonley playhouse, it was intended as a neighborhood kindergarten, and was partly built on its Olive Hill site before Barnsdall, impatient with cost overruns, halted construction. Of interest as it relates to Doheny is the clear advance in angular planning that it demonstrates; diagonal segments of the plan are smoothly integrated into bridging elements that link terraces and pools into a single, persuasive composition (fig. 37).

Similar to La Miniatura, both the Storer and Freeman houses were relatively small and compact, and contained compartmented spaces that contrasted with the more open plans of Wright's earlier

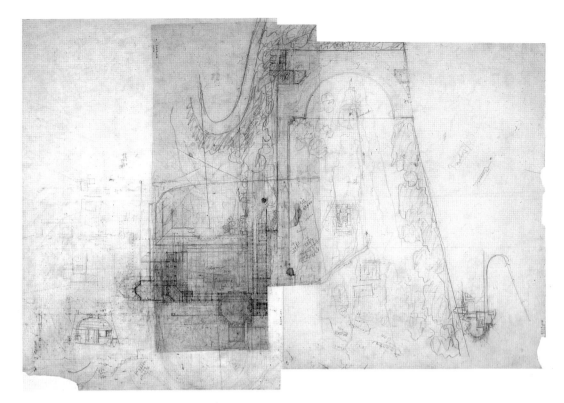

35
Frank Lloyd Wright. *Aline Barnsdall
House. Beverly Hills, California. Plot plan.*
1923. Pencil on tracing paper, assembly
of three fragments, 22 x 28 in.,
21 x 26 in., 14 x 26 in. The Frank Lloyd
Wright Foundation, 2009.001, 005, 016

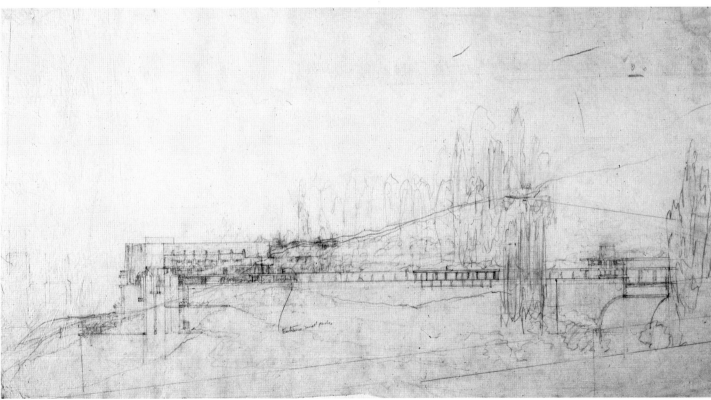

36
Frank Lloyd Wright. *Aline Barnsdall
House, Beverly Hills, California. Elevation.*
1923. Graphite and colored pencil on
wove paper, 12 x 27 in. The Library
of Congress, Washington, D.C., Gift of
Donald D. Walker, 152.59

37
Frank Lloyd Wright. *Community
Playhouse (The Little Dipper), Olive Hill,
Los Angeles. Perspective with pool.* 1923.
Pencil and colored pencil on tracing
paper, 15½ × 26¼ in. The Frank Lloyd
Wright Foundation, 2301.008

38
Frank Lloyd Wright. *John Storer House,
Los Angeles. Perspective.* 1923. Pencil
and colored pencil on tracing paper,
8⅜ × 17¼ in. The Frank Lloyd Wright
Foundation, 2304.002

work. Their constricted sites were steeply sloped
and midway up hills, like Doheny's House 'B.' Wright
placed each house close against its bordering road,
which ran along the bottom of the Storer site and
at the top of the Freeman. In perspective views of
the Storer house, he emphasized its composition as
a series of walled terraces that stepped up to join
the hill behind with the house itself (fig. 38). It is a
strongly urban scheme of concentrated masses; on
one plan, he noted "Palazzo!" perhaps in reference
to this quality.[90] Like an open pavilion, the central
two-story block – containing reception and dining
areas below and the major living space above –
amplifies the continuity of the terraces, which seem
to surround the house on every side and to open
from every level. The regularly spaced piers defining
the line between interior and exterior spaces
initiate a pattern of enclosure by discontinuous elements; a similar pattern had been suggested in the
grouped columns of the Martin house (Buffalo,
1904), and Wright later developed this approach in
the Cudney and Jones houses. As was often the
case in Wright's domestic architecture, the resulting
ambiguity mitigated any sense of a single, formal
entrance. Inside the Storer house, changing floor
and ceiling levels intensify spatial variety. In the high-
ceilinged living space, for example, French windows
open to terraces that extend the linear axis of
the room; these are placed not beneath low, protective overhangs, as would have been typical of his
earlier work, but instead rise up within the tall
central portion of the ceiling, where they beautifully
amplify the openness they celebrate. Not atypically
for Wright, he derived elements of the scheme from
an earlier, unbuilt project: the Lowes house (Eagle
Rock, California, 1922). Yet in the few months separating the similarly organized designs, he had moved
decisively from the conventional frame and stucco
construction of the earlier proposal to a mature
statement of textile blocks.

The Freeman house is the smallest of the block
series, illustrating Wright's contention that even
modestly scaled dwellings could be spatially rich (fig.
39). In an early sketch, Wright drew the curved
roadway as part of the compact composition, and
balanced its profile with a semi-circular terrace
below, in plan not unlike that of the Barnsdall Beverly Hills project. Its concrete blocks are complexly
patterned, appearing heavier than those of the ear-

lier houses, so that the fully glazed corner windows – built with mitered glass – contrast powerfully with their masonry frames. From the time of his earliest Oak Park designs Wright had tended to emphasize diagonal axes within rooms by clustering major openings near corners rather than within the central portions of enclosing walls – even the George Blossom house (Chicago, 1892), with its classicizing details, shows this. The corner windows of the Freeman house – especially the one opposite the entrance to the main room – express this with renewed force.

By virtue of its exaggerated length and prominent site, the Ennis house, of all the block houses, comes closest to evoking the image of Doheny. Visible for a great distance from below, its massive retaining walls seem to embank the entire slope of the hill along which it is placed (fig. 40). The house is treated as a series of clustered units, or suites, that are connected on the main upper level by an extended loggia. Wright welcomed the accompanying differentiation of elements: "The dining room associated with terraces is one mass. The living room with bedrooms attached, another mass. . . . A little study will show how each separate room makes its own characteristic contribution to the whole mass."[91] On the side of the house overlooking the city, a series of narrow terraces that step down the slope at the far end balance the loggia on the opposite side and further emphasize the building's linearity. At the other end of the house, another, larger terrace serves as an arrival court for automobiles, which enter under a bridged extension of an upper level. The court is connected in turn to a garage and service quarters, which complete the composition.

The larger size of the Ennis house allowed a more effective integration with the roadway than had been possible in the earlier houses, for the two elements are more balanced in scale, and the approach up and around the house facilitates a more dramatic, architecturally ordered progression. Problems of cost and structural stability – not to be unexpected in so unusual a design – prolonged construction and led to changes unsupervised by Wright. From his viewpoint, these seriously compromised its design; as he protested to the client regarding one such change, "[I] earnestly beg you not to destroy interweaving of blocks at window

39
Frank Lloyd Wright. *Samuel Freeman House, Los Angeles. Aerial perspective.* 1924. Pencil and colored pencil on tracing paper, 10¾ x 21⅞ in. The Frank Lloyd Wright Foundation, 2402.001

40
Frank Lloyd Wright. *Charles W. Ennis House, Los Angeles. Perspective and plan.* 1924. Ink, pencil, and colored pencil on tracing paper, 10¼ x 39 in. The Frank Lloyd Wright Foundation, 2401.003

heads.... The effect of level heads would stupidly destroy the grace and beauty of entire design."[92] Yet in its essentials the Ennis house forms a fitting conclusion to his work in Los Angeles during the 1920s.

Broader aspects of Wright's proposals for Los Angeles seem to anticipate significant shifts in American society later noted by J. B. Jackson. One such shift pertains to horizontality and a sense of changing landscape; as Jackson wrote, "It is evident that Americans now perceive their environment in a new and as yet undefined manner. It is evident that increased mobility, and even more, an increased experience of uninterrupted speed – whether on the highway or the ski slope or on the surface of the water – bring with them a sharpened awareness of horizontal space and the eventual transformation of many landscapes."[93] Jackson further urged that some means be devised of combining such qualities of mobility with more fixed and stable components of the environment to define a new landscape appropriate to our world.[94]

Wright, in considering American society some fifty years earlier, had seized upon similar aspects of horizontality and mobility. Among several statements in this regard he wrote, "The citizen of the near future preferring horizontality – the gift of his motorcar, and telephonic or telegraphic inventions –

will turn and reject verticality as the body of any American city."[95] Like Jackson, Wright recognized these changes as inevitable, but he was even more forthright in welcoming them and was perhaps the first to engage their potentialities in a positive, architectural sense, as his Doheny proposal shows. Wright's later writings suggested continued study; "Complete mobilization of the people is another result fast approaching," he wrote, adding, "The great highways are in process of becoming the decentralized metropolis."[96] In his utopian Broadacre City, highways, buildings, and land were to be joined in one composition as they had been in Doheny: "The ground will determine the shape and even the style of the buildings in the Broadacre City, so that to see where ground leaves off and the buildings begin would require careful attention.... Architecture and acreage will now again be seen together as landscape, as the best of architecture has ever been."[97]

In Wright's idealized landscape, fixity and mobility were thus to be acknowledged in a single composition, as Jackson would later enunciate. Wright saw the two natures as inherent in humanity: "The cave dweller became the cliff dweller and began to build cities.... His swifter, more mobile brother devised a more adaptable and elusive dwelling place, the folding tent.... The cave dweller's human counterpart cultivated mobility for his safety.... As ingrained instinct of the human race now, in this far distance

41
Panorama of Lake Tahoe from the tavern wharf. ca. 1906. Pillsbury Picture Co. The Library of Congress, Washington, D.C., 93845487

of time, are both these primitive instincts. . . . Gradually, the body of mankind, both natures working together, has produced what the body of mankind calls civilization."[98] Such attitudes are not far removed from Emerson, who had written, "Motion or change, and identity or rest, are the first and second secrets of nature."[99]

Lake Tahoe Summer Colony

During the summer of 1923, while La Miniatura was under construction and Wright was perhaps still hoping for some response from Doheny, he embarked upon another speculative venture for a site on Lake Tahoe.[100] Mobility was again fundamental to his concept, although it was not the mobility of the automobile and integrated roadways, but instead of the houses themselves, for he envisioned floating cabins of changeable position that would bring the lake more fully within the scheme.

The site was indeed extraordinary and must have excited his imagination. With cool, green mountains and limpid alpine lakes, it was far different in character from Los Angeles. Emerald Bay, where the project was to be, lies at the southwest corner of the lake and is highly regarded for its special beauty. The area had begun to be developed with luxurious hotels and summer homes during the 1880s, and was much favored by wealthy Californians.[101] Not far to the east of Emerald Bay, Hotel Tallac – known as "the Saratoga of the Pacific" – had been built in 1898. It was later razed, and the castellated extravaganza proposed to take its place in 1915 was never built, but many of the elegantly rustic lodges erected during the early 1900s survive in an enclave known as the Tallac Estates.[102] Farther east was Camp Richardson, an 1880s logging camp that had been rebuilt as a lodge in the early 1900s and continues, in 1995, to operate. There were more hotels in the nearby town of South Lake Tahoe, such as Al Tahoe, built in 1907, and many had long piers extending far out into the lake (fig. 41). The pier at Timber Cove was one thousand feet long, and the Bijou's over eighteen hundred. Although a road circling the southwest corner of Lake Tahoe had been completed in 1913 and provided comparatively easy access by automobile (fig. 42), luxurious steamers continued, in the 1920s, to provide the favored means of transport.

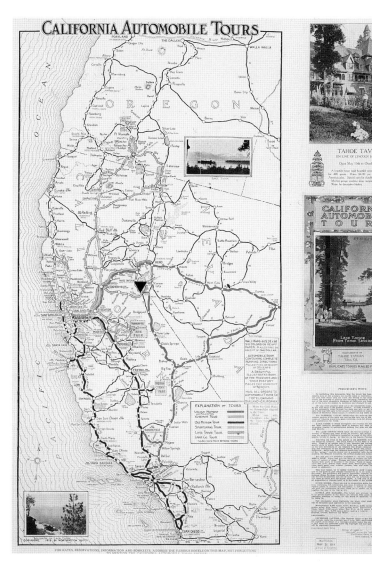

42

California Automobile Tours; Tahoe Tavern on Line of Lincoln Highway. . . . April 1914. The Library of Congress, Washington, D.C., Map Division. Compliments of Tahoe Tavern, Tahoe, California. Black triangle indicates Lake Tahoe site

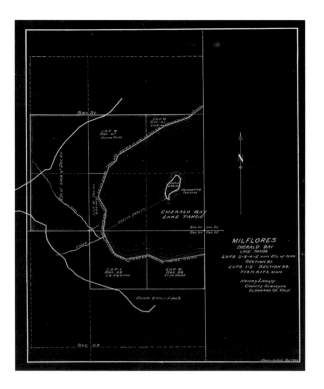

44

*Milflores Lot Plan, Emerald Bay, Lake
Tahoe, California.* 1922. The Frank
Lloyd Wright Foundation, 2205.050

The proposed site of Wright's development
comprised some two hundred acres enclosing the
head of the Emerald Bay, and it included Lake
Tahoe's only island, generally known as Fannette, but
at other times called Emerald, Coquette, Baranoff,
Dead Man's, and Hermit's island, suggesting that it
was much fancied (fig. 43). It is a small but prominent feature, rising some 150 feet above the water
from a base of roughly three hundred by five hundred feet, its area about the size of a city block.
Surrounding the bay are heavily wooded mountains
towering nearly three thousand feet over the lake.
Granite cliffs at the higher elevations give way to
natural terraces edged with boulders on the lower
slopes, and these, in turn, lead to a narrow beach
of white sand. Spring-fed rivulets and waterfalls provide a continuous, soothing sound of falling water.

In 1923, the property was owned by Jessie
Armstrong (fig. 44), and she and her mother, both
deeply attached to the place, had come to call it
Milflores. Her father, William H. Armstrong, had
acquired the property in 1892 from Lucy Kirby, the
widow of Paul T. Kirby, a fellow Mason from Virginia
City. That year Armstrong deeded the property to
his wife, Margaret Jane, and she, in turn, transferred
ownership to her unmarried daughter in 1917.[103]
During the 1880s the Kirbys had developed the site
as a resort of detached cabins, and these Jessie and

43

Frank Lloyd Wright. *Emerald Bay, Lake
Tahoe, California. Aerial view.* 1923.
Graphite on gelatin print, 9 x 21 ⅞ in.
The Frank Lloyd Wright Foundation,
2205.052

her mother used as a summer retreat. After selling to Armstrong, Lucy Kirby remarried and stayed close by on property she had maintained near the mouth of the bay. There she and her new husband, the widower Russell Cowles Graves, established Emerald Bay Camp, which, under different owners, operated well into the twentieth century.

How Wright was first drawn to the site is uncertain, but correspondence regarding its purchase suggests speculation, further confirmed by Jessie Armstrong's recollection that, at the time of his first and apparently only visit, he "had even begun to form his plans for how he would develop the property if this company took it over."[104] She does not name the company, but correspondence in December 1923 confirms that negotiations for the purchase were under way. Frank P. Deering, a San Francisco attorney who had assisted the Armstrongs in their own acquisition of the property, reported to E. E. Prussing, the Los Angeles attorney representing Wright's interests, that the owners were asking $150,000.[105] Wright was still discussing terms in May 1924 when he telegraphed his son Lloyd that Jessie Armstrong seemed to be cooperating.[106] Given his financial circumstances, Wright's optimism must reflect hope of outside support, perhaps from the Armstrongs themselves, and it would not have been unthinkable for him to have offered his talents as collateral.

Jessie Armstrong remembers meeting Wright at the nearby Emerald Bay Camp landing as he arrived by steamer from Tahoe City, and she ferried him in the family's small boat to their own camp for lunch. Transportation available at the time would have made this short visit possible. He probably arrived on the *Tahoe* (fig. 45), described as the most elegant of the lake's ships, and returned on the steamer that circled in the opposite direction — usually the almost equally elegant *Meteor*.[107] From

Jessie Armstrong's account, Wright clearly performed in his usual style, charming both mother and daughter with compliments and drawings. What drawings he brought is unknown, but he took them away with him, so they are possibly among those in the Frank Lloyd Wright Archive.

The focal point of the development was to be an inn built over the bay itself. Wright gave it special prominence by placing it not near the shore, where one would expect, but adjacent to the island, where it would have appeared appealingly isolated. In the sketchy site plan and elevation that survive (fig. 46), it is shown on the western side of the island, near its northern tip, and is connected to the mainland by a network of piers that bridge across the bay to a prominently projecting feature on the shore known as Parsons Rock. The distance between island and shore at this, its narrowest point, is under one thousand feet, so Wright's would not have been the longest such pier on the lake.

The main room of the inn was to be connected to the island by the transverse wing of the dining room and by clustered piers and pavilions that defined water courts within their precincts. Angled bay-windows shown on the plan together with steeply pitched roofs, rows of dormers, and massive chimneys seem appropriate to the image of a mountain lodge. While the inn itself would almost certainly have been supported on piles, Wright treated the piers in the manner of a pontoon bridge, delineating the floating metal boxes on which they, in turn, were to float as projecting triangular elements, so they became an articulating feature of the plan. As shown in elevation, the vertical standards rising from each pontoon, and the open pattern of angled tie-rods forming a balustrade, would have created a diaphanous enclosure sympathetic to the liquid transparency of the bay.

45
Emerald Bay, Lake Tahoe, Steamer at Pier. Photograph ca. 1910. Prints and Photographs Division, Library of Congress, Washington, D.C., PAN US GEOG-CALIF, No. 325

Along the shore and on the lower slopes of the mountains, Wright planned a series of individual cabins. No site plan survives that would locate these, and probably none was ever drawn; as in the Doheny project, his designs were clearly intended as prototypes that could be varied to meet specific demands. He again proposed his system of concrete blocks, but to be made of Tahoe's white sand rather than the reddish granite of Los Angeles, and limited to the retaining walls of terraces and the lower walls of the buildings, so their appearance was considerably varied from his Los Angeles proposals. The upper levels of the lodges were to be of stained boards, and the steep roofs of copper with a crystalline pattern of standing seams.[108]

What Wright called the Lodge type cabin was the simplest of the houses in terms of its geometry, shown along the edge of one of the site's flatter segments (fig. 47). A more finished perspective shows how effectively he refined his Tahoe vocabulary by adding angled bays, complicated roof profiles, and varied terraces (fig. 48). Bedrooms are placed within a two-story enclosure, expressed as a bay window, that projects on one side. It is linked to the house's central core, which rises from the highest terrace, at the center of the composition (fig. 49). A living room at the front would have overlooked Emerald Bay from an elaborately angled window, and behind that, framed by two massive

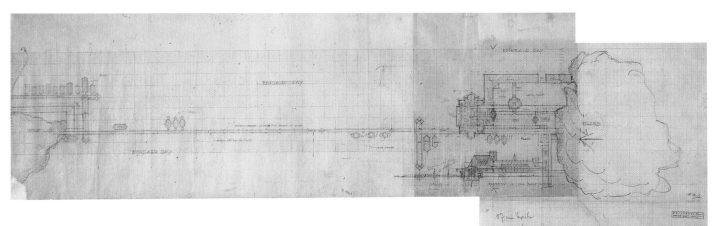

47
Frank Lloyd Wright. *Lake Tahoe Summer Colony, California, Lodge Type Cabin. Perspective and plan.* 1923. Graphite and colored pencil on Japanese paper, 20½ × 13¾ in. Canadian Centre for Architecture, Montréal, Gift of George Jacobsen and of the CCA Founders Circle, in his memory, 1994

46
Frank Lloyd Wright. *Lake Tahoe Summer Colony, California. Site plan and partial elevation showing inn and piers.* ca. 1923. Pencil and crayon on tracing paper, 17 × 62½ in. John Lloyd Wright Collection, Avery Architectural and Fine Arts Library, Columbia University, New York

48

Frank Lloyd Wright. *Lake Tahoe Summer Colony, California, Lodge Type Cabin. Perspective and plan.* 1923. Pencil and colored pencil on tracing paper, 21⅜ x 14⅞ in. The Frank Lloyd Wright Foundation, 2205.001

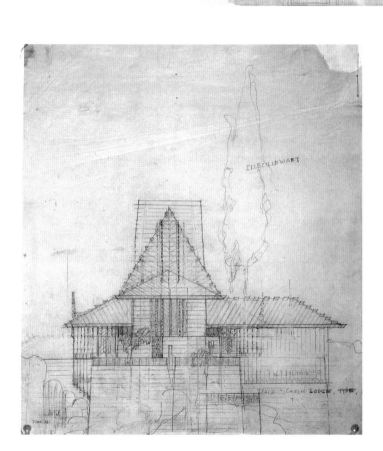

49
Frank Lloyd Wright. *Lake Tahoe Summer Colony, California, Lodge Type Cabin. Plan.* 1923. Pencil and colored pencil on tracing paper, 20 ¾ × 15 ¾ in. The Frank Lloyd Wright Foundation, 2205.024

chimneys, is what Wright identified as a "sun court" with the kitchen behind. Continuing the line of bedrooms on the opposite side of the living room is a second cluster of bedrooms (fig. 50), placed in an extended wing that helps define a stone entrance court behind. The court, in turn, was to be edged along its back by a rock garden. Steps shown on the opposite side would have provided links to paths leading down the mountain.

Wright called a second prototype the Big Tree or Wigwam cabin, an obvious allusion to its peaked roof that recalls Indian tepees and echoes the shapes of local trees (fig. 51). It is compactly planned, with four square rooms joined at the center by a massive fireplace (fig. 52). This cluster is rotated forty-five degrees on its terraced base, adding angular complexities. The windowed tip of each room projects over its base, like the bedroom enclosure of the Lodge type, and the outer corners of the base are developed in different ways, with those at the front to be used as terraces and those at the back as service spaces. Again, to judge by the elevation and perspective, the cabin would have looked out over the lake from the high vantage point of one of the area's small plateaus.

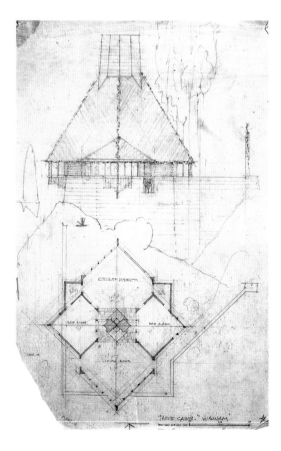

50
Frank Lloyd Wright. *Lake Tahoe Summer Colony, California, Lodge Type Cabin. Elevation.* 1923. Pencil and colored pencil on tracing paper, 16 × 14 in. The Frank Lloyd Wright Foundation, 2205.022

52
Frank Lloyd Wright. *Lake Tahoe Summer Colony, California, Wigwam Cabin. Plan and elevation.* 1923. Pencil and colored pencil on tracing paper, 17 ⅛ × 10 ½ in. The Frank Lloyd Wright Foundation, 2205.019

TAHOE CABIN - B'S TEPE TYPE.

2205.026

51
Frank Lloyd Wright. *Lake Tahoe Summer
Colony, California, Wigwam Cabin.
Perspective.* 1923. Pencil and colored
pencil on tracing paper, 16 x 15 ⅜ in.
The Frank Lloyd Wright Foundation,
2205.026

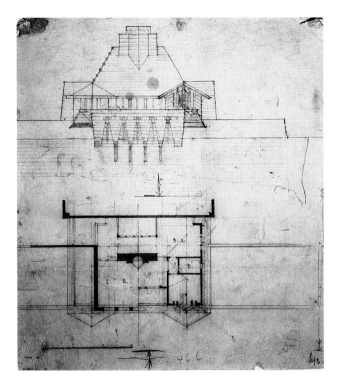

Drawings for a third prototype, the Shore cabin, confirm that it would indeed be best placed along the flatter areas of the site adjacent to the bay (figs. 53, 54). It is more extended in plan than the other two, with walled terraces stretching out from each side of a central, steeply roofed enclosure (fig. 55). The spaces within are arranged in a U-shaped cluster opening out to the lake, and the windowless wall along the back would retain the likely hill behind. At the center, focusing on a massive fireplace, is a double-height living room, and behind the fireplace, small rooms – presumably service spaces – overlook a small court at the rear. At the front of the living room, in a one-story space below a roof terrace, are corbeled openings looking out to the lake. On the second floor, paired bedrooms are placed along each side, cantilevered over supporting walls below, somewhat in the manner of a ship's bridge.

55
Frank Lloyd Wright. *Lake Tahoe Summer Colony, California, Shore Type Cabin. Plan and elevation.* 1923. Pencil on tracing paper, 15 ¼ x 13 ⅛ in. The Frank Lloyd Wright Foundation, 2205.018

53
Frank Lloyd Wright. *Lake Tahoe Summer Colony, California, Shore Type Cabin. Perspective sketch.* 1923. Pencil on tracing paper, 5 x 11 ¾ in. The Frank Lloyd Wright Foundation, 2205.007

54
Frank Lloyd Wright. *Lake Tahoe Summer Colony, California, Shore Type Cabin. Perspective and plan.* 1923. Pencil and colored pencil on tracing paper, 18 ¾ x 15 ¾ in. The Frank Lloyd Wright Foundation, 2205.003

LAKE CABIN - *whitewood Blocks*
Steel Band (copper covered projected)
{ SHORE TYPE

Block technique
Taliesin

In the drawing: TAHOE CABIN / FIR TREE TYPE

56

Frank Lloyd Wright. *Lake Tahoe Summer
Colony, California, Fir Tree Cabin.
Perspective and plan.* 1923. From H. de
Fries, *Frank Lloyd Wright: Aus dem
Lebenswerke eines Architekten* (Berlin:
Ernst Pollak, 1926), p. 50. Canadian
Centre for Architecture, Montréal

A fourth prototype, the Fir Tree cabin, survives in reproduced drawings (figs. 56). Like the Wigwam, its plan is complex (fig. 57). From a central, loosely octagonal core containing living room and kitchen, bedrooms extend forward on each side. These are placed atop an angular terrace and have steeply pitched roofs with lower hipped bays, similar in detail to the other cabins.

On the plan for the Lodge cabin are notes listing prototypes being contemplated for the colony; these correspond somewhat to the surviving drawings, but suggest that other types were also being considered, and that names were in flux. A recently discovered sheet of sketches in Wright's hand gives hints of one: what might be called a Bridge cabin (fig. 58). Linear in plan and less symmetrical than the others, it was to span a shallow chasm, thus joining two hill-like portions of the terrain. It would have been a powerful form, but more difficult than the others to locate.

On the site plan showing the inn, Wright indicated some twenty-two barges moored along the piers. These were intended as floating cabins, like houseboats, that could be moved about the bay, thus bringing the lake itself into special play. Wright suggested that utility connections be located at various points so each cabin, when moored, could be provided with electricity and telephone; each was also to have a radio.[109]

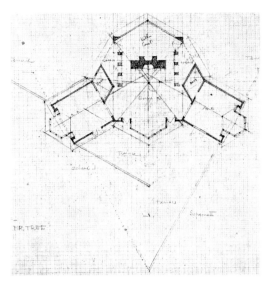

57
Frank Lloyd Wright. *Lake Tahoe Summer Colony, California, Fir Tree Cabin. Plan.* 1923. From H. de Fries, *Frank Lloyd Wright: Aus dem Lebenswerke eines Architekten* (Berlin: Ernst Pollak, 1926), p. 51. Canadian Centre for Architecture, Montréal

58
Frank Lloyd Wright. *Lake Tahoe Summer Colony, California. Perspective sketches and plans.* 1923. Graphite on Japanese paper, 17 × 14 in. The Library of Congress, Washington, D.C., 152.22

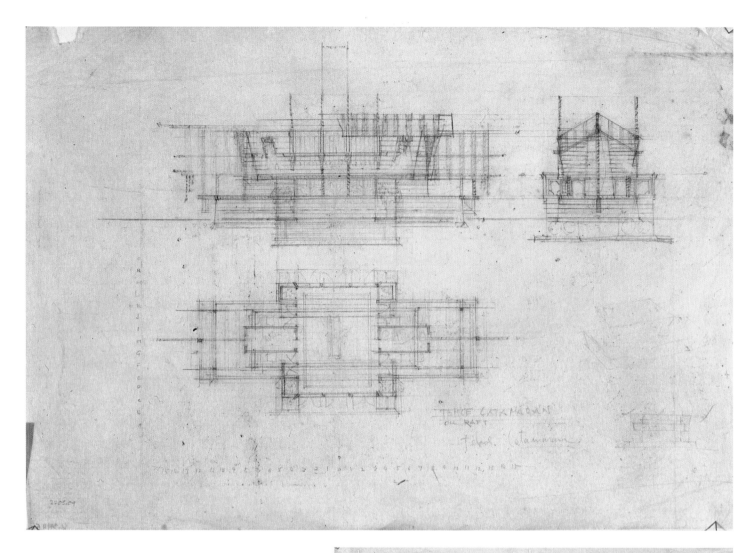

60
Frank Lloyd Wright. *Lake Tahoe Summer
Colony, California, Catamaran Barge. Plan
and elevations.* 1923. Pencil on tracing
paper, 10⅞ × 15⅞ in. The Frank Lloyd
Wright Foundation, 2205.009

59
Frank Lloyd Wright. *Lake Tahoe Summer
Colony, California, Catamaran Barge.
Perspective and plan.* 1923. Pencil on
tracing paper, 16¾ × 17¼ in. The Frank
Lloyd Wright Foundation, 2205.021

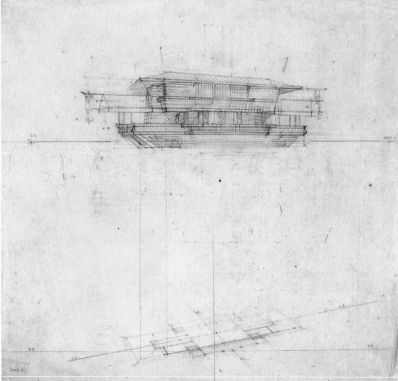

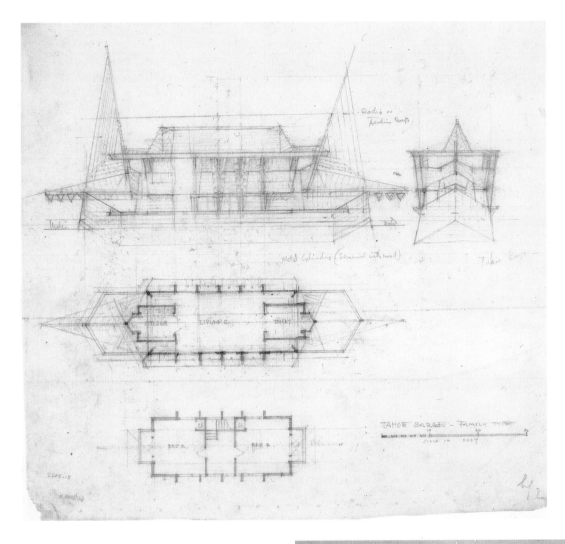

62
Frank Lloyd Wright. *Lake Tahoe Summer Colony, California, Family Type Barge. Plans and elevations.* 1923. Pencil on tracing paper, 13 x 13 ½ in. The Frank Lloyd Wright Foundation, 2205.015

61
Frank Lloyd Wright. *Lake Tahoe Summer Colony, California, Family Type Barge. Perspective and plan.* 1923. Pencil on tracing paper, 15 ⅛ x 18 ⅛ in. The Frank Lloyd Wright Foundation, 2205.020

Like the individual lodges, the floating cabins were classified by type. The Catamaran barge was most conventional in terms of its geometry, with long, narrow rooms and extended decks emphasizing its linear nature (figs. 59, 60). The Family barge had more complicated shapes better suited to movement through water, with angled ends that functioned as prows and established a geometric pattern that was carried into the end bays of the lower service spaces. Similar to the Catamaran barge, it was to have two decks, with living spaces below and sleeping quarters above. Wright experimented with different roof configurations, ranging from relatively simple to more interwoven (figs. 61, 62). In the latter, the angled planes of upper and lower roofs were augmented by diaphanous compositions suggestive of wings that Wright noted as "Radio or Aeolian Harp," presumably a radio antenna.

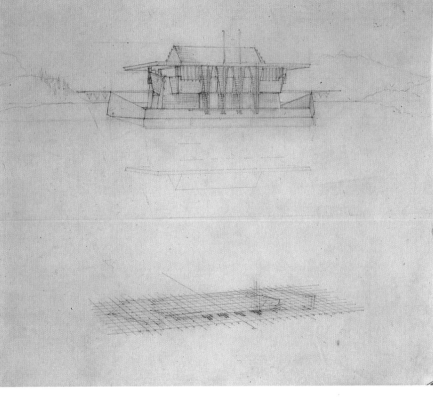

63
Frank Lloyd Wright. *Lake Tahoe Summer Colony, California, Fallen Leaf Barge. Perspective.* 1923. Pencil and colored pencil on tracing paper, 6½ × 11⅜ in. The Frank Lloyd Wright Foundation, 2205.002

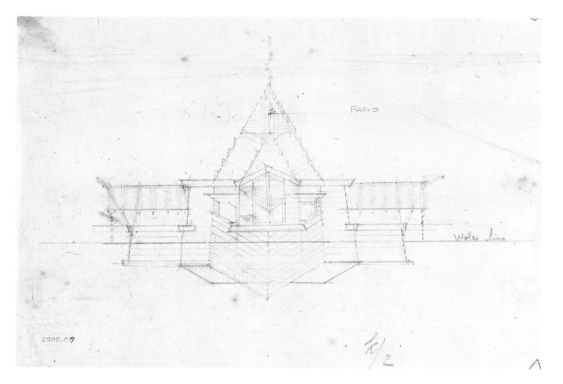

64
Frank Lloyd Wright. *Lake Tahoe Summer Colony, California, Fallen Leaf Barge. Elevation.* 1923. Pencil on tracing paper, 6½ × 9¼ in. The Frank Lloyd Wright Foundation, 2205.005

A third barge, the Fallen Leaf, developed geometric themes of the Wigwam cabin, with square shapes superimposed in plan (figs. 63–65). Again the angled terminals at each end would have facilitated movement. Over the central space of this essentially one-room cabin was a peaked roof with a richly faceted pattern and, again, a multi-wired radio antenna. A fourth type, the Barge for Two, is significant in recording what seems to be Wright's first use of a fully hexagonal module (figs. 66, 67). Not only the bays but also the spaces throughout are so shaped, resulting in a fully hexagonal plan. Above the cabin, kitchen, and open deck of the main level was to be a "sheltered deck – for sleeping."[110] Linear projections at each end, echoing similar exaggerations of the extended roofs below, would have emphasized the movement of the barge. Again a radio antenna – developed as a fin at the back of the sleeping deck – adds a special note of diaphanous enclosure.

Wright superimposed an outline of the Lake Tahoe summer colony over an aerial photograph of the site, reflecting his broad, inclusive vision of landscape and facilitating the depiction of his knowing manipulation (fig. 68).[111] The manner of presentation is significant, for it shows a new awareness of the vast scale at which he was working, a scale beyond the range of conventional perspectives. In these years those conventions, too, seem challenged by a new approach, for vanishing lines of panoramic views that were relatively contained within the frames of earlier drawings gradually expand beyond their usual borders, and multiple points of view seem superimposed, as in the Doheny perspectives. It seems as if not only the broad landscape but an entire continent were contained within his vision. His use of an actual photograph to support that vision anchors it within a tangible realm.

At Lake Tahoe, the shape of the small island would have been intensified by the sympathetically scaled inn and, through its connection to the shore, brought into stronger alliance with the surrounding mountains whose shapes it echoed. Unlike extended piers elsewhere on the lake, Wright's lead to specific points of reference, reinforcing order through connection and framing a portion of the bay for recreational pursuits. Had he continued to plan, bringing the individual cabins more firmly into the composition, they would no doubt have further structured their setting. Perhaps he had them in mind when, a few years later, he described general thoughts for a new world architecture: "Homes? Growing from their site in native materials, no more 'deciduous' than the native rock ledges of the hills, or the fir trees rooted in the ground, all taking on the character of the individual in perpetual bewildering variety. . . .The city? Gone to the surrounding country."[112] In contrast to these stabilizing elements, the floating cabins would have provided an element of gentle mobility. As they changed position, shifting compositions of their forms would have added special dynamism. Again systems of movement were integrated into one single, all-embracing vision.

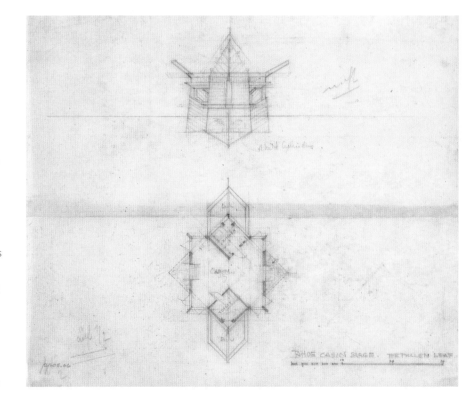

65
Frank Lloyd Wright. *Lake Tahoe Summer Colony, California, Fallen Leaf Barge. Plan and elevation.* 1923. Pencil on tracing paper, 9½ x 10¾ in. The Frank Lloyd Wright Foundation, 2205.006

66

Frank Lloyd Wright. *Lake Tahoe Summer
Colony, California, Barge for Two.
Perspective.* 1923. Pencil and colored
pencil on tracing paper, 9 ¾ × 14 ⅜ in.
The Frank Lloyd Wright Foundation,
2205.004

68

Frank Lloyd Wright. *Lake Tahoe Summer
Colony, California. Perspective sketch
on photograph.* From H. de Fries, *Frank
Lloyd Wright: Aus dem Lebenswerke
eines Architekten* (Berlin: Ernst Pollak,
1926), p. 46. Canadian Centre for
Architecture, Montréal

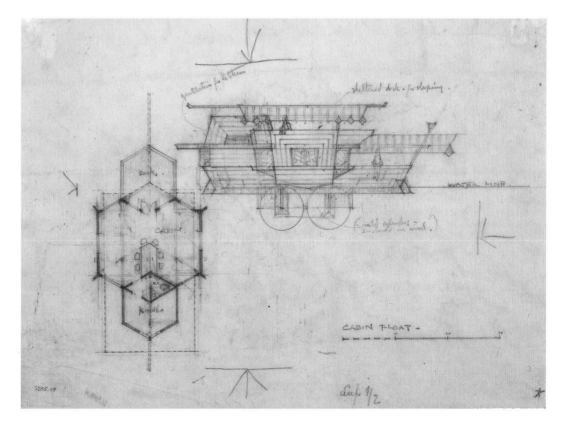

67

Frank Lloyd Wright. *Lake Tahoe Summer
Colony, California, Barge for Two. Plan
and elevation.* 1923. Pencil on tracing
paper, 9¼ × 11¾ in. The Frank Lloyd
Wright Foundation, 2205.008

Wright's Tahoe vocabulary reflects obvious sources. For example, similar developments in the Adirondacks had long incorporated steeply hipped roofs, massive chimneys, angled bays, broad terraces and porches, and expansive interiors with open, high ceilings. The famed Ausable Club, established near Keene Valley, New York, in 1892, is one of several such enclaves that focus on a lake and employ such devices.[113] Its component parts, too, are not unlike those of the Tahoe project; individual lodges – some privately owned – are part of a master plan focusing on a centrally located hotel and restaurant. There are no floating cabins, but theatrically rustic camps, located on a private lake and accessible only by specially designed boats, are a major feature of the complex. Closer to the Tahoe site, R. C. Reamer's Old Faithful Inn (1903) at Yellowstone National Park is one of several well-known establishments reflecting a similar Adirondack vocabulary, and again it is designed to emphasize a connection between building and landscape.[114] In his proposal, Wright updated the architectural vocabulary, much as he would the Tudor image of his 1895 Nathan G. Moore house in Oak Park when he rebuilt it in 1923 (after the original had been heavily damaged in a fire). Period details are abstracted, so that textures and the very density of ornamental detail are not reduced but instead detached from specific sources. The effect is distantly evocative of another time while firmly expressive of its own, more modern age.

In naming one cabin "Wigwam," Wright pointed to American Indian themes as another source of inspiration. This did not go unnoticed by Jessie Armstrong, who recalled that Wright "had the plans drawn for the Campoodi Indian-type architecture for a home for mother and me on some site."[115] The Washoe tribe that had lived in the Tahoe area had built tepees of branches, and surviving photographs show them in relation to the conical pines of the area.[116] Again, it seems, Wright was looking to indigenous building as a source for an American architecture evocative of place, now turning from the Pre-Columbian forms of Mexico that helped inspire his designs for Los Angeles to the native tents and related dwellings that had been built in the Northeast. At the time, the terms "wigwam" and "tepee" were interchangeable, and both could refer to the familiar conical tent. Illustrations of "long wigwams" are even closer in form to the roof configurations that Wright developed for Tahoe.[117] One could even imagine that Wright found it possible to combine aspects of both Mexican and American prototypes in his own reinterpretation of origins; illustrations of Pre-Columbian temples recall the Tahoe lodges, and the idealized dwellings that these temples represented, with roof profiles similar to Indian dwellings, may have suggested a common root (fig. 69).[118]

In terms of Wright's later career, his incorporation of angled elements, especially in the floating cabins, held more promise than the stylistic motifs that can be discerned in the details. As discussed earlier, he had long incorporated such angled elements as bay windows. With Doheny's House 'C' and more persuasively with Tahoe's Fir Tree and Wigwam cabins, he began to explore angled geometries as a means to shaping whole volumes, at first in plan, then in section as well. With the Barge for Two, combinations of angled and orthogonal geometry give way to a scheme based entirely on hexagonal shapes, and a new configuration of space is brought into focus. It would form the basis for some of Wright's most significant work in the years to follow, and its roots can be traced back in details of his earlier work.

Modest hexagonal elements appear in Wright's work at least as early as 1903, in a plan for the Francis W. Little house (Peoria, Illinois), yet at first he tended to employ such elements more regularly in decorative adjuncts of his buildings, as the chairs of the Imperial Hotel illustrate.[119] With the Barge for Two, a more decisive step is taken. Such shapes are by no means new to architectural decoration, or even to isolated details of plan, but they are less common as an underlying theme of spatial organization, so that to find even simplistic adaptations of the form it is necessary to turn to such comparatively remote prototypes as the hexagonally shaped port at Ostia, added during the reign of Trajan, or the forecourt of the Sanctuary at Baalbek, begun in the early first century and completed ca. 250. Wright himself indicated his Froebel toys were a source, as summarized in the autobiography he began to write in 1926: "Now came the geometric by-play. . . . the box with a mast to set up on it, on which to hang with string the maple cubes and spheres and triangles, revolving them to discover subordinate forms. . . . And the exciting cardboard shapes. . . . Smooth triangular shapes. . . . cut in rhomboids with which to make designs on the flat tabletop. What shapes they made naturally if only you would let them! . . . Shapes that lay hidden behind the appearances all about. . . . Here was something for invention to seize and use to create."[120] Later he returns to this theme: "That early kindergarten experience with the straight line; the flat plane; the square; the triangle; the circle! If I wanted more, the square modified by the triangle gave the hexagon — the circle modified by the straight line would give the octagon. Adding thickness, getting 'sculpture' thereby, the square became the cube, the triangle the tetrahedron, the circle the sphere. These primary forms and figures were the secret of all effects, not merely efflorescent or fluorescent, which or what ever got into the architecture of the world."[121] He thus suggests a more elemental aspect of varied geometries than mere pattern, and it was this quality that he began to explore in the 1920s.

In the end no investors for his Lake Tahoe project came forward, and the venture ended much as Doheny was ending at the same time, with little but fragmentary drawings to suggest what might have been. As Jessie Armstrong speculated, "he had peculiar ideas of architecture; everyone didn't respond to them."[122] She sold Milflores to the First National Bank of Los Angeles in 1928, reportedly for $250,000, and the bank, by prior arrangement, sold the property to Mrs. Lora Josephine Moore

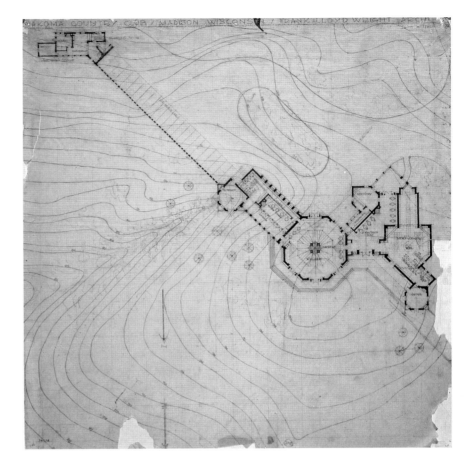

Knight in 1929.[123] Mrs. Knight, an heiress of considerable means, built the medievalizing confection known as Vikingsholm on a site near the Armstrongs' camp, and this house, where the Armstrongs were later guests, became part of a state park in 1953.

Late in 1923, while he still held hopes for Tahoe's realization, Wright took advantage of a commission for the Nakoma Country Club to explore the vocabulary in greater detail.[124] The clubhouse he proposed was adjacent to a golf course and part of the residential suburb of Nakoma, located a few miles west of Madison in Wright's native state of Wisconsin. The octagonal elements of its plan are less daring than his angular proposals for Lake Tahoe, but its scale is larger than Tahoe's individual cabins, and it is dramatically sited so that one long wing — planned as an enclosure for parking automobiles — bridges a shallow ravine (fig. 70). Except for this passive reference to the automobile and a conventional driveway, however, roadways are not integrated into the design. Responding to the Indian theme of the development's name, Wright centered his scheme upon a steeply roofed octagonal room

70
Frank Lloyd Wright. *Nakoma Country Club, near Madison, Wisconsin. Site plan.* 1924. Pencil on tracing paper, 23 ⅞ × 23 ¼ in. The Frank Lloyd Wright Foundation, 2403.028

that he called a "wigwam" in plan and furnished with a central campfire. Preliminary perspectives suggest the extended line of the building and depict an interplay of Tahoe-like roofs; Wright has noted both "wigwam" and "tepee" on the drawing, affirming the interchangeability of the terms in his mind at the time (fig. 71).[125] He again suggested concrete block for the masonry elements of the building, though in some drawings native limestone is also proposed.

In a letter to the directors of the club protesting their criticism of his proposal for a sculpture basin at the entrance, Wright offered clear views of how his approach in relating built forms to the land could lead to a more expressive landscape:

At your invitation I have earnestly tried to put a piece of noble and quiet architecture in your landscape. The emphasis should rest upon the architecture *because all the importance that can be given to it as such will be insignificant enough in the big scale of "out of doors." Yet, fear has crept in among you and a subsequent desire to obliterate the architecture reducing the contrast of the shining plateau and more shadowed pool to a couple of naturalistic sunken-pools, the stone memorials thus rising from a pair of depressions. That not only leaves bare concrete roadways still the dominant feature of Nakoma land-scape, but turns a noble piece of architecture into a mere landscape banality.*[126]

Obviously Wright grasped the scale of the site and the need for an architectural statement that would have discernible, even symbolic presence within its broad expanse. The "contrast of the shining plateau and more shadowed pool" are rendered in an early perspective, and on that drawing, in his own hand, Wright noted his intended meaning: "Nakoma 'Basin' – Stone memorial to *Nakoma* – 'Woman' (domestic); Stone memorial shaft to Nakomis – 'Plateau' – Nakomis 'warrior' (dramatic)" (fig. 72).[127] While the sentiment is now somewhat difficult to embrace, his words confirm a belief in the expressive potential of a designed landscape. Unpersuaded, the directors rejected his pleas and Wright resigned from the commission.

Isolated elements of the Tahoe proposal found their way into a few later designs. He suggested a scheme of floating bridges supported on pontoons for the 1933 Century of Progress Exposition in Chicago, and he included a floating barge as a dining room at Auldbrass (a plantation for Leigh Stevens near Yemassee, South Carolina, begun in 1938). Auldbrass was built, but without its floating component. For the E. A. Smith house (Piedmont Pines, California, 1939) he revived the vocabulary of Tahoe's individual cabins, but that, too, remained unbuilt.

Created within the brief span of a few months in 1923, Wright's proposals for Doheny and Tahoe demonstrated an ability to effect significant change. These designs differ not only from his earlier work but also from each other in their contrasting responses to specific settings. In this they offer generalized prototypes of the sort that form a convincing basis for Wright's later critique of the International Style, which he believed was seriously flawed in its failure to accommodate such response. Wright's designs also expand on his statement of 1908 that "there should be as many kinds (styles) of houses as there are kinds (styles) of people."[128] As designs related to Doheny and Tahoe illustrate, he sought types that could be adapted with minor adjustments to suit groupings of clients. In this his work remained firmly governed by principles, an aspect not always understood by certain of his enthusiastic but less disciplined followers, who could too easily mistake the irrational novelty of their work as reflecting Wright's approach.

The A. M. Johnson Desert Compound

In designing a large residential complex for A. M. Johnson on the edge of Death Valley, Wright began his long association with the desert. Stimulated by new terrain, he sought forms responsive to its stark beauty and of sufficient dimension to provide visible structure in its vast, seemingly scaleless spaces. Later commissions provided opportunities to develop the prototypes he initiated, and the desert came to hold special fascination, leading to the building of Taliesin West near Scottsdale, Arizona, beginning in 1938.

Except for a few scattered tourist accommodations and mining operations, Death Valley was unoccupied when Wright began his work there. The earliest permanent settlements had been established near the borax mines at Ryan, where operations started not long after 1849, when California-bound prospectors in wagon trains had

71

Frank Lloyd Wright. *Nakoma Country
Club, near Madison, Wisconsin.
Perspective.* ca. 1924. Graphite and
colored pencil on tracing paper,
13 ¼ x 27 ¹¹⁄₁₆ in. The Library of
Congress, Washington, D.C., Gift of
Donald D. Walker, 152.37

72

Frank Lloyd Wright. *Memorial Gateway
to Nakoma Country Club, near Madison,
Wisconsin. Perspective showing club
in distance.* 1924. Pencil and colored
pencil on tracing paper, 11 x 8 in.
The Frank Lloyd Wright Foundation,
2405.011

begun to cross the valley. The central area of the
valley – more than two hundred square miles surrounded by bare, rocky mountains – is still largely
barren (fig. 73). Yet the very extremes of the place
added to its imagined exoticism, and by the early
1920s it had become a tourist objective. At first
travelers arrived by train, disembarking at Death
Valley Junction and camping out or staying at
Ryan.[129] By the early 1920s, adventurous travelers
were making the trip by automobile. There were
few roads, but in 1921 the Automobile Club of
Southern California posted signs, which made it
possible to navigate across the desert.[130] Within a
year many of these signs had disappeared, and those
surviving were described as "the only evidence of
civilization for miles in any direction," especially in
the "uncharted, perilous, and treacherous northern
section," words well chosen to inspire the enthusiasm of the hardy.[131] Getting to the edge of the
valley was facilitated by any number of roads and
highways then being built, part of a growing fascination with transcontinental travel by automobile; the
Lincoln Highway between San Francisco and New
York, for example, was charted between 1916 and
1919, consisting primarily of roads already in existence but not so mapped. Increasingly travel by
automobile to remote and previously inaccessible
places was becoming popular.[132] Reflecting this
spirit, a typical photograph of the period is cap-

tioned, "'Terror of the desert' fast diminishes in
Southern California as auto highway now crosses
former arid and death defying waste."[133] Even
advertising was affected; the sequential Burma
Shave advertisements first appeared in 1925.[134]

Johnson's interest in Death Valley had begun earlier.
Born to a prosperous Ohio family and trained at
Cornell as a mining engineer, Albert Mussey Johnson
(1872–1948) was involved in his family's various
mining and power interests until injuries suffered
in an 1899 train accident made sustained travel difficult.[135] He moved to Chicago and gradually assumed
control of the National Life Insurance Company,
reportedly earning between $750,000 and $1 million
annually during the 1920s. His interests in mining
continued, however, and he came into contact with
Walter E. Scott (1872–1954), better known as Death
Valley Scotty, a colorful, entrepreneurial, publicity-
prone prospector who had performed with the
Buffalo Bill Wild West Show. Johnson began to
invest in Scotty's mining exploits, and in 1905 they
traveled across Death Valley together, allegedly in
search of Scotty's elusive mine.[136] Johnson found
the area to his liking and around 1915 began to buy
property near Scotty's camp, acquiring some fifteen hundred acres over the next twelve years.[137]
Johnson's land lay not in Death Valley itself but along
Grapevine Canyon, which led northeast out of the

valley near its northern end (fig. 74). There, a little over a mile from the valley and about three thousand feet higher in elevation, he selected his own camp site. It was protectively enclosed by mountains and contained springs supplying abundant water (around two hundred gallons per minute).

By 1921, Johnson had something more permanent in mind. He wrote to Scotty, "We could fix up a very nice place on the Grapevine Ranch. I rather think it would be better to put up a number of separate houses out of stone and cement rather than all in one, but to fix them up right we should have some pipe, as you suggest, and bring our water down from the upper spring, which would give us plenty of water and plenty of pressure, and we could also have a little power for electric light at night."[138] The need for a truck to bring building supplies from the nearest railroad station at Bonnie Clare, Nevada (some twenty miles farther east), was discussed, and Johnson reminded Scotty, "I want to fix up the ranch so that I will have a place to come in and rest up and recuperate."[139] In 1922, construction began on three blocky, stucco-faced, wood-frame buildings: the main house, two stories and thirty-two by ninety-six feet; a garage, and a cookhouse (fig. 75).[140] Scotty, ever seeking publicity, allowed, or perhaps encouraged, local newspapers to describe the project as his and to speculate on its purpose. This might have suited Johnson, who permitted the claims to go unchallenged and may well have been amused by the deception. In July of 1923, one article reported Scotty as building a $150,000 home in the desert "for an unknown purpose"; others refer to the project as Scotty's, but suggest that Johnson is the real backer.[141] By October of 1923, the buildings were described as nearly completed, but as only the first components of "a mysterious project in Grapevine Canyon" that Scotty estimated would cost $500,000; he also reported that Johnson – now acknowledged as his backer, but still not the primary resident – planned to visit the site in November.[142] By December it was reported that something was "about to break at the ranch," but there was no description or mention of any architect.[143]

Specifically how Wright became involved with the project is not known; he may even have volunteered his services in an effort to secure the commission. There is no record of any formal

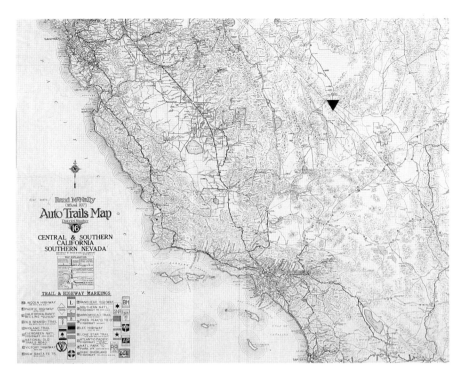

74
Rand McNally Official 1923 Auto Trails Map, District Number 1916. 1923. The Library of Congress, Washington, D.C., Map Division. Black triangle indicates A. M. Johnson site

75
Scotty's Castle, Grapevine Canyon, Death Valley, California. Photograph ca. 1922. U. S. National Park Service, Death Valley National Park

agreement with Johnson, and surviving drawings reflect only preliminary layouts. He was, however, definitely commissioned to design a far larger building for Johnson: the new headquarters for the National Life Insurance Company in Chicago.

In January 1922, Johnson had purchased a large site on Chicago's north side, where he contemplated building "a huge building" into which he would move his company.[144] Alfred MacArthur, who worked for Johnson from 1907 to 1928 and rented space in Wright's partially vacated Oak Park house from around 1911 to 1918,[145] may well have recommended the architect to Johnson. He was one of Wright's loyal admirers who later recommended Wright to Gordon Strong. Johnson formally requested that Wright undertake the design of National Life in July 1924, but in the letter he refers to preliminary sketches for the commission that Wright had already prepared. Documents suggest that discussions regarding the office building were underway by February 1924.[146] At the time, Wright was staying at the Beverly Hills Hotel in Los Angeles, and it was from that hotel, as Johnson later recalled, that they began their trip together into Death Valley.[147]

Johnson, like Wright, was an avid automobile enthusiast, and the idea of a trip across the desert to Johnson's ranch must have been appealing. It was undertaken in the grand style Wright would have appreciated; he and Johnson were in the lead car (a Dodge) followed by a Mrs. Jordan in a Jordan automobile manufactured by her husband. Others in the party included Harold McCourtney and Johnson's chauffeur, and, in Mrs. Jordan's car, Mrs. Nancy Brush Perkins, whose father, of the Brush Motor company, claimed the invention of the arc light. Apparently the two women had no need of a chauffeur; they were described as close friends who had recently made a daring journey together across the Sahara.[148] Recounting the adventure, Wright said "Nature staged a show for us all the way."[149] The trip would have taken a few days, and along the way they stopped one night at Deep Springs College, in a high desert valley several miles north of Death Valley but almost equally remote. An early road map of the area shows Deep Springs to be along the most direct route from Los Angeles to Grapevine Canyon, with the last portion of the journey over a lesser, "unimportant road," probably a dirt trail.[150]

Deep Springs College was founded in 1917 by L. L. Nunn (1859–1925), an old acquaintance of Johnson who had also been active in mining and power interests and had enlisted Johnson as one of the school's backers.[151] The original buildings, which in 1995 look very much as they must have in 1924, resemble designs by Wright's Chicago followers, and the routine of the school, where students divide their time between study and various household or farming tasks, parallels Wright's later development of the Fellowship at Taliesin. Each of the visitors lectured during their brief stay; Wright recounted the story of the Tokyo earthquake and his Imperial Hotel.

While at Deep Springs, Wright was asked to design a house for Martin Sachse, a master mechanic who had emigrated from Germany in 1920, at the age of twenty-seven. Within a year of his arrival in the United States he was hired by Nunn to work at the college, but later went in search of other work in Los Angeles, where he met his future bride. In November 1923, he agreed to return to Deep Springs when Nunn promised to build them a house.[152] Letters from Sachse to his fiancée (whom he was to marry on August 6, 1924) describe Wright's arrival at Deep Springs, which seems to have been on March 1 or 2, 1924.[153] Later that month he was hopeful of discussing details of the house with Wright, who, he thought, was still at Johnson's ranch, but by April 23 he had given up hope of receiving any plans, and moved instead into one of the ranch houses on the property that Nunn made available.[154]

It was naive of Sachse to have expected drawings so quickly. Wright tended to wait until his ideas were firmly in mind before making such a commitment, and this often took a few months. Preliminary drawings for the house that remain in Wright's archive may have been made after Sachse had grown impatient and Nunn had lost interest; understandably, Wright himself seems to have been little involved in the small commission (he later thought it had been for an Albert Sachse and designed in 1922, but he remembered it had been for a place called Deep Springs[155]). A small, cubic structure, its massing is not unlike the Los Angeles block houses, but Wright's notes on the elevation record its construction as sand block and plaster on wood studs (fig. 76). Recessed upper planes of the house were to be faced with colored tiles in white mastic, and awnings extending at the sides were to be blue or white. The plan is T-shaped; along one axis are two bedrooms and service spaces, and along the other a living room and ornamental pool. There is little sense of specific response to the site; the only exceptions are Wright's repeated notation of "sand" in the area around the house and his designation of walled compounds at the back and sides. These seemed more a means of managing an otherwise over-expansive site – as shown, the walls were too low to serve any working purpose, such as keeping out grazing livestock. The compound at the back is noted as being green and raised six inches above the desert, thus clearly establishing a plane of plantings distinct from the surrounding wilds.

Any indecisiveness in the Sachse proposal is more than corrected in Wright's proposal for A. M. Johnson, where the sense of protective compound expands to define an entire valley. "When we arrived at Death Valley," Johnson later wrote, "there were some very plain buildings and I was thinking at that time of improving them . . . Mr. Wright made some sketches of his ideas as to the character of improvements that might be made on the place."[156] This suggests a typical pattern by which Wright – or, indeed, any enterprising architect – would move to secure a commission. The drawings that survive were probably done later; the first record of their completion is a local newspaper article of December 1924, which identified Wright as the architect for Johnson's expanded project and described it as "a veritable Eden of repose for mind and body," reporting that "Mr. Wright has spent the greater part of the fall and early winter in drafting the rough design."[157]

Wright sketched directly over photographs to record his concept; as with his Tahoe proposal, use of the photographs not only facilitated his presentation, but seemed essential in establishing the grand scale of the shaped landscape he envisioned (figs. 77, 78). He developed a series of corbeled concrete block walls that stretched almost one thousand feet

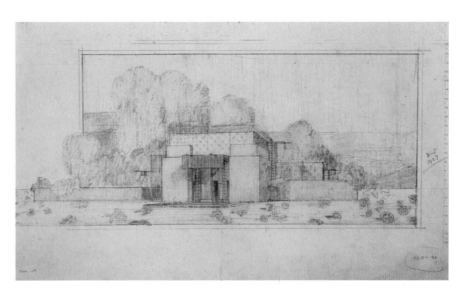

76
Frank Lloyd Wright. *Martin Sachse House, Deep Springs, California. Perspective.* ca. 1924. Pencil and colored pencil on tracing paper, 14 ½ x 24 ½ in. The Frank Lloyd Wright Foundation, 2204.001

77

Frank Lloyd Wright. *A. M. Johnson
Desert Compound, Grapevine Canyon,
California. Perspective sketch.*
ca. 1924. Pencil and colored pencil on
photograph. 11 x 13⅞ in. The Frank
Lloyd Wright Foundation, 2306.022

78
Frank Lloyd Wright. *A. M. Johnson*
Desert Compound, Grapevine Canyon,
California. Perspective sketch.
ca. 1924. Pencil and colored pencil on
photograph, 11 x 14 in. The Frank
Lloyd Wright Foundation, 2306.033

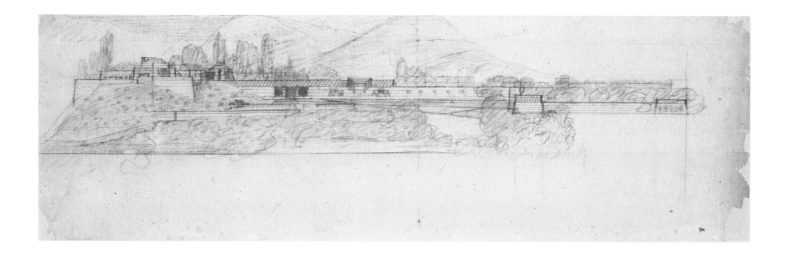

79

Frank Lloyd Wright. *A. M. Johnson Desert Compound, Grapevine Canyon, California. Elevation.* ca. 1924. Graphite and colored pencil on Japanese paper, 9 ⅜ x 30 ⅞ in. The Library of Congress, Washington, D.C., Gift of Donald D. Walker, 152.71

across the site, incorporating the existing buildings into a single composition that embanked the low hill on one side and bridged north over an intervening ravine to a second hill farther within the canyon (fig. 79). There he placed the main house, rotating its component parts so that a second axis, angled at approximately sixty degrees, was established (fig. 80). His siting was brilliant. Johnson's older buildings contributed little to the site and overlooked disappointing views; Wright's proposed house was placed so that it could look directly down Grapevine Canyon toward Death Valley, thus giving reason to the location of the ambitious complex. His composition also reinforces the larger frame of the surrounding mountains, for the axis of the house would have paralleled the range of massive mountains on the far side of the canyon, thus bringing them more obviously into the composition.

Wright also planned a new, more forceful approach to the complex. Instead of the original road that meandered uncertainly along the rim of the low valley in the foreground, he proposed an angled embankment directly across the valley to an opening within the lower wall of the building (fig. 81). Again the result would have been sympathetic to the topography by reinforcing the line of the canyon, and the stronger link with the canyon would in turn have brought the complex more within the ambit of Death Valley. The opening toward which the proposed roadway led was placed between the two hills that Wright's composition would have joined, and this opening led in turn under the bridging element of the building and farther up a ravine that continued behind. The road also joined actively with the transverse axis of the compound, for at the head of the ravine it ramped up around a central pool and back to the higher elevation of the house. As Wright developed the design, this roadway was continued through the house to a platform projecting on the north. There, a dramatic view down the canyon would have been obtained. Like a Japanese stroll garden, the design offered a sequence of framed views to distant features, but in this instance the journey was to be made by automobile rather than on foot. As envisioned, the processional movement would have contributed to the integration of the building complex with its site by making the visual experience of that site an essential component of its architecture.

The large circular fountain indicated within the circle of the roadway, fed from the nearby spring, was developed as the apparent source of water. From the fountain, a channel led down to the front wall of the compound, and as it passed through the wall was developed as a series of cascading pools. These, in turn, related to a series of diagonal irrigation canals that spread across the flat valley in the immediate foreground. Similar to the diagonal lines of green Wright noted in the Japanese landscape, these, too, were life giving, and brought an even larger part of the site into his composition. On site plans, notes indicate that alfalfa and other crops would be planted in this patterned, cultivated plain, a truly managed area defined in clear distinction to the less planned terrain at its perimeter. Wright was developing similar, if less dramatic, patterns at Taliesin. The need for cultivation at Johnson's compound was real, for government regulations required such use of the land in order to establish ownership over older claims.

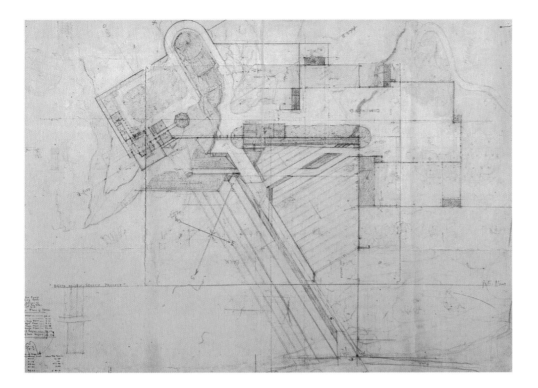

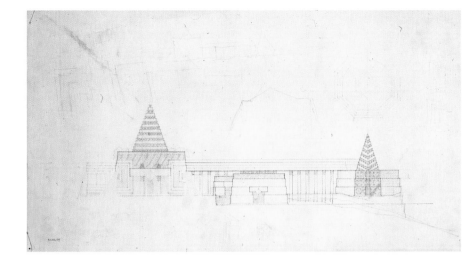

82

Frank Lloyd Wright. A. M. Johnson
Desert Compound, Grapevine Canyon,
California. Elevation and plan sketches.
ca. 1924. Pencil on tracing paper,
15 × 26 ¾ in. The Frank Lloyd Wright
Foundation, 2306.004

The existing buildings were greatly expanded in Wright's scheme and were assigned a variety of uses: plans indicate an enlarged garage, spaces for chickens, dogs, crafts, and cooking in addition to facilities for staff and guests. These buildings are shown joined at the back, near the lower slopes of the hills behind, by a network of walls that enclose what Wright labeled as courts, sand garden, and a major compound. The resulting low-walled terraces would have been cut partly into the hill in a manner that reinforced their geometric form and established a clear area of managed terrain. These cuts would have been balanced by fill used to embank the edges of terraces at the front of the composition, and they were shaped to establish a clear visual boundary.[158] Central to the composition was an octagonal element that effected a smooth transition from the axes of the original buildings to the angled axis of the new dwelling Wright envisioned. Perspectives (such as fig. 81) show design variations of this central element, some flat-roofed and some with a low spire and the suggestion of a stepped roof. The main living area of the house, positioned at the far corner, where it would enjoy the best view, is shown with a prominent hipped roof, presumably corbeled masonry, like the roof of Sullivan's Ryerson Tomb in Chicago's Graceland Cemetery

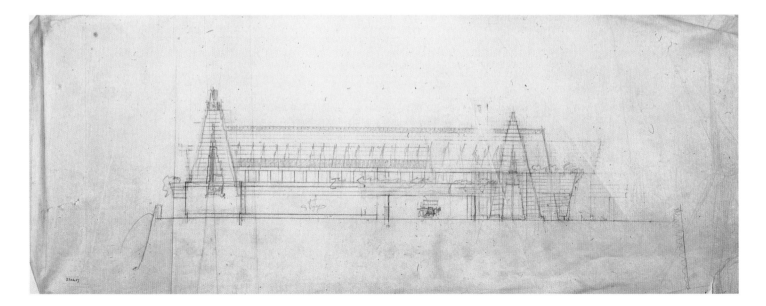

83

Frank Lloyd Wright. A. M. Johnson
Desert Compound, Grapevine Canyon,
California. Elevation showing bridge.
ca. 1924. Pencil on tracing paper,
12 ½ × 30 ⅛ in. The Frank Lloyd Wright
Foundation, 2306.007

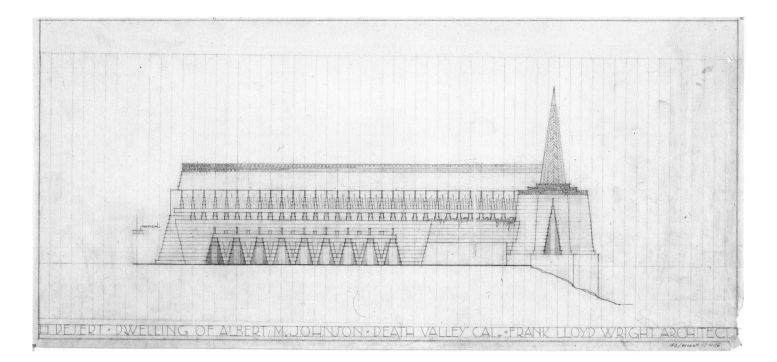

DESERT · DWELLING · OF · ALBERT · M. JOHNSON · DEATH · VALLEY · CAL · FRANK LLOYD WRIGHT ARCHITECT

(1887). Wright had sketched a similar form in the foreground of his second Doheny panorama (see fig. 8). The existing building that Johnson had used as a house is incorporated within the front wall of the lower wing to the right of the new house, articulated with a raised center portion and by corbeled windows flanking large openings at the center; it seems to have been earmarked as a guest house. Details throughout recall decorative bandings and faciated profiles that Wright had developed at Doheny.

As Wright developed the compound's new house at larger scale, the block walls were shown with more intricate banded patterns and with crestings of rich geometric ornament (fig. 82). Doors and tall windows tend to be corbeled, resulting in triangular shapes, and the walls themselves are inclined as a further reflection of corbeled construction (fig. 83). The octagonal element became increasingly emphasized as a focal device, receiving a tall, openwork spire that comes close to recalling a medieval flèche (fig. 84). As the spire grew, the roof of the living area correspondingly diminished in height, so that a clear (but changed) hierarchy was maintained. In what appear to be the final plans, three major components – separated at ground level – are joined at a second level by a system of bridges (fig. 85). At the corner of the L-shaped composition, the open pavilion housing living and dining spaces – nearly one hundred feet long and two stories tall – is expanded by terraces and pools that retain the edge of the hill and lead out toward

84
Frank Lloyd Wright. A. M. Johnson *Desert Compound, Grapevine Canyon, California. Elevation with spire.* ca. 1924. Pencil on tracing paper, 32 × 15¼ in. U. S. National Park Service, Death Valley National Park

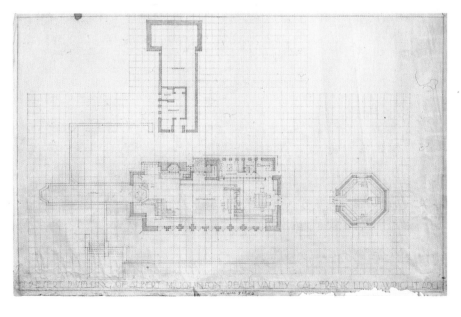

85
Frank Lloyd Wright. A. M. Johnson *Desert Compound, Grapevine Canyon, California. Plan.* ca. 1924. Pencil on tracing paper, 33 × 22 in. U. S. National Park Service, Death Valley National Park

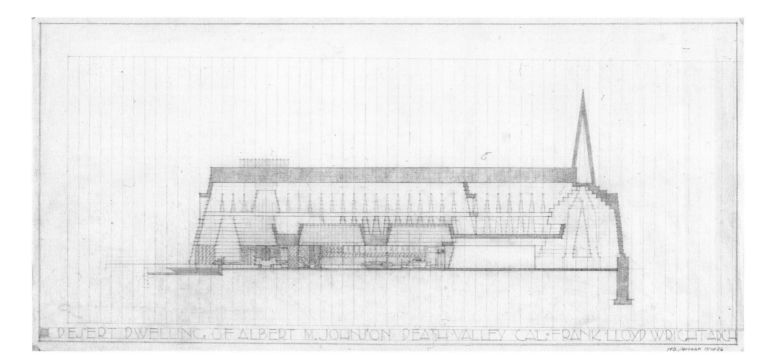

DESERT DWELLING OF ALBERT M. JOHNSON DEATH VALLEY CAL: FRANK LLOYD WRIGHT ARCH

86
Frank Lloyd Wright. *A. M. Johnson
Desert Compound, Grapevine Canyon,
California. Section showing furniture.*
ca. 1924. Pencil on tracing paper,
32 × 14 ¼ in. Courtesy U. S. National
Park Service, Death Valley National Park

major views. Behind, a smaller service wing is built into the slope of the hill, and the octagonal, terraced platform at the outer end of the main pavilion serves as a terminal of the extended layout. The seeming independence of these elements in plan is, of course, an illusion, for they are fully integrated into a single structure at the second level. Bridges not only join the three elements, defining porte-cochères and sheltered terraces below, but also stretch across the living pavilion in two places, creating an interior volume of special complexity (fig. 86).

On several drawings, the octagonal element is noted as a chapel, an understandable reflection of the Johnsons' devotion to religious causes. On what seem to be the final plans, however, the octagonal element is fitted out as a library, and this is how it was identified in a newspaper account.[159] The Johnsons may have felt a private chapel ostentatious, at least in terms of public announcement. For Wright the distinction probably mattered little; the element was essential to the ensemble whatever its use, particularly in its final phase when the added height would have reinforced its compositional function as a pivot. This reflects Wright's attention to elements that related to the larger scale of the site rather than to specific requirements of any building program; for example, the detached pavilion of the Coonley house seemed to have no essential function, nor did a similarly detached ele-

ment of the Henry J. Allen house (Wichita, Kansas, 1917); restoration architects for the latter have assumed a tea house, but its actual purpose is uncertain. At Auldbrass Plantation, as at the Johnson desert compound, Wright also inserted a hexagonal element as a pivotal device; the client wondered what it was for – a tea house? – an aviary? – but realized Wright was determined to build it whatever its use, and acquiesced.[160]

Unlike Wright's more understanding clients, the Johnsons built nothing. Officially cost was cited as the deciding factor; Johnson, while praising Wright as "one of the most able architects and one of the most original and unique of any architects we have had in America," claimed he was reluctant to invest the several hundred thousand dollars Wright's scheme would have cost, admitting at the same time that he eventually spent much more on what was later built.[161] Obviously Wright's design failed to inspire confidence. Witnesses recalled Johnson complaining of its sepulchral appearance – given the coldness of developed drawings prepared for the house, this is not altogether unfair.[162]

Johnson's wife may have had even stronger feelings. Bessie Morris Penniman, from Walnut Creek, California, had briefly attended Stanford University before transferring to Cornell, where she met her future husband; they shared a commitment to religious causes, and were married in 1896. Earlier, while still at Stanford, she had come to know Matt Roy Thompson, a fellow student who studied engineering and became a contractor. According to Thompson's son, his father was briefly engaged to the future Mrs. Johnson. They remained in touch after her marriage to Johnson and, when Wright's designs were put aside, Thompson was hired to add to the buildings that Johnson had earlier erected.[163] For some observers, the vaguely Spanish motifs that he developed resembled the buildings that Mrs. Johnson and Thompson had known at Stanford University. He resurfaced the existing house, built a second, similarly shaped building behind, joined them with a courtyard, and over the years added other elements that included a chimes tower (on the approximate site of Wright's projected chapel) and a gigantic swimming pool (unfinished; fig. 87). Working with him was the designer Charles Alexander MacNeilledge, who had remodeled the Johnsons' Chicago house; Martin D. de Dubovay, an artisan who designed some of the furniture and other decorative elements; and Dewey Kruckeburg, a landscape architect who acceded to Johnson's request for exotic plants.[164] Johnson deeded the castle together with other major assets to the Gospel Foundation (which he had established) in 1947; after Johnson's death in 1948, Scotty remained at the castle until his death in 1954. The Foundation, which was dissolved in 1989, sold the castle to the National Park Service in 1970, and it is now open to the public.[165]

Wright apparently developed another unusual design while working on the Johnson commission. He later annotated the elevation, "Study for desert dwelling for F.LL.W," and dated it 1921, characteristically assigning an improbably early year; as Henry-Russell Hitchcock noted while attempting to sort out the chronology for his pioneering study, *In the Nature of Materials*, Wright's memory "is rather vague as to exact dates."[166] The house is similar in size to the Sachse project and is obviously intended for a desert setting, but it is more sensitively planned for that harsh climate. Like the Johnson desert compound it appears to be of masonry construction — probably concrete block — and has strongly delineated horizontal courses and downwardly stepped openings (fig. 88). As in both the Johnson and Sachse designs, low walls extend out to

87
Aerial view of A. M. Johnson House (Scotty's Castle) designed by Matt Roy Thompson, Grapevine Canyon, California. 1936. Spence Air Photos. The Library of Congress, Washington, D.C., Prints and Photographs Division, Lot 3175, H1585

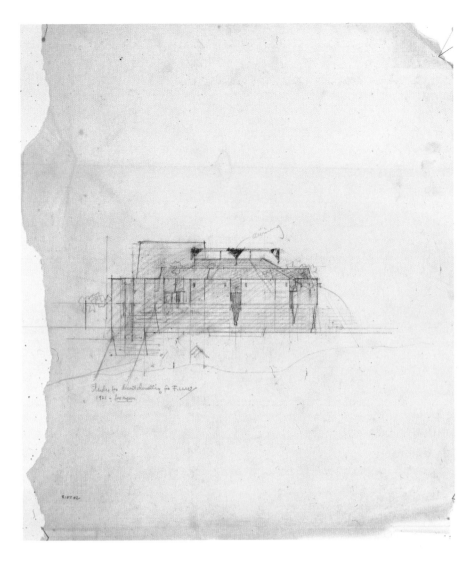

88
Frank Lloyd Wright. *Desert Dwelling for
Frank Lloyd Wright. Elevation.* ca. 1924.
Pencil and colored pencil on tracing
paper, 18¾ × 15½ cm. The Frank Lloyd
Wright Foundation, 2107.002

enclose precincts near the house, and one is labeled
"desert compound" (fig. 89). But unlike both those
designs, here Wright created a special room in clear
response to the desert: a "cool patio," octagonal
in shape with a pool at the center and an oculus
above "open to the sky" and shaded by an awning.
At the perimeter, stepped lines suggest an insulating
earth berm.

By 1924, Wright had clearly been drawn to the
desert as a place of special significance, and he may
have planned the studio as a personal retreat to
be located on a part of Johnson's ranch that might
come to him in conjunction with the commission.
Later designs develop similar architectural themes:
both the Owen D. Young house (part of the San
Marcos project, unbuilt, 1928–29) and the Harold
C. Price house (Paradise Valley, Arizona, 1954)
included cool patio rooms with oculi, not unlike a
Roman atrium. In the Price house, a retirement
dwelling, the desert setting is indeed celebrated by
an architectural enclosure that frames but does not
exclude. Like the larger and earlier Johnson compound, the Price house celebrated its desert location.
In the Johnson compound, the vast terraced elements would have been sympathetic to the natural
terraces of Death Valley itself, and the gentle slopes
near its retaining walls recall the valley's gravel fans
(fig. 90).[167] In this design, Wright intensified landscape elements, and as the natural fans and terraces
give perceptible scale to the immensity of Death
Valley, so, too, do his abstracted reflections of specific place.

The Gordon Strong Automobile Objective

In his proposal for the Johnson desert compound,
Wright had continued to show how roadways
could intensify relationships between buildings and
their surroundings, with mobility itself emerging as a
manifestation of human habitation. However uncertain the commission, it was sufficient to engender a
proposal that went beyond either Doheny or Tahoe
in suggesting how a special kind of architectural
unity could be achieved at a scale appropriate to
the twentieth century. Gordon Strong offered an
unambiguous commission, and automobiles were to
be incorporated as a major feature at the client's
request, providing Wright with a remarkable opportunity to further develop his ideas.

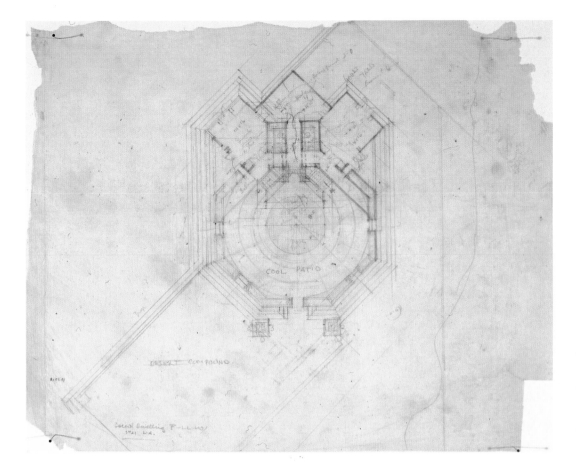

89
Frank Lloyd Wright. *Desert Dwelling for Frank Lloyd Wright. Plan.* ca. 1924. Pencil on tracing paper, 15 ⅜ × 18 ⅜ in. The Frank Lloyd Wright Foundation, 2107.001

90
Aerial view of Death Valley, California, looking east from Bad Water to Dante's View. 1936. Spence Air Photos. The Library of Congress, Washington, D.C., Prints and Photographs Division, Lot 3175, CL 21073

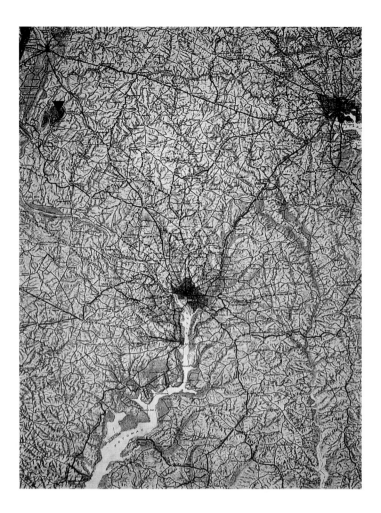

Like A. M. Johnson, Gordon Strong (1869–1954) was born in the Midwest to wealthy parents. He followed his father in combining a career in law with real-estate speculation, and in 1900 founded his own company in Chicago, devoting himself to the development and management of office buildings and amassing a considerable fortune.[168] In 1902, while exploring areas around Washington, D.C., he reportedly became captivated by Sugarloaf Mountain and began to buy up the tracts of land that comprised its undeveloped setting (figs. 91, 92). His father's death in 1911 prompted more specific action; as a condition of the will, a large portion of the estate went to establish the Henry Strong Educational Fund, and Gordon Strong capitalized on his control of the fund by establishing a school for boys on the property.[169] To house the school he began construction that same year on a large and elaborate house designed by Percy Ash of Philadelphia. Only one wing had been completed when, a few years later, legal action by one of his sisters led to a redistribution of the estate, and funds for the school were greatly diminished.[170] The completed wing became a home for Strong and his wife, Louise.

91
USGS highway map. 1922. The Frank
Lloyd Wright Foundation, 2305.037.
Black triangle indicates Sugarloaf
Mountain site

92
Property in Frederick County, Maryland,
of Mr. Gordon Strong. Plot plan. 1909.
Print, 21 x 17 in. The Frank Lloyd
Wright Foundation, 2505.038

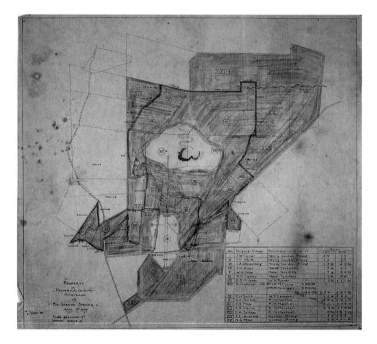

At an elevation of 1,282 feet, Sugarloaf, in Frederick County, Maryland, is the highest peak in the area and a commanding presence among the low, rolling hills (fig. 93). According to legend, it was named by hunters who noted its resemblance to the shape of sugar loaves then in common use as a means of packaging. It served as a landmark during the French and Indian War and as a lookout during the Civil War.[171] At its base lies rough, stony land unsuitable for agriculture.[172] Near its summit, the mountain is capped by a massive layer of white quartzite, which has formed steep cliffs on the west and south sides; a lower layer, stained purple, projects to form additional ledges on the upper slopes.[173]

After the First World War, Strong began to consider other possibilities for the development of Sugarloaf Mountain, and during the summer of 1924, with Alfred MacArthur, met with Wright at Taliesin. The specifics of what they discussed or how Strong was led to Wright seem not to have been recorded, but the presence of MacArthur suggests that he was the intermediary. MacArthur would have been known to Strong through marriage to one of Strong's nieces,[174] and had, as earlier sug-

gested, already led his employer, A. M. Johnson, to Wright. Given their mutual interests and prominence in the Chicago business community, Johnson and Strong must have been known to each other, and Johnson might have promoted Wright. Clearly Strong was consulted about the design of the National Life Insurance Company building; in his first letter to Wright, dated September 2, 1924, Strong offers advice on the layout of high-rise office buildings while mentioning that another letter would follow regarding "our Sugar Loaf, Maryland, project."[175]

By late September 1924, Strong had fixed upon a challenging program that he conveyed in the form of a contract; signalling agreement, Wright countersigned.[176] Strong wanted to erect "a structure on the summit of Sugar Loaf Mountain" that would "serve as an objective for short motor trips," primarily from Washington and Baltimore, each a relatively short drive away. The degree of use he imagined was impressive: parking for two hundred to five hundred cars within the structure itself, and parking for an additional one thousand cars on the gently sloped area immediately north of the

93
View of Sugarloaf Mountain, Maryland, after 1911. Stronghold Incorporated

summit. People were expected to drive out for the day, mostly for picnics; light refreshments would be provided as well as a restaurant. The enjoyment of views from the mountaintop was to be a primary feature, and for this purpose Wright was to provide what Strong specified as "three sorts of space": open terraces, covered galleries, and interior areas with generous windows; "the element of thrill, as well as the element of beauty" were to be part of the experience. The structure itself was to have its own summit with 360-degree views, and it was to include "overhanging salients" on the cliffs. Two dance floors were to be provided, one inside and one out, and a few bedrooms (approximately thirty, including staff accommodations) in addition to kitchen facilities and other services. Strong also specified what he wanted in the way of appearance: "(a) To be striking, impressive, so that everyone hearing of the place will want to come once. (b) To be beautiful, satisfying, so that those coming will want to come again, periodically, indefinitely. (c) To be enduring, so that the structure will constitute a permanent and creditable monument, instead of proving a merely transitory novelty."

For preliminary sketches (including changes that Strong reserved a right to request) Wright would be paid $1,500, and the sketches would become Strong's property. When Strong had raised at least $20,000 from outside investors, Wright would be paid an additional $1,500, and if Wright's design was judged satisfactory, Strong would "use all reasonable efforts" to convince his investors to retain Wright as architect (for the standard fee of ten percent of construction costs, less the $3,000 he would have received by that time).

Wright must have been greatly pleased to be working for two of Chicago's wealthiest businesspeople and to be involved with buildings of such scale — a skyscraper for Johnson (which would remain unbuilt) and an extraordinary recreation facility for Strong. With these fees, together with what he might earn from Johnson's desert compound (which he was then also designing), he might well have dreamed of raising sufficient capital to invest in his Tahoe venture. The very nature of the Strong commission would also have held special appeal, for in addition to reflecting his own fascination with automobiles

and his love of nature, it was more democratic in spirit than his other work of the time. Europeans had noted Wright's work as being primarily for the wealthy,[177] as if, in America, a practicing architect could easily choose his clients. Now he had the chance to demonstrate a true sense of social equality, for by then automobiles were relatively cheap, and in the Washington area as in Los Angeles ownership was widespread, so that his design would be accessible to a broad segment of the populace. Parkways were being developed then as scenic drives, facilitating the use of automobiles for recreational purposes,[178] and the idea of an automobile objective on Sugarloaf Mountain must have seemed surprisingly realistic.

On September 27, 1924, Strong proposed to take Wright and Alfred MacArthur with him to visit the site.[179] Wright was effusive in his thanks for the few days he and "the meteoric Alfred" spent there, saying Strong deserved "the best of everything in this life."[180] By early November, Wright was thinking of a large, angular garage; he sketched it in a sand dune near the Wisconsin River at Taliesin to show Eric Mendelsohn, who was visiting at the time. Mendelsohn described it as having "a fantastic superstructure" and drew a corresponding sketch to illustrate a current project of his own; in accord with his distinguished German practice at the time, it was contrastingly curvilinear.[181] As Mark Reinberger has reasoned, the parking structure could only have been the project for Gordon Strong.[182]

It pleased Mendelsohn that Wright knew of his work; he had learned of it, Mendelsohn wrote, through Richard Neutra. Neutra had worked for Mendelsohn in Germany from 1921 to 1922 before going to the United States with the objective of working for Wright, and this he briefly did, from August 1924 until the following February.[183] Wright came to identify Mendelsohn's work with curvilinear forms. Writing later of the nature of concrete, he described it as "a plastic material, that as yet has found no medium of expression that will allow it to take plastic form"; Wright's approach had been to discipline that plasticity through the use of his specially designed, richly patterned concrete blocks, but he recognized that a larger potential existed, and as a worthy example of what he termed "the purely 'plastic' structure" he cited Mendelsohn's

Einstein Tower (Potsdam, designed 1917–20, constructed 1920–21).[184] As Wright developed his design for Sugarloaf, it is difficult not to assume that he was influenced by Mendelsohn's work, and that he determined to develop a parallel approach that would be distinctively his.

A few days after Mendelsohn's departure, Wright invited Strong and his wife to Taliesin for Thanksgiving; Alfred MacArthur would also be there, and Wright promised that he would "try to have something on the mountain top by then."[185] Wright was spared the immediate necessity of committing his ideas to paper, however, for Strong replied that work would prevent him from accepting. In the same letter, Strong recommended information on ramped parking structures that he remembered having read: ramps should be sloped between fifteen and twenty percent, widths varied depending on whether the ramp were straight or curved, and so on.[186] The information corresponds exactly to an article on ramped parking structures that had recently appeared and that is almost certainly its source.[187] In that article, well illustrated with diagrams and photographs of existing structures, the ramp is shown to be more efficient than the elevator in multi-story parking structures and praised as "nothing more or less than an artificial hill, and consequently. . . man's first means of moving from one level to another." A helical form "in which the whole floor of the garage slopes" is described as the latest and most efficient development. The article was readily available to Wright and may have helped him determine his own design.

Within a week of receiving the information on ramped structures, Wright questioned the scale of the site plan he had been sent. A sometimes acrimonious debate with Strong unfolded over the next two months, and it became clear that a variety of errors had contributed to a confusing situation, one that would be more amusing if not for the critical question of dimensions, for Wright believed the summit to be approximately four times larger in area than did Strong. In the midst of the debate, and somewhat to Strong's consternation, Wright announced that he had his scheme in mind: "You wanted something *rational* but *unforgettable* and reasonably *economical*. Well, this would be the talk of the world – as is the Leaning Tower of Pisa, the Hanging Gardens of Babylon, King Solomon's Temple, King Tutankhamens tomb, etc. etc. And it is all delightfully simple and sensible. It is fearfully difficult to draw on account of the curving ramps and eats up office time like a devouring dragon. . . .With all its simplicity it is a difficult thing to draw – more so than to build eventually."[188] Alarmed, Strong urged Wright to stop work until the scale was verified and a plaster model of the site was completed. Wright replied that his scheme would be "applicable to the mountain top" whichever of the two debated scales it was.[189] Eventually Strong was proven correct and Wright adjusted his design accordingly.[190]

A preliminary sketch by Wright that must be one of the first he drew is indeed astonishingly simple in appearance while remarkably complicated in its implications: a helical spiral placed at the edge of the mountain (fig. 94). A roadway circles clockwise in four circuits to the top, where a crossover allowed cars to return back down a descending ramp contained within the structure. The diagrammatic plan indicates a columned structure, and in both plan and perspective a thin, metallic spire rises from an open well at the center. A section and elevation in Wright's hand, together with other diagrammatic plans, show this spire rising from deep within the central well, with spaces for parking along the descending interior ramp (fig. 95), and he has noted key dimensions: the spiral structure was to be one hundred feet tall and 270 feet across at its base.

Given his presumed familiarity with curvilinear structures, Neutra would have been a logical choice among Wright's assistants to develop the scheme, and two surviving plan diagrams of the first scheme appear to reflect his hand.[191] They accommodate Strong's program remarkably well. On one plan – apparently the lower level, with an indication of plantings and pools at the perimeter – "coming cars" approach the spiral ramp from the upper right, and "garage going cars" – presumably heading for the one-thousand-car parking area specified by Strong – exit at the lower left (fig. 96). A dance hall is placed at the center, with a foyer leading to an entrance terrace at the upper left, and at the lower right are steps labeled "auditorium." A bridge across the dance hall links to a water garden and overlook at the upper left. In the second plan – probably the

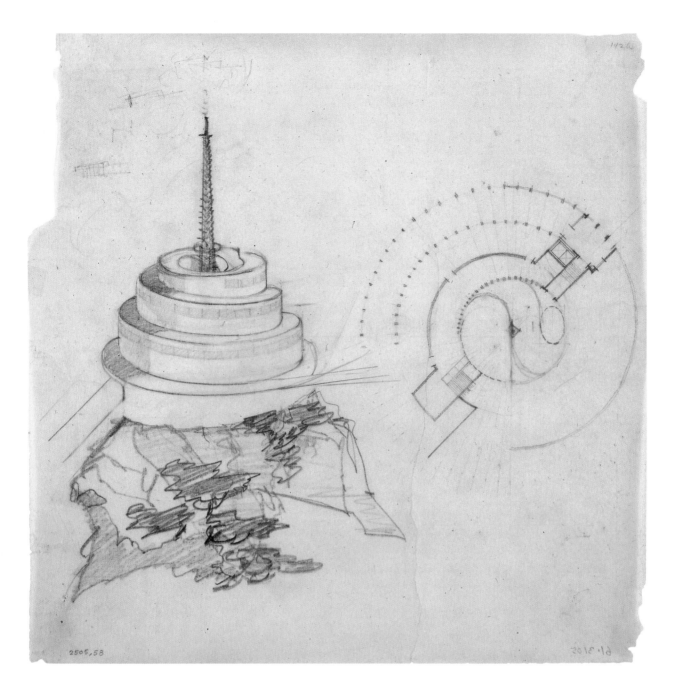

94
Frank Lloyd Wright. *Gordon Strong
Automobile Objective, Sugarloaf
Mountain, Maryland. Perspective sketch
with spire and plan.* 1924. Pencil on
tracing paper, 11 ⅜ × 11 in. The Frank
Lloyd Wright Foundation, 2505.058

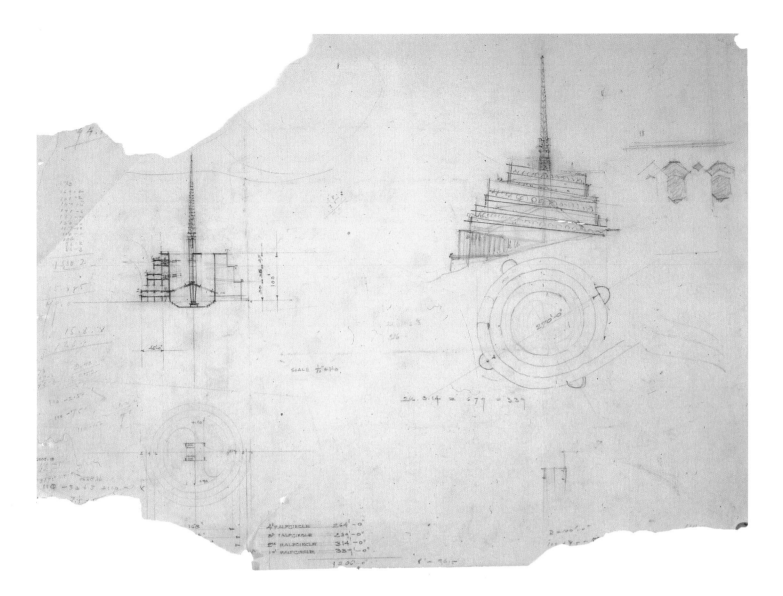

95
Frank Lloyd Wright. *Gordon Strong Automobile Objective, Sugarloaf Mountain, Maryland. Section and plan sketches.* 1924. Pencil on tracing paper, 14 ¾ × 20 ⅛ in. The Frank Lloyd Wright Foundation, 2505.018

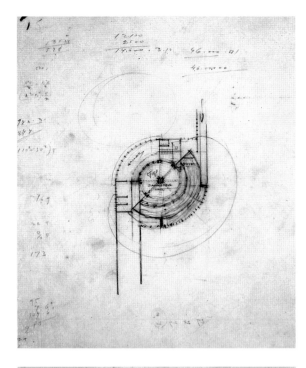

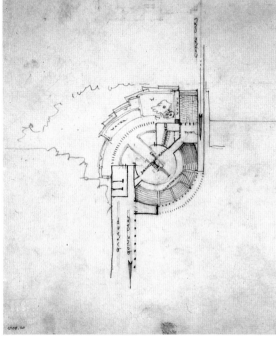

97
Frank Lloyd Wright. *Gordon Strong
Automobile Objective, Sugarloaf
Mountain, Maryland, Upper Level, with
Gallery and Stage. Plan.* 1924. Pencil
on tracing paper, 13 × 10 in. The Frank
Lloyd Wright Foundation, 2505.019

96
Frank Lloyd Wright. *Gordon Strong
Automobile Objective, Sugarloaf
Mountain, Maryland, Lower Level, with
Ramps, Terrace, Dance Hall, and
Auditorium. Plan.* 1924. Pencil on tracing
paper, 13 × 10 in. The Frank Lloyd
Wright Foundation, 2505.020

upper level (fig. 97) — a gallery and stage are located
at the upper left, and the diagonal struts shown
bracing the spire in section are depicted as dotted
lines immediately above, where, presumably, they
would also serve to frame a glazed roof.

The purpose of the spire is uncertain; like the
octagonal element in the Johnson desert compound,
it may have been something Wright wanted as part
of the composition whatever its function. Some have
suggested that it was a mast for dirigibles, believ-
able in terms of events at the time — the transcontinental flight of the *Shenandoah* in October 1924
had inspired the building of many such masts — but
as rendered, it seems structurally lacking for this
purpose. It is more likely a radio tower — such towers
were also much in the news at the time, especially
following the greatly heralded broadcast of national
election returns in November 1924.[192]

Two other sketches of the first phase are
similar in form and, like the others, sufficiently generalized as to position so that, as Wright claimed, the
exact size of the mountain's summit was not critical.
One sketch, apparently unpublished until now (fig.
98), remains with Gordon Strong's papers (see
n. 175). It is the only drawing to show the structure
in relation to the entire mountain and is remarkably
Mendelsohnian, as if Wright were determined to
show that he, too, could produce such ravishingly
beautiful images. The other sketch (fig. 99) is more
generalized as to location and shows only three
loops rather than four; there is no spire, and the
ascending ramp is cantilevered over the descending
ramp below, as Wright would develop in later
phases of the design.

During the weeks that followed Wright developed
his concept. More drawings survive than is usual
in these years of Wright's career, suggesting that he
indeed had difficulty in resolving details of such
complicated shapes. It was his first major essay in
circular geometry. In earlier designs, such elements
had been modestly scaled or incorporated within
conventional layouts, or they had been restricted
to decorative features, as the murals at Midway
Gardens. For his automobile objective, they became
the fundamental basis of form. The geometry
was as natural a choice for the movement of automobiles as his hexagonal forms had been for the
movement of barges; in both instances, major

98
Frank Lloyd Wright. *Gordon Strong Automobile Objective, Sugarloaf Mountain, Maryland. Perspective sketch with cover sheet.* 1924. Graphite and colored pencil on Japanese paper, 21½ × 32⅜ in. (with mat). Stronghold Incorporated

99
Frank Lloyd Wright. *Gordon Strong Automobile Objective, Sugarloaf Mountain, Maryland. Perspective sketch without spire.* 1924. Pencil on tracing paper, 10¾ × 8⅜ in. The Frank Lloyd Wright Foundation, 2505.023

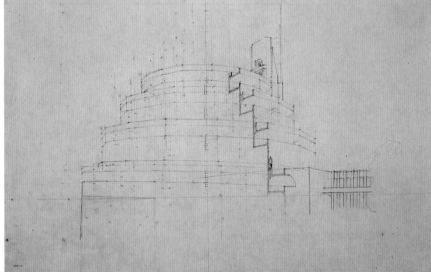

100
Frank Lloyd Wright. *Gordon Strong
Automobile Objective, Sugarloaf
Mountain, Maryland, Segmented Ramp.
Perspective*. ca. 1925. Pencil on tracing
paper, 19 × 16 in. The Frank Lloyd
Wright Foundation, 2505.054

101
Frank Lloyd Wright. *Gordon Strong
Automobile Objective, Sugarloaf
Mountain, Maryland, Segmented Ramp.
Perspective with section*. ca. 1925.
Pencil and colored pencil on tracing
paper, 16 × 25 in. The Frank Lloyd
Wright Foundation, 2505.015

themes of Wright's later career were initiated, and spaces new to architecture resulted.

As the design evolved, the dance hall at the center was replaced by a single large stage and the vertical accent of the central mast was shifted to a stair tower at the side. In one variation he translated the curved ramps into polygonal segments (figs. 100, 101), but he quickly returned to a fully circular form. The structure remained one of continuous ramps supported on freestanding columns. In some drawings the roof of the stage was given an elaborate profile (fig. 102), and in others he suggested placing glass Luxfer prisms within portions of the ramps and dome.[193] In addition to the auditorium, other facilities included restaurants, lobbies, and various services. As in the first scheme, parking is indicated within the structure along the descending ramp. Wright now fixed the position of the structure with exactitude, placing it on the southern edge of the summit. Linear walkways link the central rotunda to nearby features of the site, and approach ramps lead up from the gently sloping northern face of the mountain (fig. 103). Adjoining the lobby of the theater, a long, curved gallery opens out above the steep cliffs on the south; its piers were developed as a special feature in the perspectives.

Wright invited Strong to come to Taliesin and review his plans in April 1925. Irritated to be called away from work for such a time-consuming journey, Strong insisted that Wright send the drawings to Chicago for his inspection, reminding him that he had been generous in setting no deadlines for completion and could wait a bit more, if necessary.[194] Wright felt slighted by Strong's businesslike response, wanting to explain the scheme in person; he offered to deliver the drawings to Chicago himself. Before a meeting could be arranged, Taliesin burned for the second time, on April 20. Understandably, Wright delayed his trip, writing to Strong that it was "really too painful . . . to see anyone I like or who likes me."[195]

During the months that followed, Strong waited patiently while Wright continued to rework his design. He devised a better, more integrated scheme in which the central dome was expanded to fill much of the interior of the ramped structure. One drawing compares the two sections; erasures

102

Frank Lloyd Wright. *Gordon Strong
Automobile Objective, Sugarloaf
Mountain, Maryland, Theater. Section.*
1925. Pencil on tracing paper,
14 × 20⅞ in. The Frank Lloyd Wright
Foundation, 2505.029

103

Frank Lloyd Wright. *Gordon Strong
Automobile Objective, Sugarloaf
Mountain, Maryland, Theater. Plan.* 1925.
Pencil on tracing paper, 17 × 26 in.
The Frank Lloyd Wright Foundation,
2505.011

104

Frank Lloyd Wright. *Gordon Strong
Automobile Objective, Sugarloaf
Mountain, Maryland, Planetarium Look-
ing Southwest, Theater Looking
Southeast. Sections.* 1925. Pencil on
tracng paper, 19 × 42 in. The Frank
Lloyd Wright Foundation, 2505.034

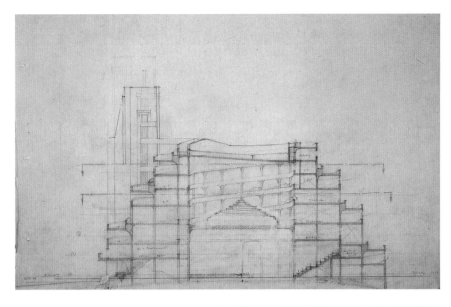

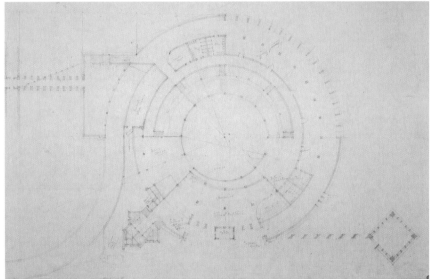

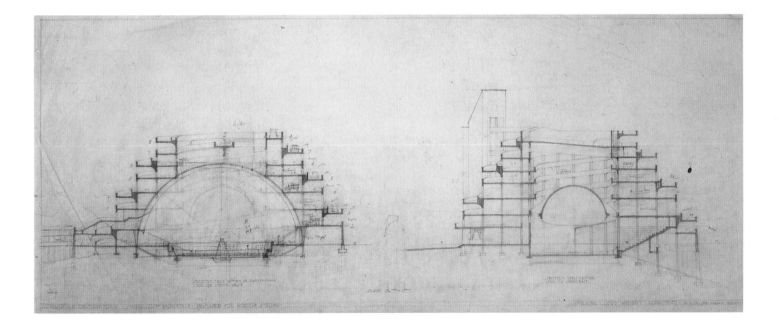

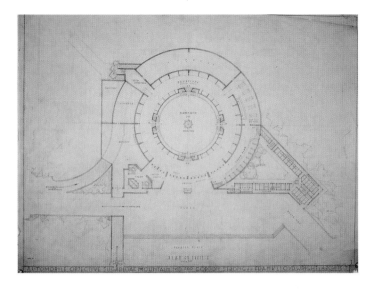

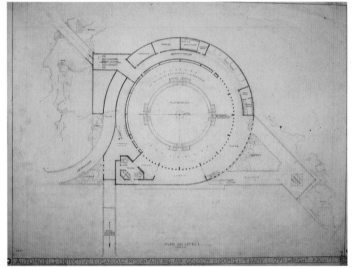

105
Frank Lloyd Wright. *Gordon Strong
Automobile Objective, Sugarloaf
Mountain, Maryland, Level 0. Plan.* 1925.
Pencil on tracing paper, 24 ¾ × 31 ⅞ in.
The Frank Lloyd Wright Foundation,
2505.041

106
Frank Lloyd Wright. *Gordon Strong
Automobile Objective, Sugarloaf
Mountain, Maryland, Level 1. Plan.* 1925.
Pencil on tracing paper, 24 ¾ × 31 ⅞ in.
The Frank Lloyd Wright Foundation,
2505.042

show that Wright had reworked an earlier drawing
of the theater scheme to achieve this end (fig. 104).
Although the drawing does not conform in size
or title with the final presentation drawings Wright
developed, he must have shown it to Strong to
help explain the changed program he proposed,
for it was the title of this drawing, "Automobile
Observatory," rather than the next and more pervasive title of "Automobile Objective," to which
Strong referred in later correspondence.

With a diameter of 150 feet, the dome was
now a major, centralized feature. The disparate
structures of a separate, small dome within a hollow
spiral were now made one, and the architectural
ambiguity of stepped seats crowded beneath a portion of a ramp gave way to a majesterial, unified
volume. Wright suggested the domed space be
used as a planetarium, and this idea must have held
special appeal. The crowning feature of the summit
now contained a major representation of the cosmos
itself; like an Indian stupa complete with provision
for ritual circumambulation, it united earthly and
celestial worlds. Yet in place of the visible central
axis of that perhaps coincidental prototype, Wright
substituted a small garden on the very top of the
structure, an intensification of worldly nature. The
proposed optical projector for the planetarium was
also timely; the first such instrument had only been
completed in Germany in 1924 and had been formally inaugurated in Munich with much fanfare in
March of 1925.[196]

In late August 1925, Wright telephoned Strong's
office to arrange the promised meeting. Strong suggested gathering a small group of friends for the
event "as a tribute to an artist rather than an entertainment for a client."[197] Flattered, Wright agreed, and
invitations were sent to five Chicago colleagues.[198]
A few days later Wright presented his scheme; he
was no doubt cognizant of the importance of convincing Strong and other backers of its validity, and
had expended special effort in preparing his set
of some thirteen drawings. Within the context of
Wright's practice, this was unusually complete for
such an early stage of a design (figs. 105–113).

The siting of the structure and its general configuration had not changed from the earlier theater
scheme, but internal arrangements were substantially different. Automobiles would approach from
the lower slopes to the north, ramping up and

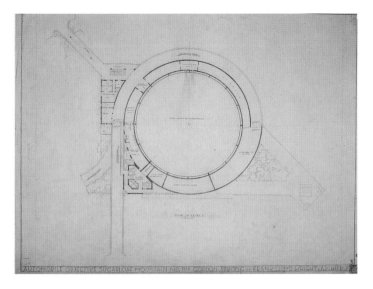

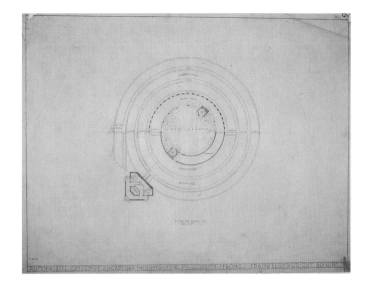

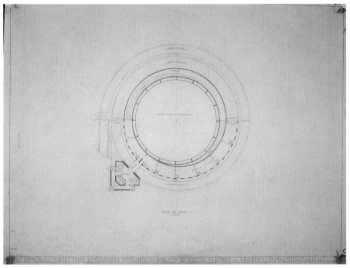

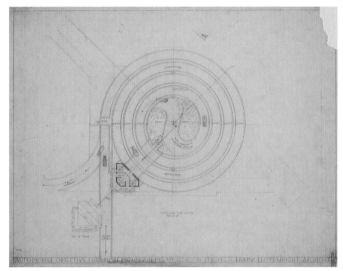

107
Frank Lloyd Wright. *Gordon Strong Automobile Objective, Sugarloaf Mountain, Maryland, Level 2. Plan.* 1925. Pencil on tracing paper, 24 ¾ × 31 ⅞ in. The Frank Lloyd Wright Foundation, 2505.043

108
Frank Lloyd Wright. *Gordon Strong Automobile Objective, Sugarloaf Mountain, Maryland, Level 4. Plan.* 1925. Pencil on tracing paper, 24 ¾ × 31 ⅞ in. The Frank Lloyd Wright Foundation, 2505.045

109
Frank Lloyd Wright. *Gordon Strong Automobile Objective, Sugarloaf Mountain, Maryland, Level 7. Plan.* 1925. Pencil on tracing paper, 24 ¾ × 31 ⅞ in. The Frank Lloyd Wright Foundation, 2505.048

110
Frank Lloyd Wright. *Gordon Strong Automobile Objective, Sugarloaf Mountain, Maryland, Top Level. Plan.* 1925. Pencil on tracing paper, 24 ⅜ × 31 ½ in. The Frank Lloyd Wright Foundation, 2505.049

past a stair tower to begin their circular ascent (see fig. 105). At the top, passengers could step out on a roof terrace over the stair tower to contemplate from a stationary position the view that they had just experienced during their drive (see fig. 110). From the terrace, they could descend directly down the tower, or stroll along the inside of the ramp on a special walkway raised above the adjacent automobile ramp so that views out over the landscape would be unimpeded (see fig. 109). From the walkway, or from bridges that linked the tower with the main structure, they would move past a dazzling array of lounges and restaurants, all opening to the views through windows above the walk itself (see fig. 108). Near the bottom, two additional bridges led to special overlooks: on the southeast, to a terrace built over a large rock outcropping (see fig. 106), and on the northwest, across a natural chasm to a second summit (see fig. 107). This last prospect was to be further dramatized by a pool and waterfall that Wright proposed. Returning from these overlooks, visitors would enter through lobbies to a grand esplanade encircling the base of the dome and overlooking the planetarium floor directly

below. There, surrounding the optical projector, was to be a circular gallery containing aquaria and natural history exhibits (see fig. 105).

Cars descending from the top circled back under the cantilevered ascent ramp with views out over a low balustrade; no view-obstructing columns were needed. Near the bottom, cars exited on a curved ramp that led under the approach and to remote parking (see fig. 107). Additional parking was provided immediately to the north of the building's ground-level loggia, which could be entered directly without need of making the ascent (see fig. 105). In the final scheme, all parking within the spiral structure had been eliminated. The developed height of the structure was approximately 112 feet above the summit, and retaining walls on the steep southern slopes extended down an additional thirty feet. The main spiral was over 190 feet across at its base, and with the added bridges extended more than four hundred feet across the summit.

Perspectives suggest the monumentality of the scheme. The stair tower and bridges effectively moderated its circular form, serving to integrate it both visually and physically with the precipitous terrain. Characteristically, Wright had not shied from a difficult site, but instead placed the structure on the very edge of the summit so that it seemed to complete it. The bridge over the chasm extended this sense of structured land by reconnecting and strengthening elements of the terrain. Never one to be bound by narrow interpretations of his own or anyone else's rules, he had placed the building on the hill, but still made it very much of the hill; indeed, he made it the hill itself. It was a building devoted to the movement of both automobiles and people; the spiral not only symbolized that movement, but contained it, much as the linear bridges provided esplanades to connect pedestrians with the natural surroundings they had come to behold. In two perspectives that were part of the presentation set, a draftsman rendered the mountainside with a crystalline imagery, as if aware of its quartz underpinnings (see figs. 112, 113). Both perspectives and elevations show the concrete walls punctuated with a fretwork of angular openings; these had been sketched on the very first perspectives, and were one means by which Wright gave character to a material that, he said, "aesthetically . . . has neither song nor story."[199]

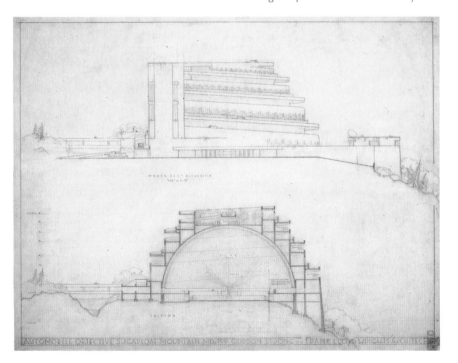

111
Frank Lloyd Wright. *Gordon Strong Automobile Objective, Sugarloaf Mountain, Maryland. Elevation and section.* 1925. Pencil on tracing paper, 24¾ x 31¼ in. The Frank Lloyd Wright Foundation, 2505.050

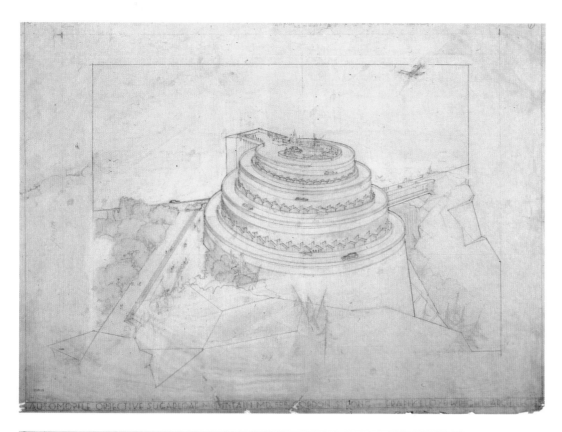

112

Frank Lloyd Wright. *Gordon Strong Automobile Objective, Sugarloaf Mountain, Maryland. Aerial perspective.* 1925. Pencil and colored pencil on tracing paper, 21 ¼ × 31 ¼ in. The Frank Lloyd Wright Foundation, 2505.052

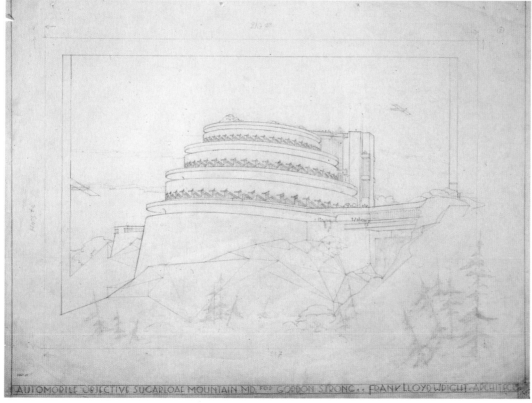

113

Frank Lloyd Wright. *Gordon Strong Automobile Objective, Sugarloaf Mountain, Maryland. Perspective from below.* 1925. Pencil and colored pencil on tracing paper, 32 × 25 in. The Frank Lloyd Wright Foundation, 2505.053

114
Frank Lloyd Wright. *Gordon Strong
Automobile Objective, Sugarloaf
Mountain, Maryland. Perspective.* 1925.
Pencil and colored pencil on tracing
paper, 19 ⅞ × 30 ⅛ in. The Frank Lloyd
Wright Foundation, 2505.039

Several perspectives show evidence of having been reworked (for example, fig. 114); apparently the taller stair tower and gallery piers of the second scheme have been erased to bring the design into conformity with Wright's later thinking. Significantly, he changed the structure from one of point supports to one of thin shell construction, with the ramps and continuous fin walls partly supported by the dome itself. An inner shell shown in section (see fig. 111) might signal the presence of strengthening ribs, but could also represent the projection screen for the observatory. It was a daring structure without exact precedent. Spectacular concrete bridges designed by the Swiss engineer Robert Maillart (1872–1940), such as the Valtschielbach Bridge (1925),[200] suggest a similar structure in section, and perhaps such a structure could be rotated to create the three-dimensional equivalent that Wright now suggested, but he was pushing the technology of his times to its very limits and perhaps beyond. Whether it could have been built as designed, and what its cost might have been, were not, however, to be determined.

The immediate reactions to Wright's presentation were not recorded, but Wright waited anxiously for Strong's response. He offered to make changes if requested and, clearly in financial need, added that he was "carrying on my house-building under great difficulties. No doubt a foolish thing to do. But I must do it."[201] More than a week after the presentation Strong wrote that he had "not yet come to any definite opinions . . . but . . . the perspectives are very attractive bits of artistic work."[202] Fearful of this implication, Wright responded that he hoped Strong would "not let the 'artistic' character of the sketches prejudice you against the scheme" and added more about the difficulties of trying to rebuild his house, ending his letter with the plea, "If ever a feller needed a friend – I need one now."[203]

By mid-October, Strong had decided against Wright's proposal. He criticized it as an "automobile observatory. . . . without any relation to its surroundings. . . . highly formalized and standardized." Clearly not in accord with Wright's appreciation of the recreational potential of the automobile, he complained that things were reversed, and that the cars should be on the inside and the people on terraces outside. No doubt particularly insulting to

Wright was Strong's claim that he had adapted the Tower of Babel for his design; Strong added that while he would offer no opinion as to whether or not Wright was the world's greatest architect, he was willing to promote him as the "world's greatest archaeologist and philologist."[204] Wright's response, understandably bitter, also offered further explanations. To counter the assertion of inspiration from the Tower of Babel, he reminded Strong of the commonality of the helix as demonstrated by such everyday examples as the screw, the spiral spring, a snail shell, and the egg beater, and he described his concept as "the natural snail-crown of the great couchant lion . . . grown up from his mountain head, the very quality of its movement, rising and adapting itself to the uninterrupted movement of people sitting comfortably in their own cars in a novel circumstance with the whole landscape revolving about them, as exposed to view as though they were in an aeroplane."[205] Affirming his belief in the automobile as a theme underlying the design, he added that an automobile objective "should make a novel entertainment out of the machine itself" and, perhaps sincerely, offered to redesign the project as Strong had suggested, with the cars inside and people on outer terraces.[206] Strong, it seems, did not reply.

Wright, in suggesting his own precedents, demonstrated the universality of the spiral. He might also have mentioned other adaptations of the form to buildings, for while the Tower of Babel survived only in the form of fanciful illustrations, other examples were real. In particular the Russian Constructivists had experimented with its potential; most impressive was Vladimir Tatlin's design for a Monument to the Third International (1919–20). Wright would surely have been drawn to its design.[207] As Ford Peatross has discovered, other proposals had been made for spiral parking garages, notably one by Konstantin Melnikov. Spiral buildings were thus not unprecedented at the time, but Wright's was probably the most daring.

As to earlier examples, Wright, with his love of mythologies surrounding the *Arabian Nights*, must have had a high regard for the ziggurat-inspired minaret at the Great Mosque of Samarra (842–846). It provided a point of departure for his Monument to Haroun-al-Rashid (Baghdad, 1957, unbuilt; fig.

115; monument is at lower tip of island), and he acknowledged shaping the natural island proposed as a setting for the monument to enhance its image.[208] Some have suggested that he might have been influenced by a Pre-Columbian watch tower; a drawing depicting its spiral form had indeed appeared in 1856, but in an obscure publication.[209] If Pre-Columbian inspiration lies behind the Gordon Strong automobile objective, it would probably have been general rather than specific; certainly early illustrations of the great pyramids at Teotihuacán suggest a similarly commanding completion of landscape, and drawings of circular towers on the San Juan River show circular forms poised above high cliffs.[210]

Overlooks that Gordon Strong built along the road up Sugarloaf Mountain suggest the more conservative image he may have had in mind for his automobile objective. He had begun these before hiring Wright and continued them after; low-walled stone terraces with rustic touches, they suggest little of the challenge or excitement he had specified in his contract with Wright.[211] Throughout their correspondence, in fact, he seemed increasingly irritated by Wright's artistic nature and what he called Wright's "curious fancy for impossibilities"; in particular, Wright's Taliesin office – so distant from

the city – seemed to Strong a sign of Wright's poor business sense.[212] Wright, in turn, came to see Strong as the sort of real-estate magnate who built efficient but inhumane buildings of the sort that were ruining life in cities.[213]

Wright, of course, continued to develop ideas of spiral architecture. In 1929, he asked Strong to return his original drawings so that he might rework them for publication, explaining, "it seems something of the kind is contemplated on the other side, in France, only in that case, it is a *museum*. Some interest has arisen in this idea as I have worked it out for you and I have been asked many times to see it."[214] Some minor changes were indeed made to the drawings, most notably the extension of the stair tower to restore a vertical accent (fig. 116), and a rendered set of prints was returned to Strong together with the Mendelsohnian sketch, which Wright fashioned into an ornament for the cover sheet.[215] Le Corbusier's design of 1928–29 for a spiral museum must have been what Wright meant, and he was clearly determined to show that he had done it first. Fourteen years later, he had his opportunity in the commission for the Guggenheim museum, in which the spiral was exploited to create one of the most significant interiors in the history of architecture. It remained a form linked with movement, not only of the people descending the

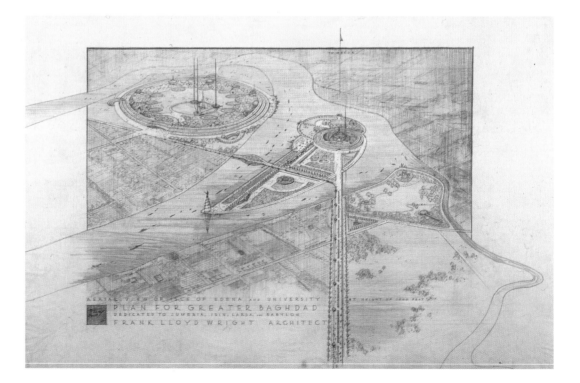

115
Frank Lloyd Wright. *Project for Greater Baghdad. Aerial perspective.* 1957. Pencil and colored pencil on tracing paper, 36 × 53 in. The Frank Lloyd Wright Foundation, 5733.008

116
Frank Lloyd Wright. *Gordon Strong
Automobile Objective, Sugarloaf
Mountain, Maryland. Perspective.* 1925,
with later revisions. Graphite and
colored pencil on Japanese paper,
21 ½ × 32 ½ in. The Library of
Congress, Washington, D.C., Gift of
Donald D. Walker, 152.16

ramp inside, but also as it related to the vehicular traffic without; renderings feature the presence of automobiles moving along Fifth Avenue as the most vivid element of its setting, and in the nearly forty years that have elapsed since it was completed, it is indeed the context that has remained the least changed, for many neighboring buildings have either been replaced or significantly altered. Wright's automobile entrance, now sadly transformed into a gift shop, had emphasized that connection.

Wright continued to explore the potential of the spiral in later designs, most notably the Pittsburgh Point Park project (1947) and the scheme for greater Baghdad (1957); in both instances, he conceived an architecture of extraordinary scale, one in which roadways and parking garages were manipulated to shape and bring greater unity to their urban settings. His belief in automobile objectives as a desired feature of modern life must have reinforced his approach; he described the communal center of his ideal Broadacre City as an automobile objective and wrote, "golf courses, racetrack,

117
Furnace Creek Inn, Death Valley, California. Photograph 1936. The Library of Congress, Washington, D.C., Prints and Photographs Division, Lot 3175, H1588

zoo, aquarium and planetarium will naturally be found at these places grouped in architectural ensemble with a botanical garden."[216] About resorts he said, "natural places of great beauty – in our mountains, seasides, prairies and forests – will be developed as automobile objectives. . . . from end to end of the country in various national circuits."[217]

San Marcos in the Desert

The mid-1920s were bleak years for Wright. Following Strong's rejection of the proposed automobile objective, Johnson, already working with someone else in planning his desert compound, decided not to proceed with Wright's skyscraper design. Hopes for Tahoe faded, and Doheny seems never to have had any chance of realization. Personal crises compounded professional setbacks: his loss of Taliesin when the Bank of Wisconsin foreclosed in September 1926, and his bizarre arrest on charges of violating the Mann Act in October of that year, the result of vengeful action by Miriam Noel, from whom Wright was seeking a divorce, and the former husband of the woman he intended to marry, Olgivanna Lazovich Milanoff. Near desperation, Wright sought loans from friends; to Jens Jensen, a close associate whom he had earlier praised as "a true interpreter of the peculiar charm of our prairie landscape," he wrote in November 1927, "I am a stranger in a strange land."[218] Echoing this plea a month later to the noted essayist and critic Alexander Woollcott, he wrote, "more and more a stranger, in my own land."[219] Before he could regain full control of Taliesin or effectively develop his few commissions of the time, he was ordered by the Bank of Wisconsin in January 1928 to vacate Taliesin, leaving him even more vulnerable to the vicissitudes of his tumultuous life.

Within a few weeks of temporarily losing Taliesin, things gradually began to improve. He was asked by Albert Chase McArthur (1881–1951), a former apprentice at Oak Park (from 1907 to 1909) and the son of a former client (Warren McArthur), for technical advice related to the design of the Arizona Biltmore. This hotel was intended to set a new standard for luxury in the Phoenix area and was solidly backed by McArthur's brothers, Charles H. and Warren, Jr., who had been active as investors in Phoenix since 1910.[220] Albert McArthur was to

be the building's architect and wanted to use Wright's
system of concrete blocks; he and his brothers
offered Wright a generous fee to consult on its
design. Ordinarily an offer of such secondary respon-
sibilities would not have appealed to an architect
of Wright's standing, but in his circumstances at the
time the opportunity was welcomed, and he went
immediately to Phoenix in early 1928 to work on
its design, staying until May of that year. The varying
degrees of skill reflected in the completed buildings,
ranging from distinguished to ordinary, suggest that
Wright contributed more to selected elements
than he ever claimed. Surely it was out of gratitude
to his former apprentice that he never challenged
McArthur's role as architect.[221]

By the late 1920s, desert tourism was becoming
increasingly appealing, and the dry, hot climate –
judged beneficial to health – drew ever more
visitors. Death Valley had shared in this popularity;
Wright may well have noted the opening of the
luxurious Furnace Creek Inn in February 1927.
Designed by Albert C. Martin, its long, low wings
were architecturally undistinguished, but its expansive scale and terraced levels must have been
appealing (fig. 117).[222] Near Phoenix, Alexander J.
Chandler (1859–1950) had opened his San Marcos
Hotel in 1913. By then a prominent investor in
the Phoenix area, Chandler had moved to Prescott
in 1887 to work as a veterinary surgeon for the
Arizona Territory but he soon turned to real-estate
investment and in 1912 founded the new town
of Chandler some twenty-four miles south of
Phoenix.[223] The hotel, designed by Arthur Benton
in a vaguely Spanish Colonial manner, was one of
several buildings Chandler erected.[224] In 1928,
wanting to compete more effectively with other
developments in the area – most notably the Arizona Biltmore – he decided to build a new luxury
resort on land some nine miles west of Chandler,
at the foot of the Salt River Mountains (figs. 118,
119). Not unexpectedly he contacted the famous
architect who was advising on the design of the
Biltmore and thus close at hand. He and Wright met
to discuss the venture in February 1928. Discussions
continued during March, and by April 5 Wright had
secured the commission. He telegraphed the news
to Darwin D. Martin, his former client who had
remained loyal during lean times and who by then

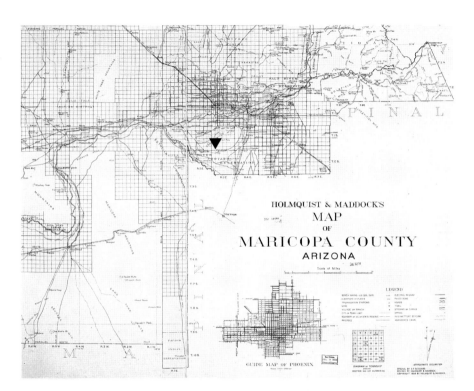

118
Map of Maricopa County, Arizona.
From *Holmquist & Maddocks Map of
Maricopa County Arizona* (1926).
The Library of Congress, Washington,
D.C., Map Division. Black triangle
indicates San Marcos in the Desert site

had loaned Wright a considerable sum of money.[225] To his son John he was even more enthusiastic: "Phoenix seems to be the name for me too. I came here to help Albert establish the textile-block in his Biltmore Hotel job. . . . Now I have a job of my own. Dr. Chandler . . . has given me the 'San Marcos in the Desert' to build with the blocks. A half-million dollar hotel project of a very fine character. He has fourteen-hundred acres of the most perfect mountainous desert in existence. . . . He is an ideal client – a gentleman and interested in . . . the preservation of Arizona desert beauty." After urging his son to join him in working on the project, Wright continued, "This is a great region for a young man. It is going to be the playground of the United States soon. . . . It looks as tho I was well started now for the last lap of my life and work."[226] Already familiar with the desert, and with ideas no doubt partly in mind even before receiving the commission, Wright worked quickly, and by April 30, still lacking the topographical surveys and aerial photographs he had requested, he wrote Chandler that his design had "taken shape definitely."[227]

In its general form, the San Marcos site, like that of Doheny, Tahoe, and Johnson, is positioned somewhat in the manner of a harbor, with immediate views to a protected foreground and framed views to a greater vista beyond. From the base of the Salt River Mountains, the immediate view is to a broad, flat plane with hills bordering each side; through a wide gap between these hills are views to the greater desert beyond. Wright emphasized this prospect in positioning his building, as he had in the earlier projects, thus reinforcing a residential typology in which protective elements of the visible surroundings were balanced with an openness suggesting limitless space. In a way it enlarges a pattern long noted of Wright's early houses, in which the fixity of the central hearth symbolized an anchor balanced by a loose, open perimeter supportive of human freedom.[228]

In its basics Wright's scheme was remarkably simple. Automobiles would have approached up toward, then under, the building along the diagonal line of a natural ravine. The building was thus to bridge this ravine, joining separate parts of the land into one composition (fig. 120). Paralleling the line of the ravine, flowing pools would have made the building itself seem a source of water. The entrance to the hotel was at the center of the complex, beneath the major public spaces that were contained within the bridging element (fig. 121). A richly faceted organ tower rising behind this central element would have reinforced the importance of its location, much as the vertical spire of the Johnson compound amplified its point of entrance by automobile.

119
View of Ocatilla site, Arizona. ca. 1929.
The Frank Lloyd Wright Foundation,
2702.0081

SAN MARCOS IN THE DESERT · · ALEXANDER CHANDLER · FRANK LLOYD WRIGHT · ARCHITECT · PERSPECTIVE FROM GATE LODGE

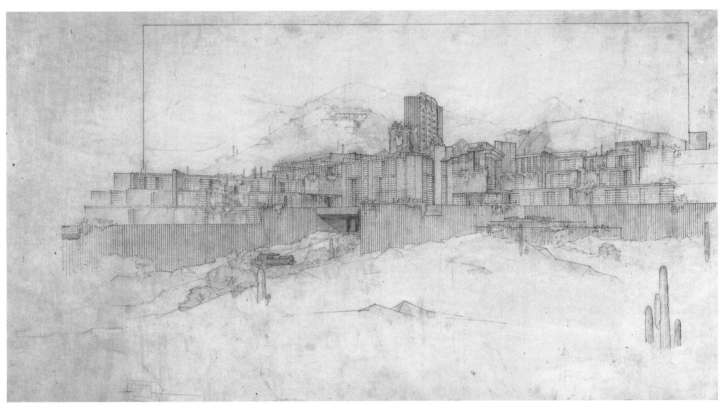

120
Frank Lloyd Wright. *San Marcos in the Desert, Arizona. Perspective.* 1928. Pencil and colored pencil on tracing paper, 16 x 54 ¾ in. The Frank Lloyd Wright Foundation, 2704.047

121
Frank Lloyd Wright. *San Marcos in the Desert, Arizona. Perspective showing entrance.* 1928. Pencil on tracing paper, 21 x 36 in. The Frank Lloyd Wright Foundation, 2704.049

From the central core, long, low wings containing private suites stretched out on each side, terracing the natural slope of the hills (fig. 122). The angles of the existing contours, and, indeed, the very desert setting itself, suggested triangular shapes to Wright, and with these he infused his plan with a rich angularity that, by comparison, had only been suggested in his earlier work of the decade (figs. 123, 124). By such angles the earth itself was brought into greater play with the building forms, as Wright had already begun to suggest in replanning Taliesin; in one plan for Taliesin, as if the decision were instantaneous, an entire section of the sheet was cut and rotated to a new position, achieving a similar connection between building and place.

Wright summarized essential details of San Marcos in describing effects he wanted his son Lloyd to emphasize in a major rendering; the design was "an architectural theme based on the triangle. . . .the mountains. . .rising behind – triangles. The cross sections of the Suhuaro and all other desert plants – triangles"; and he urged Lloyd to depict "the character of the site with desert-growth and the rock-masses as they are – the building horizontally drifted between the rock ledges that terminate it – belonging to all *naturally*." The plantings on the terrace were to contrast sympathetically with the local plants of the desert, and Wright envisioned them as "gay in color – flowering vines combined with tall spikes that harmonize, or brilliantly contrast with the desert garden." Finally, the building's color was to "be that of the desert, lit that is. . .by atmospheric changes."[229] Lloyd Wright's rendering (fig. 125), and others that relate to it, show how effective these features were in achieving a unified, massively scaled yet informally shaped landscape of building, roadway, and terrain. The sharply drawn lines of the terraces, and their

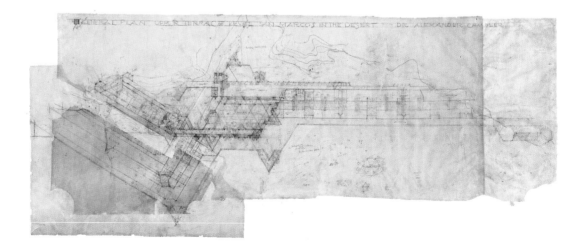

122
Frank Lloyd Wright. *San Marcos in the Desert, Arizona. Elevation.* 1928. Pencil and colored pencil on tracing paper, 12 x 60 in. The Frank Lloyd Wright Foundation, 2704.006

123
Frank Lloyd Wright. *San Marcos in the Desert, Arizona. Plan.* 1928. Pencil and colored pencil on tracing paper, 22 x 51 ¾ in. The Frank Lloyd Wright Foundation, 2704.004

124
Frank Lloyd Wright. *San Marcos in the Desert, Arizona. Plan.* 1928. Ink and pencil on tracing paper, 17 ¼ × 32 ¼ in. The Frank Lloyd Wright Foundation, 2704.052

125
Frank Lloyd Wright; Lloyd Wright, delineator. *San Marcos in the Desert, Arizona. Aerial perspective.* 1928. Watercolor, 25 × 65 in. The Frank Lloyd Wright Foundation, 2704.048

triangular terminations carried out into the desert (fig. 126), make a clear division between the wild and the cultivated. As each level of rooms steps responsively back along the slope it adjoins, the roof terraces multiply, so that, as in the Doheny project, an architectural composition of connected terraces is achieved (fig. 127). The horizontal drifting that Wright described alludes clearly to the natural topographic features he saw in Death Valley and used to advantage there, too. The powerful joining of topography effected by the main building is echoed by smaller, less detailed bridges that step up the ravine as it continues up the mountain draw behind (see fig. 122), recalling Bruno Taut's Expressionist visions of an Alpine architecture (fig. 128).[230] Farther still up the mountain, to the left, another building – its design also left undeveloped – suggests a continued structuring of the site (see fig. 126).

With the San Marcos design, Wright left the predictable symmetries of conventional monumentality far behind. It was no little achievement at a time when most architects relied on rules of the Ecole des Beaux-Arts, as had Wright himself in work of the previous decade. Sensing his achievement and the reason for it, he wrote, "Out here obvious symmetry soon wearies the eye, stultifies imagination, closes the episode before it begins. So, there should be no obvious symmetry in building in the desert, none in the camp."[231] Clearly the site itself had inspired a response of special significance to Wright: "There could be nothing more inspiring on earth than that spot in the pure desert of Arizona. . . . As I saw this desert resort it was to embody all that was worthwhile that I had learned about a natural architecture."[232] For Wright, it broadened his rediscovery of an American architecture that he had begun with Doheny: "The Arizona desert itself was architectural inspiration. . . . Is this not what we mean by an 'indigenous architecture'?"[233]

Fundamental to Wright's conception were the means by which it would be realized. With San Marcos, he seized the opportunity to develop the full potential of his textile-block system, realizing – at least on paper – a true mono-material building.

126
Frank Lloyd Wright. *San Marcos in the Desert, Arizona. Aerial perspective.* 1928. Pencil and colored pencil on tracing paper, 27½ x 68½ in. The Frank Lloyd Wright Foundation, 2704.198

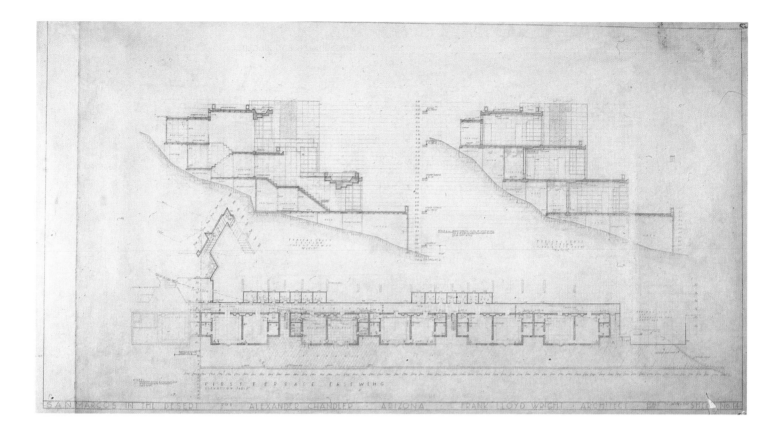

127

Frank Lloyd Wright. *San Marcos in the Desert, Arizona, East Wing First Terrace. Plan and sections.* 1929. Pencil on tracing paper, 30 × 54 ½ in. The Frank Lloyd Wright Foundation, 2704.103

128

Bruno Taut. *Weg zum Kristallhause im Wildbachtal* (Ascent to the Crystal House, Wildbachtal). ca. 1918. Print, 9 × 9 ⅞ in. Akademie der Künste, Sammlung Baukunst, Bruno-Taut Archiv

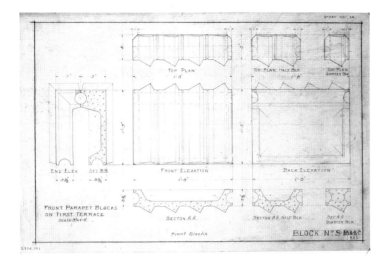

129

Frank Lloyd Wright. *San Marcos in the Desert, Arizona. Details, scoriated parapet blocks.* 1929. Pencil on tracing paper, 12 × 18 in. The Frank Lloyd Wright Foundation, 2704.141

Some 120 different block types were designed, many richly patterned (fig. 129). They were to form not only the walls and provide finished interior and exterior surfaces, but structure floors and ceilings as well. He devised an ingenious system of precast concrete pans that would create a coffered ceiling within and, when positioned, provide the formwork for a structural grid of poured concrete ribs above, achieving a lamella structure of considerable strength. Precast concrete tiles were to complete the floor above, and cavities left within portions of the floors as well as within the walls would provide necessary spaces for utilities. Not all the blocks were to be concrete. Some he planned as glass, recalling a similar device in the Arizona Biltmore, but here significantly developed. They were to be placed as triangular points on certain hexagonal columns and as collars between selected vertical and horizontal surfaces; designed to conceal electric lights behind, they would have caused the structure itself to seem a source of light, and the solid realities of mass to dissolve into luminescent bands (detail, upper left, fig. 130).[234]

Embossed concrete blocks were placed to augment desired effects of massing. Their patternings were to be most intense within the public spaces and on the surfaces of the faceted tower rising behind the central block of public rooms (see fig. 130). On the top level, the dining room was to have a richly faceted ceiling of copper and glass

130

Frank Lloyd Wright. *San Marcos in the Desert, Arizona. Section.* 1929. Pencil on tracing paper, 31½ × 54⅛ in. The Frank Lloyd Wright Foundation, 2704.106

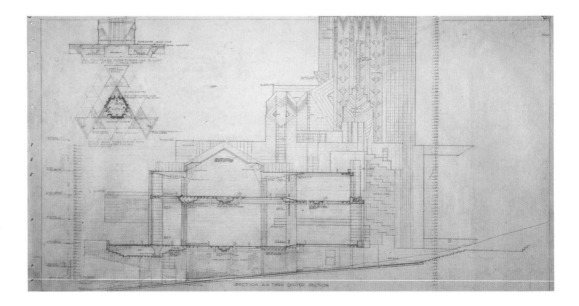

131

Frank Lloyd Wright. *San Marcos in the Desert, Arizona, Dining Room. Interior perspective.* ca. 1928–29. Pencil and colored pencil on tracing paper, 17⅜ x 33⅞ in. The Frank Lloyd Wright Foundation, 2704.199

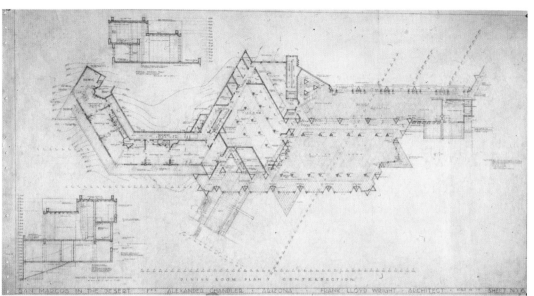

132

Frank Lloyd Wright. *San Marcos in the Desert, Arizona, Central Building. Plan.* 1929. Pencil on tracing paper, 30 x 54⅜ in. The Frank Lloyd Wright Foundation, 2704.095

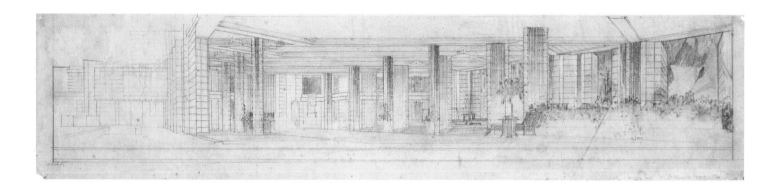

133

Frank Lloyd Wright. *San Marcos in the Desert, Arizona, Lobby. Interior perspective.* ca. 1928–29. Pencil and colored pencil on tracing paper, 7¼ x 30½ in. The Frank Lloyd Wright Foundation, 2704.051

(figs. 131, 132); it recalled the similarly rich interior of the dining room at the Imperial Hotel. The dining room and tower completed a sequence of vertical ascent from the porte-cochère entrance within the ravine through the two-story lounge between (fig. 133). In contrast, the three levels of terraced rooms extending to each side emphasized horizontality; it was no casual horizontality, but an echo of the desert itself, with patterned blocks arranged to animate the lines themselves. "Every straight horizontal line in San Marcos in the Desert is a dotted line," Wright wrote; "every flat plane gros-grained like the sahuaro itself. The building itself an abstraction of cactus life in masonry shells made more cactus than any cactus."[235] For Wright, the dotted, or fretted, line suggested the essence of desert light; through pattern, he planned to animate the forms of his building so that its lines were uniquely reflective of its setting. With time he came to sense broader applications of such animated lines:

134
Ocatilla, Arizona. View of main entrance with sample blocks on left. 1929.
The Frank Lloyd Wright Foundation, 2702.0050

In organic architecture the hard straight line breaks to the dotted line where stark necessity ends and thus allows appropriate rhythm to enter in order to leave suggestion in proper values. This is modern. . . . Eye-weary of reiterated bald commonplaces wherein light is rejected from blank surfaces or fallen dismally into holes cut in them, organic architecture brings the man once more face to face with nature's play of shade and depth of shadow seeing fresh vistas of native, creative human thought and native feeling presented to his imagination for consideration. This is modern.[236]

Only a partial mock-up of the blocks was constructed, but as photographed it suggests the effects Wright envisioned across an entire landscape of structured form (fig. 134).

As in Los Angeles, Wright intended for the blocks to be partly made from the gravel-like material of the area's decomposing rock. This, too, reinforced expression of place. Writing of the nature of concrete "on the Phoenix plain of Arizona," he explained his reasoning: "The ruddy granite mountain-heaps grown 'old,' are decomposing and sliding down layer upon layer to further compose the soil of the plain. Buildings could grow right up out of the 'ground' were this 'soil,' before it is too far 'rotted,' cemented in proper proportions and beaten into flasks or boxes."[237] For Wright, stone and its derivations held special meaning as a form-giving element natural to place, and within the desert, stone and its natural forms were made manifest. He described the San Marcos site as a "vast battleground of titanic natural forces," reflecting his sensitivity to its very creation.[238] Buildings in alignment with its natural forms responded to the scale of the earth itself:

Stone is the frame on which [man's] Earth is modeled, and wherever it crops out — there the architect may site and learn. . . . As he takes the trail across the great Western Deserts — he may see his buildings — rising in simplicity and majesty from their floors of gleaming sand — where organic life is still struggling for a bare existence: we see them still, as the Egyptians saw and were taught by those they knew. . . . For in the stony bonework of the Earth, the principles that shaped stone as it lies, or as it rises and remains to be sculptured by winds and tide — there sleep forms and styles enough for all the ages, for all of Man.[239]

With design drawings essentially completed by June 1928, Wright left Phoenix for La Jolla, where he remained as a result of financial crises that prevented his return to Taliesin before October. By that time he had married Olgivanna Milanoff, and things at last seemed well in control. During the fall he continued to refine technical details of San Marcos. The Arizona project occupied him fully; he wrote to Woollcott, "I don't know whether you have seen Arizona, but Arizona seems to me the most beautiful part of this earth and the most unspoiled. . . . It is the place of all places where it would be best to build buildings of this new block-system."[240] He wanted to return there to prepare working drawings and supervise testing of the textile blocks, and he convinced Chandler that it would be cheaper to house his family and staff of fifteen near the site in a "sightly camp of wood and canvas" rather than pay for hotel accommodations.[241] To this Chandler agreed. In January 1929, Wright selected a low mound on Chandler's property where he could look north across the broad plain to the rising slopes of the building site, and within a few days the camp was built. Justifying its cost to his ever worrisome banker, he described it as "army style with cots. . . . We did this at once and in three days were all sleeping and eating in it, although cold and dirty. . . . The camp will have cost, completed and furnished, about $2,600."[242]

Wright called his camp Ocatilla after the cactus he so admired, and with low board walls he defined an angled enclosure apart from the surrounding desert (fig. 135). The cabins, raised on posts at the edges of the mound, were built with horizontal board-and-batten walls and angled canvas roofs; these have been compared to migrant workers' cabins with which Wright was probably familiar,[243] but they worked so radical a transformation on that primitive prototype as to render the comparison insignificant. In a letter to Franz Aust, he described them as "desert ships" and added, "No man is really qualified as a director of landscape until he has soaked this desert into his system."[244] The mobile, impermanent image was one that stayed with him; a month later, he wrote, "We have constructed light desert-ships — a small village here in the desert . . . constructed of box boards, 2 x 4s, and canvas."[245] Near the center of the enclosure, Wright set aside space for a communal campfire, marking human occupation in a time-honored manner (fig. 136). He seemed almost to welcome the spartan life, and he repeated the reinvigorating exercise in the building of Taliesin West. Ocatilla itself was to be short-lived; with working drawings for San Marcos completed, Wright left for Taliesin in late May 1929; in June, much of the camp was destroyed by fire, and what remained gradually fell into ruin and disappeared. Yet briefly it demonstrated how Wright approached the land even when no permanent structure was contemplated: as a place that could reach higher definition through understanding use.

135
Ocatilla, Arizona. View from garage. 1929. The Frank Lloyd Wright Foundation, 2702.032

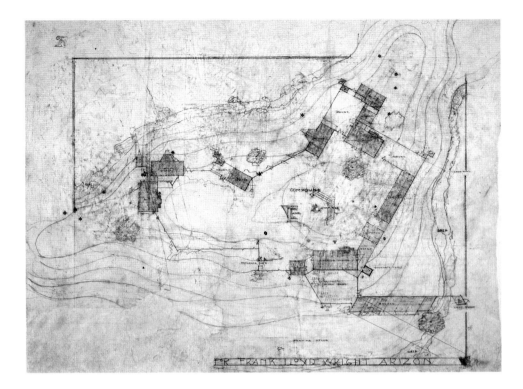

In these years Wright began a pattern of cross-country travel by automobile that augmented his understanding of mobility as an essential component of the new American landscape. After one such trip in the summer of 1929, from Phoenix to New York and back to Taliesin, he wrote, "I know more about my country now than I ever knew before."[246] The scale of what he saw affected him, too; increasingly he spoke of a "new standard of space measurement – the man seated in his automobile."[247] The horizontal line of San Marcos, an intensification of the horizontal line of the desert, now seemed extended to the horizontal line of the entire nation, like the molecular interweaving of steel cable: "The highway is becoming the horizontal line of Freedom extending from ocean to ocean tying woods, streams, mountains, and plains together by way of the regional field for building. All human occupation expanding and adding beauty of feature to the great national environment."[248]

The continued promise of San Marcos seemed to sustain his exuberance. To assure workable details he consulted with Paul Mueller, the trusted builder who had worked with him to realize some of his greatest achievements: Unity Temple, Midway Gardens, and the Imperial Hotel.[249] He was surrounded by admiring assistants from Europe and Japan, and he began to reestablish contacts with former associates and clients.[250] Favorable estimates

for San Marcos were obtained,[251] and two commissions for individual houses that would be designed as an extension of the complex were received: one for Wellington and Ralph Cudney, Chicago brothers who, with their families, were friends of Wright; and a second for Owen D. Young, one of the nation's more prominent industrialists, who must have seemed a likely backer of the entire project.[252] Wright was also working on an additional commission for Chandler: the San Marcos Water Gardens, a smaller resort of detached units in the town of Chandler.

The Young and Cudney designs illustrate Wright's continued exploration of block construction adapted to a desert setting. In its general layout, the Young house resembled the Sachse project, but with the oculus of Wright's own desert studio added, for its major room, indicated on the drawings as a solarium, was to be open at the center (fig. 137). By aligning the blocks of its walls on a diagonal grid, Wright developed unusual triangular massing, and windows identical in shape and size to the individual blocks animated its massiveness (fig. 138). In the Cudney house, Wright developed variations of hexagonal geometry; it was an intensification of shapes of the main hotel, effectively rendered to suggest a pattern of vibrating lines that appear to rise up out of the desert itself (figs. 139, 140). By October 1929, all seemed in order and

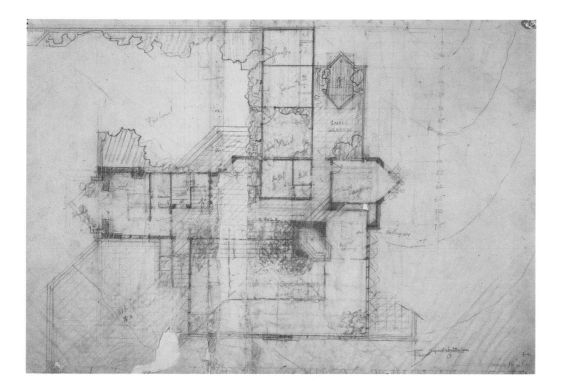

137
Frank Lloyd Wright. *San Marcos in the Desert Complex, Arizona, Owen D. Young House. Plan.* ca. 1928–29. Pencil and colored pencil on tracing paper, 18 × 26 in. The Frank Lloyd Wright Foundation, 2707.007

PERSPECTIVE VIEW

SAN MARCOS IN THE DESERT. MOUNTAIN COTTAGE FOR MRS. OWEN D. YOUNG   FRANK LLOYD WRIGHT. ARCHITECT

138
Frank Lloyd Wright. *San Marcos in the Desert Complex, Arizona, Owen D. Young House. Perspective.* ca. 1928–29. Pencil on tracing paper, 24 × 32 in. The Frank Lloyd Wright Foundation, 2707.002

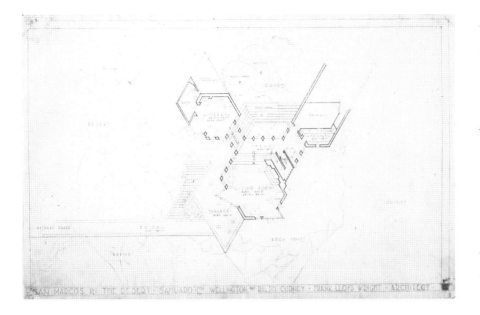

Wright expected contracts for construction to be quickly negotiated. The beginning of the Great Depression that month, however, doomed the project. For a while both Wright and Chandler remained hopeful that financing could still be secured, but by July 1931, any chance of realization seemed over.[253]

Ironically, another commission that Wright had regarded as comparatively modest became his only design of the period to be realized. It was a house in Oklahoma for his cousin, Richard Lloyd Jones, publisher of the *Tulsa Tribune*. Jones had begun discussions with Wright late in 1928, and by April of the following year the design had taken shape. Again Wright employed a triangular module, and like a grand version of the Cudney house, its plan extended in gentle angles across a broad site. Tulsa was no desert, but its climate could be nearly as harsh, and the flat, unrelieved site, which sloped gently toward the distant Arkansas River valley, must have seemed even less protected than those in Arizona. In appearance, the house recalled a fortress, and it was planned with rows of block piers that were joined with glass to define interior spaces or left open to define garden enclosures and inte-

140

Frank Lloyd Wright. *San Marcos in the Desert Complex, Arizona, Wellington and Ralph Cudney House, Upper Level. Plan.* ca. 1928–29. Pencil and colored pencil on tracing paper, 21 ¾ × 32 ¾ in. The Frank Lloyd Wright Foundation, 2706.004

139

Frank Lloyd Wright. *San Marcos in the Desert Complex, Arizona, Wellington and Ralph Cudney House. Perspective and partial plan.* ca. 1928–29. Graphite and colored pencil on tracing paper, 26 ¹³⁄₁₆ × 35 ¹⁄₁₆ in. (irreg.). Canadian Centre for Architecture, Montréal

142

Frank Lloyd Wright. *Richard Lloyd Jones House, Tulsa, Oklahoma, Ground Floor. Plan.* 1929. Pencil on tracing paper, 21 × 30 in. The Frank Lloyd Wright Foundation, 2901.005

141

Frank Lloyd Wright. *Richard Lloyd Jones House, Tulsa, Oklahoma. Aerial perspective.* 1929. Colored pencil on tracing paper, 17 ¼ × 47 ½ in. The Frank Lloyd Wright Foundation, 2901.002

rior divisions (figs. 141, 142). Jones disliked the triangular shapes, and during the summer of 1929 Wright translated his plan into one based on more conventional rectangles. Jones next questioned the rows of piers that seemed to block views; Wright explained, "If you take the proper view-point your whole living room wall becomes a window with vertical mullions. All the walls become such. You have an outlook in every direction."[254] Indeed, as a continuation of an idea first explored in the Martin house and carried further in the Storer, solidity gave way to an essay of point supports that united wall and window as a single, space-defining entity. It effected a more permeable connection with its site, as Wright also explained, and provided special enclosures outside: "There is nothing more charming than a sequestered garden....This garden is not walled but screened, just as all your rooms are

143
Aerial view of Richard Lloyd Jones
house under construction, Tulsa,
Oklahoma. ca. 1930–31. The Frank
Lloyd Wright Foundation, 2902.0021

not walled but screened."[255] The house was built at last, a final demonstration of Wright's textile block system. Its construction was problematic; Bruce Goff, then a young architect practicing in Tulsa, volunteered his services as supervisor, and later recalled that unforeseen details required frequent modification of Wright's prefabricated system.[256] After that Wright used blocks more conventionally. But in the Jones house he at least succeeded in showing how truly monumental forms might be achieved with relatively modest means, and that such monumentality, properly handled, could give structure to a somewhat featureless site (fig. 143).

By the time the Jones house was completed, almost a decade had passed since Wright's final return from Japan in 1922. For an architect of his standing, at the height of his creative powers, he had received comparatively few commissions – certainly an insufficient number to fully engage his talents. Those he did receive suggest the range of his vision; in addition to suburban prototypes of potentially vast scale, he proposed an equally distinguished series of buildings for urban settings: these include skyscraper proposals for the National Life Insurance Company in Chicago (1924), the St. Mark's Tower apartments for New York (1929), and the smaller but equally sophisticated Noble apartments in Los Angeles (1929). Other commissions elicited proposals for buildings of remarkable geometric richness that were largely self-contained, ranging in size from the gigantic Steel Cathedral envisioned for New York's Central Park (1926) to the small pavilions for the Egyptian resort Ras El Bar (1932).[257] Of those very few commissions of the period that were actually built, the Jones and Ennis houses were easily the largest.

In 1932, with the publication of two seminal books, *An Autobiography* and *The Disappearing City*, and with the founding of the Taliesin Fellowship, Wright's career entered a new phase. With his commission for the Wiley house that same year, he initiated the renowned series of Usonian houses; these were built inexpensively of readily available materials.

Several larger commissions of the 1930s provided opportunities for continued investigations of suburban and related urban prototypes. At Fallingwater

(Bear Run, Pennsylvania, 1936), he demonstrated how building, roadway, earth, and water could be shaped as one integrated landscape that enhanced underlying qualities of place. He worked at larger scale at Auldbrass plantation (near Yemassee, South Carolina, begun in 1938) and Florida Southern College (Lakeland, Florida, begun in 1938), integrating movement systems as part of an architectural framework that created an ordered, visible pattern where little had existed before. In his proposal for Monona Terrace (Madison, Wisconsin, 1939, unbuilt), the idea of road architecture was carried further; local streets were integrated into a single, powerful form that projected out over the surface of the water, its shape the exact opposite of the more passive Wolf Lake project of many years before.[258] At Taliesin West (near Scottsdale, Arizona, 1938), he gave architectural scale to a vast desert setting, orienting major axes of the complex to distant features of the surrounding countryside so that a grand unity was achieved. Judging by the large areas of cut and fill required to bring this special composition into being, it was clearly no easy feat, as Anne Spirn describes in her essay.

During the last decades of his life, Wright worked at increasingly larger scales. For example, in his proposal for the Huntington Hartford sports club and cottage group (Hollywood, 1947, unbuilt; fig. 144), an expansive landscape comparable to Doheny was organized according to a single, integrated vision. The park-like edge of Pittsburgh was given coherent architectural form in his visionary scheme for Point Park (1947, unbuilt); bridges and gigantic parking structures were used to shape the city's edge as a single structure. In the Marin County Civic Center (San Rafael, California, begun in

144
Frank Lloyd Wright. *Huntington Hartford Cottage Group Center, Hollywood, California. Perspective.* 1948. Pencil and colored pencil on tracing paper, 19 × 36 in. The Frank Lloyd Wright Foundation, 4837.046

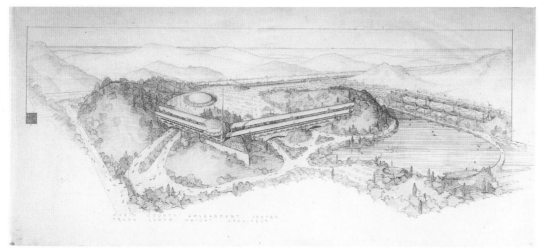

145
Frank Lloyd Wright. *Marin County Civic Center, San Rafael, California. Aerial perspective.* 1957. Ink, pencil, and colored pencil on tracing paper, 34½ × 74⅜ in. The Frank Lloyd Wright Foundation, 5746.001

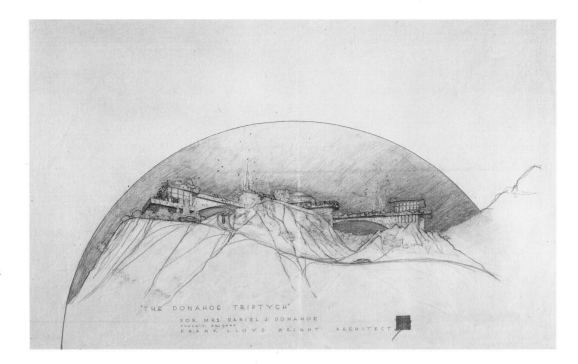

146
Frank Lloyd Wright. *Mrs. Helen
Donahoe House, Paradise Valley, Arizona.
Perspective.* 1959. Pencil and colored
pencil on tracing paper, 36 x 58 in.
The Frank Lloyd Wright Foundation,
5901.020

1957; fig. 145), the California site was reconnected
in a similar manner, there as proof that a suburban
landscape could have visible, memorable form.

Even small projects could be affected by this
quest for large-scale unity: the Donahoe house
(Paradise Valley, Arizona, 1959, unbuilt; fig. 146) was
designed with bridges joining three hills, shaped to
celebrate arrival by automobile. An integrated roadway was to spiral up and around the central hill,
passing beneath bridging terraces that linked the
central house to two outlying guest houses. From a
parking court at the terminus of the road, a more
formal pedestrian ramp continued up and around
the house itself to a glass-domed "sky parlor" at its
top, Wright's replacement for the original summit
that an over-zealous developer had flattened.[259]
His last sketches for the Donahoe house are dated
only a few days before his death, affirming his determined pursuit of a unified suburban landscape. In
these and other designs, however bold, Wright's
underlying principles remained consistent.

In several of Wright's statements, cosmic elements
are mentioned as an essential part of the landscapes he described. Other than these widely
separated quotations – and several have been
included here – he left only glimpses of the deeper
meaning he intended. Given the seriousness of his
approach, it seems fair to assume that his use of
such terms was no mere window-dressing, but

referred instead to his particular view of architecture and its essential contribution to landscape.
Therefore a few brief speculations follow.

Wright's beliefs in the primacy of nature lay at
the base of his principles. Edgar Kaufmann, jr., has
shown how those beliefs contributed to his philosophy of an organic architecture:

*[Wright] saw human life as one of the processes of
nature, not as some exceptional form of creation.
Within nature people are active, adapting nature to
suit their wants; they contribute feedback within the
natural system. Similarly, he saw architecture as a
natural process of human life, in turn nourishing its
parent system. Thus to Wright architecture, humankind,
and nature were joined in a grand dynamic continuity,
and continuity within architecture indicated that
people were aligning themselves – as he believed
they should – with the natural forces of life.*[260]

Wright, who regarded architecture as the mother
of the arts, unhesitatingly believed that artists (and
therefore architects) were best positioned to
express such human ideals:

*All the wisdom of science, the cunning of politics, and
the prayers of religion can but stand and wait for the
revelation – awaiting at the hands of the artist "conventionalization," that free expression of life-principle
which shall make our social living beautiful because*

organically true. Behind all institutions or dogmatic schemes, whatever their worth may be, or their venerable antiquity, behind them all is something produced and preserved for its aesthetic worth; the song of the poet, some artist vision, the pattern seen in the mount.[261]

For the architect in particular, geometry was critical to expression, and for Wright such geometry was Euclidian. As he readily acknowledged, this he had learned early on from the Froebel kindergarten system. For Wright, the ideal order of the universe was thus Euclidian by nature, and this order could be represented by combinations of Euclidian shapes organized according to a larger field of gridded modules.[262]

To what degree individual shapes held specific meaning for Wright is uncertain. Clearly he identified basic geometric shapes as carrying symbolic meaning, yet he never seemed unduly governed by that meaning, believing it more suggestive than absolute. His primary statement in this regard was in reference to Japanese prints, although broader implications have long been assumed:

There is a psychic correlation between the geometry of form and our associated ideas, which constitutes its symbolic value. There resides always a certain "spell-power" in any geometric form which seems more or less a mystery, and is, as we say, the soul of the thing. . . . certain geometric forms have come to symbolize for us and potently to suggest certain human ideas, moods, and sentiments — as for instance: the circle, infinity; the triangle, structural unity; the spire, aspiration; the spiral, organic process; the square, integrity.[263]

Elsewhere Wright seemed to qualify his own statement, suggesting limits to any overly specific interpretation: "In meticulous, abstract, geometrical analysis there will always be fascinating room for the astrological, geometrical mind. And sometimes the long arm of coincidence will find a pretty circumstance in its hand. I should say the laws lie deeper and in the realm of relativity. . . . Architectural depths are seldom if ever plumbed by geometrical devices.[264]

Wright's belief in the fundamental concept of order itself, and its realization through basic geometry, seems, however, undeniable. In his most evocative descriptions of landscape, it was this order he perceived, cosmic in spirit, architectural in nature,

often suggestive of ancient building, often experienced while in motion across it. For example, recalling his view of the Badlands of South Dakota, he observed:

What I saw gave me an indescribable sense of mysterious otherwhere — a distant architecture, ethereal, touched, only touched with a sense of Egyptian, Mayan drift and silhouette. As we came closer, a templed realm definitely stood ambient in air before my astonished "scene"-loving but scene-jaded gaze. . . . Endless trabeations surmounted by or rising into pyramid (obelisk) and temple, ethereal in color and exquisitely chiseled in endless detail, they began to reach to infinity, spreading into the sky on every side; an endless supernatural world more spiritual than earth but created out of it. As we rode, or seemed to be floating upon a splendid winding road that seemed to understand it all and just where to go. . .the sky itself seemed only there to cleanse and light the vast harmonious building scheme. . . . Here was the element, architecture, cut of the body of the ground itself.[265]

It lay with the architect to extract and clarify these forms, shaping them, when necessary, to complete imperfectly revealed order. By these means a representation of the cosmos, and a stronger connection to it, could be demonstrated.

Ungoverned wilderness, sometimes unpredictable, always uncertain, was imperfect. Through an ordered architecture that shaped and unified that wilderness or its unplanned counterparts, Wright sought, it seems, to bring these unpredictable rhythms into a regular, perceivable order, thereby reinforcing a cosmic pattern of chartable rhythms. He thus tamed the uncertain and effected a larger unity of humanity with the universe. A landscape with observable order has a quality of predictability and stability — it is life-sustaining; life is ordered and in alignment with cosmic forces.[266] For Wright, such materiality was substantiation of spirit: "Earth-dwellers that we are, we are become now sentient to the truth that living on Earth is a materialization of Spirit instead of trying to make our dwelling here a spiritualization of matter. . . .To be Gods of earth *here* is all the significance we have here."[267]

By evoking ancient architectures, Wright acknowledged his debt to a longstanding tradition of cosmic representation. In those ancient cultures in which religious beliefs were closely tied to nature, architectural complexes of a scale comparable to Wright's had been created for ritualistic purposes, and in those complexes an amplifying unity with setting was achieved, as the Funerary Temple of Queen Hatshepsut (Deir-el-Bahari, XVIII Dynasty, ca. 1480 B.C.) or the Temple of Fortuna Primigenia (Praeneste, ca. 80 B.C.) illustrate. Wright could have known of the former, but the latter was rediscovered only after the Second World War; essentially it was intuitive rather than specific inspiration that applied, contrary to Gordon Strong's clumsy accusation.[268] In contrast, later religious attitudes, particularly in the West, tended to encourage detachment from specific place and to deny or at least minimize physicality, encouraging, in turn, architectural expression through idealized geometries that were conceived without reference to location. Renaissance churches embody this achievement and could not be further from the ideal Wright sought.

Similarly, Wright resisted the detached, often neutral geometries of modernist architecture. Rather, he sought universal meaning through attachment to place, varying his geometries not only to achieve an indivisible bond with each specific location, but, more importantly, to complete that location's underlying structure, so that each place became more fully revealed as an indivisible part of an ordered cosmos. He remained sympathetic to his favorite nineteenth-century writers and to an earlier, more distant history by honoring a belief in the spirituality of nature, which led him to reexamine issues of design that had been long unstudied. Yet he invigorated this approach by incorporating the latest advances of his own era, so that mobility and a new awareness of change became part of his ideal landscape. He thus effected connections with both place and time, creating a modern architecture of profound, richly layered meaning.

Notes

I am grateful to C. Ford Peatross, who originally suggested collaborating on a Frank Lloyd Wright exhibition, and to Nicholas Olsberg, who caused it to happen. Throughout the long planning phase – more than four years – I have benefitted greatly from the active participation and constructive suggestions of noted Wright scholars Anthony Alofsin and Neil Levine. From Robert Sweeney and Anne Whiston Spirn I have also received much help.

During the course of my archival and institutional research, many individuals provided essential and greatly appreciated assistance. These include staff members of the Lake Tahoe Public Library; Elizabeth Isles, director, and Rosemary Mazzetti of the Shadelands Ranch Historical Museum, Walnut Creek Historical Society; Mary Liddecoat, retired president of the Gospel Foundation; David F. Webster, executive secretary/treasurer, Stronghold Incorporated, and Marion M. Webster; Marcia Stout, museum curator, and Blair Davenport, museum technician, Scotty's Castle Museum Collection, Death Valley National Monument; Sherwin W. Howard, president, and Jan Vleck, graduate, Deep Springs College; Alan E. Morrison, head librarian, Fisher Fine Arts Library, University of Pennsylvania; Janet Parks, curator of drawings, and Dan Karny of the Avery Art and Architecture Library, Columbia University.

I would like to thank the University of Pennsylvania for providing me with a research grant, and both the former and interim deans of the Graduate School of Fine Arts at the University of Pennsylvania, Patricia Conway and Malcolm Campbell, for permitting me to take a partial academic leave to complete my manuscript. I am grateful to Suzanne Hyndmann, my administrative assistant, and Christine Mesa and John Boyer, office assistants. Also deserving acknowledgment are two research assistants, Robert Saarnio and Evan Kopelson, both holders of the Edgar Kaufmann, jr., Fellowship in Historic Preservation at the University of Pennsylvania. I would also like to thank the students in my 1991 graduate seminar on Frank Lloyd Wright – Jeffrey L. Baumoel, Lisa M. Di Chiera, Carol A. Hagan, Joshua D. Hilton, David S. Jones, Paul H. Kapp, Thaddeus R. Kilpatrick III, Sarah P. Korjeff, Sheryl F. Mikelberg, and Ann K. Milkovich – and, Nabil Abu-Dayyeh, who shared his doctoral research.

Additional funding for research, including extensive field trips, was provided by the Canadian Centre for Architecture and the Library of Congress, sponsoring institutions of the exhibition. Many staff members of the CCA merit special recognition, including Christine Dufresne, Gwendolyn Owens, Helen Malkin, and, in particular Phyllis Lambert, founder and director; at the Library of Congress, Eileen Sheppard Gallagher, Tambra Johnson, Irene Burnham, Mary Ison and librarians in the Prints and Photographs Division, and librarians in the Geography and Maps Division. For dedicated effort in building the architectural models, special thanks are due George Ranalli, Aaron MacDonald, Julie Shurtz, Nathaniel Worden, and Yasin Abdullah; for equally dedicated effort in creating the computer models, John Danahy and Shannon McKenzie of the University of Toronto. I am especially grateful to Diana Murphy, Senior Editor, and Judith Hudson, Designer, both of Harry N. Abrams, for their many valued contributions and welcome encouragement. Additionally, I would like to thank Curtis Besinger, Brendan Gill, Richard Joncas, Mr. Kanaya (of the Kanaya Hotel, Nikko), Richard Longstreth, Paul Mayen, Joel Silver, Kathryn Smith, and Nobu and Kameki Tsuchiura (along with Yoshiuki Takaichi and Jackie Kestenbaum) for help given in many ways over the past few years.

Finally, and perhaps most importantly, I would like to acknowledge those people at the Frank Lloyd Wright Archives and others at Taliesin West without whom the exhibition would not have been possible. Among the many who provided assistance and encouragement are Penny Fowler, Indira Berndtson, Margo Stipe, Oscar Muñoz, Christopher Bernotas, and especially Bruce Brooks Pfeiffer (with a nod to Geronimo).

1 Ralph Waldo Emerson, "Art," in *Essays*, First Series (Boston and New York: Houghton Mifflin, 1903), 352. The first edition of this essay appeared in 1841.

2 Ralph Waldo Emerson, "Beauty," in *Nature: Addresses and Lectures* (Boston and New York: Houghton, Mifflin and Company, 1883), 28–29. The first edition of this essay appeared in 1836.

3 Ralph Waldo Emerson, "The Young American," in *Nature: Addresses and Lectures*, 345. The first edition of this essay appeared in 1849.

4 Emerson, "Beauty," 25.

5   William Cronon, "Inconstant Unity:
    The Passion of Frank Lloyd Wright,"
    in *Frank Lloyd Wright, Architect*, ed.
    Terence Riley (New York: The Museum
    of Modern Art, 1994), 13–14.

6   Frank Lloyd Wright, "In the Cause of
    Architecture: The Third Dimension"
    (1925), in *Frank Lloyd Wright: Collected
    Writings* vol. I, 1894–1930, ed. Bruce
    Brooks Pfeiffer (New York: Rizzoli
    in association with The Frank Lloyd
    Wright Foundation, 1992), 212. For
    quotations of Wright during the
    period under study, I have relied on
    this source, which is the latest and
    most comprehensive.

7   Frank Lloyd Wright, "The Logic of
    Contemporary Architecture as an
    Expression of This Age" (1930), in
    Pfeiffer, *Collected Writings* I, 340.

8   Letter from Frank Lloyd Wright to
    Louis Sullivan, November 30, 1922;
    The Frank Lloyd Wright Archives,
    The Frank Lloyd Wright Foundation,
    Scottsdale, Arizona (hereinafter
    FLWA).

9   Frank Lloyd Wright, "In the Cause of
    Architecture: Second Paper" (1914),
    in Pfeiffer, *Collected Writings* I, 129–30.

10 Letter from Frank Lloyd Wright to
    H. P. Berlage, November 30, 1922,
    FLWA.

11 Letter from Frank Lloyd Wright to
    Louis Sullivan, February 5, 1923,
    FLWA. He had written to his son
    Lloyd on October 5, 1922, that he
    was considering working on the West
    Coast; as quoted in Robert Sweeney's
    Chronology in this volume, 187.

12 Kathryn Smith, "Frank Lloyd Wright,
    Hollyhock House, and Olive Hill,
    1914–1924," *Journal of the Society of
    Architectural Historians* 38 (November
    1979), 31.

13 Kevin Starr, *Material Dreams: Southern
    California Through the 1920s* (New
    York: Oxford University Press, 1990),
    2.

14 G. Gordon Whitnall, "Regional Plan-
    ning Progress in the Los Angeles
    District," *The American City Magazine*
    29 (December 1923), 578–79.

15 Starr, 93.

16 Paul G. Hoffman, "The Traffic Com-
    mission of Los Angeles: Its Work on
    the Traffic Problem," *The Annals of the
    American Academy* 116 (November,
    1924), 246–50.

17 Richard Longstreth, *City Center to
    Regional Mall: Architecture, the Auto-
    mobile, and Retailing in Los Angeles,
    1920–1950* (Cambridge, Mass.:
    M.I.T. Press, forthcoming 1996). I am
    grateful to Professor Longstreth for
    allowing me access to his unpublished
    manuscript. It is claimed that the first
    drive-in restaurant opened in Dallas
    in 1921; David L. Lewis, "Sex and the
    Automobile: From Rumble Seats to
    Rockin' Vans," in *The Automobile and
    American Culture*, ed. David L. Lewis
    and Laurence Goldstein (Ann Arbor:
    The University of Michigan Press,
    1980), 129.

18 James J. Flink, *The Car Culture*
    (Cambridge, Mass., and London: MIT
    Press, 1973), 141.

19 As summarized in Christian Zapatka,
    "The American Parkways: Origins
    and Evolution of the Park-Road,"
    Lotus International 56 (1987), 96–128,
    and Bruce Radde, *The Merritt Parkway*
    (New Haven and London: Yale
    University Press, 1993), esp. 2–12
    and 115–25.

20 Among early publications illustrating
    the viaduct are *Wonderful California*
    (Chicago: C. T. and Co., 1915), not

paginated. A copy is filed with Sou-
venir Books, California, in the Prints
and Photographs Division, Library of
Congress. The Arroyo-Secco Parkway,
later renamed the Pasadena Freeway,
was finally completed in 1940.
Zapatka, 121.

21 Whitnall, 578–79; Starr, 107.

22 Among descriptions of the problem
    and proposals for its solution are
    Frederick Law Olmsted, Harland
    Bartholomew, and Charles Henry
    Cheney, *A Major Traffic Street Plan for
    Los Angeles*, prepared for the Com-
    mittee on Los Angeles Plan of Major
    Highways of the Traffic Commission
    of the City and County of Los Ange-
    les (Los Angeles: Traffic Commission,
    May 1924); Clarence R. Snethen, "Los
    Angeles Scientific Study to Relieve
    Traffic Congestion," *American City
    Magazine* 31 (September 1924),
    196–200; and Miller McClintock,
    "Interesting Features of Los Angeles'
    New Traffic Ordinance," *American City
    Magazine* 32 (March 1925), 333–35.

23 Joseph Interrante, "The Road to
    Autopia: The Automobile and the
    Spatial Transformation of American
    Culture," in Lewis and Goldstein, *The
    Automobile and American Culture*, 95.

24 Letter from Frank Lloyd Wright to
    Louis Sullivan, April 2, 1923, FLWA.

25 Frank Lloyd Wright, "An Autobiogra-
    phy" (1932), in *Frank Lloyd Wright:
    Collected Writings, Including An
    Autobiography*, vol. II, 1930–1932, ed.
    Bruce Brooks Pfeiffer (New York:
    Rizzoli in association with The Frank
    Lloyd Wright Foundation, 1992), 276.
    According to Pfeiffer, Wright began
    writing his autobiography in the sum-
    mer of 1926; 102.

26 Ibid., 279.

27 Ibid., 282.

28 Biographical information on Doheny is drawn largely from Starr, 125–27, and Robert Sweeney, *Wright in Hollywood: Visions of a New Architecture* (New York, Cambridge, Mass., and London: The Architectural History Foundation and MIT Press, 1994), 16–18.

29 Sweeney, *Wright in Hollywood*, 19.

30 For each of the five major projects under discussion – Doheny, Tahoe, A. M. Johnson, Gordon Strong, and San Marcos – I have sought to understand Wright's designs more fully by examining related evidence. Thus, paralleling my study of drawings, correspondence, and related archival documents at the FLWA and elsewhere, I have examined historical maps and geological surveys to determine routes of access available to Wright and his clients, and to verify actual topography. Visits to each of the five sites have enabled me to confirm actual views and to identify specific locations where the buildings themselves might have been located according to Wright's proposals. By these means it has been possible to construct hypothetical models suggesting a three-dimensional image of Wright's designs.

31 Frank Lloyd Wright, "Ausgeführte Bauten und Entwürfe von Frank Lloyd Wright" (1910), in *Collected Writings* I, 106.

32 Frank Lloyd Wright, "The Disappearing City" (1932), in *Frank Lloyd Wright: Collected Writings*, vol. III, 1931–1939, ed. Bruce Brooks Pfeiffer (New York: Rizzoli in association with The Frank Lloyd Wright Foundation, 1993), 89, 91.

33 Edgar Chambless, *Roadtown* (New York: Roadtown Press, 1910). The Algiers project is illustrated in Pierre Jeanneret, *Oeuvre Complète 1929–1934* (Zurich: W. Boesiger, 1935), esp. 140–143. Historical sources for Le Corbusier's design are discussed in Stanislaus von Moos, *Le Corbusier: Elements of a Synthesis* (Cambridge, Mass.: MIT Press, 1979), 204.

34 Wright, "Autobiography" 190.

35 Frank Lloyd Wright, "The Architect and the Machine" (1894), in Pfeiffer, *Collected Writings* I, 21.

36 I am grateful to Nabil Abu-Dayyeh for bringing the remote pavilion of uncertain function to my attention while he was completing his doctoral dissertation, "The Place of Dining in Frank Lloyd Wright's Houses" (University of Pennsylvania, 1993). As he noticed, its placement extends the axis of the dining room and focuses its view.

37 The powerful composition of the house as it relates to its site is described by Terence Riley in his essay "The Landscapes of Frank Lloyd Wright: A Pattern of Work," in Riley, *Frank Lloyd Wright, Architect*, 101.

38 Anthony Alofsin, *Frank Lloyd Wright: The Lost Years, 1910–1922 – A Study of Influence* (Chicago and London: University of Chicago Press, 1993), 32.

39 Ibid., esp. 4–5, 51, 88, 101. Parallels between Wright's work and Italian examples are discussed in Alexander C. Gorlin, "Frank Lloyd Wright and the Italian Villa," *A + U (Architecture and Urbanism)* 90 (October 1990), 44–56.

40 For example, Frank Lloyd Wright, *Drawings for a Living Architecture* (New York: Horizon Press for the Bear Run Foundation Inc. and the Edgar J. Kaufmann Charitable Foundation, 1959), 120. The anonymous text accompanying the illustrations is by Edgar Kaufmann, jr.

41 Wright, "Ausgeführte Bauten und Entwürfe," 104–5.

42 Ibid., 103–4.

43 Frank Lloyd Wright, "Plan by Frank Lloyd Wright" (1916), in Pfeiffer, *Collected Writings* I, 140–43. The plan is discussed by Gwendolyn Wright in her essay "Frank Lloyd Wright and the Domestic Landscape," in Riley, *Frank Lloyd Wright, Architect*, 91–93. Wright's entry in the competition for a model suburb was originally published in *City Residential Land Development: Studies in Planning, Competitive Plans for Subdividing a Typical Quarter Section of Land in the Outskirts of Chicago*, ed. A. Yeomans (Chicago: University of Chicago Press, 1916).

44 Curtis Besinger, "Working with Mr. Wright: What It Was Like" (unpublished manuscript), 373. I am grateful to Professor Besinger – long a senior apprentice at Taliesin – for sharing his research. His revised manuscript has since been published as Curtis Besinger, *Working With Mr. Wright: What It Was Like* (New York: Cambridge University Press, 1995).

45 Wright, "Autobiography," 224–25.

46 Ibid., 226–27.

47 Among the first readily available books in English on Japanese architecture was Edward S. Morse, *Japanese Homes and Their Surroundings* (Boston: Ticknor and Company 1886; reprinted, New York: Dover Publications, Inc., 1961). Detailed drawings of the Japanese buildings at the World's

Columbian Exposition, along with descriptions of their authentic historic detail, may be found in P. B. Wight, "Japanese Architecture at Chicago," *The Inland Architect and News Record* 20 (December 1892), 49–50, plate 6; and P. B. Wight, "Japanese Architecture in Chicago, Part II," The *Inland Architect and News Record* 20 (January 1893), 61, plate 5. These buildings have been analyzed more recently in Masahiro Mishima, "The Factor and the Motivation of the Hō-ō-Den's Construction in the World's Columbian Exposition in Chicago, 1893," *Journal of Architecture, Planning and Environmental Engineering* (November 1991), 151–63; continued in April 1992 issue, 107–16. Other well-illustrated articles on Japanese architecture appearing in the late 1890s include C. T. Mathews, "Eastern Asia: Or, China, Corea, and Japan," and "Japanese Architecture," *Architectural Record* 5 (1895), 288–97 and 383–92. One of the first to note Japanese elements in Wright's early work was Clay Lancaster, "Japanese Buildings in the United States Before 1900: Their Influence upon American Domestic Architecture," *Art Bulletin* 35 (September 1953), 217–24. Ties between rendering styles of Wright's office and Japanese prints are discussed in Julia Meech-Pekarik, "Frank Lloyd Wright and Japanese Prints," *Bulletin of the Metropolitan Museum of Art* 40 (Fall 1982), 48–57. Among more recent publications are Kevin Nute, "Frank Lloyd Wright and Japanese Architecture: A Study in Inspiration," *Journal of Design History* 7 (1994), 169–85, and Nute, *Frank Lloyd Wright and Japan* (New York: Van Nostrand Reinhold, 1993).

48 Ralph Adams Cram, "The Early Architecture of Japan," *The Architectural Review* (Boston) 5 (1898), 54–57.

49 Ralph Adams Cram, "The Later Architecture of Japan," *The Architectural Review* (Boston) 5 (1898), 77–80.

50 C. T. Matthews [sic], "A Temple of the Tokugawa at Nikko," *Architectural Record* 4 (October–December 1894), 191–209. In this article, Mathews also describes how Japanese buildings, in contrast to American and European examples, have foundations "not built in the ground but on the ground" so that, in the case of an earthquake, they "avoid being snapped off, and tend rather to slide." Wright's solution for the Imperial Hotel was not dissimilar. The danger of fire, and of falling roof tiles during earthquakes — seeming to predict Wright's own words in describing his approach to the hotel — was discussed in Katharine C. Budd, "Japanese Houses," *Architectural Record* 19 (January 1906), 3–26.

51 Wright's stay at the Kanaya Hotel, Nikko, is confirmed by his signatures in the register in April 1905 and December 1918. I am grateful to the hotel staff and to the present Mr. Kanaya, whose grandfather bought the original hotel and added a wing for Western visitors in 1892. Mr. Kanaya showed me the register books in September 1992 and examined the older portions of the hotel with me to determine which room Wright might have had. Wright's entries had earlier been discovered by Masami Tanigawa, who shared the information with Margo Stipe at Taliesin West, and it was Ms. Stipe, to whom I am also grateful, who first informed me.

52 Interview with Nobu and Kameki Tsuchiura, Tokyo, June 17, 1992. Mr. Tsuchiura worked with Wright on the Imperial Hotel in Tokyo, and he and his wife later worked with Wright in Los Angeles and at Taliesin. Both Mr. and Mrs. Tsuchiura remembered traveling to China with Wright and Miriam Noel so that Wright could check on the rugs. Mr. Tsuchiura also recalled working at Taliesin with Richard Neutra and Werner Moser on the Lake Tahoe summer colony and the California block houses. I am grateful to Mr. and Mrs. Tsuchiura for making the difficult journey to my hotel in Tokyo to meet with me, and for sharing their memories. I am also grateful to Yoshiyuki Takaichi of the Mainichi Newspapers for arranging the interview. The most current account of Wright's travels in Japan is Margo Stipe, "Wright's First Trip to Japan," *Frank Lloyd Wright Quarterly* 6 (Spring 1995), 21–23.

53 Frank Lloyd Wright, "The Print and the Renaissance" (1917), in Pfeiffer, *Collected Writings* I, 152.

54 Wright, "Autobiography," 244.

55 Anthony Alofsin is one of several observers who have noted the similarities between the Imperial Hotel and traditional Chinese planning. Ties between Wright's earlier work, such as Wolf Lake, and principles of the Ecole des Beaux-Arts were noted early on by Henry-Russell Hitchcock in his essay "Frank Lloyd Wright and the Academic Tradition of the Early Eighteen-Nineties," *Journal of the Warburg and Courtauld Institutes* 7 (1944), 46–63.

56 Frank Lloyd Wright, "The New Imperial Hotel, Tokio" (1923), in Pfeiffer,

Collected Writings I, 177. Neil Levine has suggested that Wright's awareness of ancient "yedo," or "searching for a way to understand and thereby express the natural history of the site," was strongly influential, and led to his identification of "the archetypal image of the 'sacred mountain' Fujiyama" as "emblematic of the place"; Levine, "The Architecture of Frank Lloyd Wright" (unpublished manuscript), 200. I am grateful to Mr. Levine for allowing me access to his impressive and comprehensive study.

57 The hotel, reportedly constructed except for its roof tiles, was intended as part of a recreational complex. See Masami Tanigawa, "Wright's Little-Known Japanese Projects," *Frank Lloyd Wright Quarterly* 6 (Spring 1995), 16–19.

58 Although designed in 1918, when Wright was in Japan, the house was built only in 1924, well after his departure. Construction was supervised by two of his Japanese assistants, Arata Endo and Makoto Minami, and it is generally assumed that many of the details reflect their contributions. Information on the house and its recent restoration as the guest house of the Yodogawa Steel Company is contained in a brochure, Masami Tanigawa, "The Yamamura House" (Ashiya Board of Education, not dated).

59 The restored house is illustrated in Michael Webb, "Historic Architecture: Wright in Japan: Preserving the Yamamura House near Kobe," *Architectural Digest* 50 (August 1993), 54–58.

60 The most complete history of the commissions is Kathryn Smith, *Frank Lloyd Wright: Hollyhock House and Olive Hill, Buildings and Projects for Aline Barnsdall* (New York: Rizzoli, 1992). Also of interest is Neil Levine, "Hollyhock House and the Romance of Southern California," *Art in America* 71 (September 1983), 150–64.

61 Frank Lloyd Wright, "In the Cause of Architecture: The Third Dimension," unpublished manuscript (Los Angeles, February 9, 1923). John Lloyd Wright Collection, folder III/2, no. 8, Avery Library, Columbia University, New York. I am grateful to Robert Sweeney for bringing this manuscript to my attention.

62 Wright, "Autobiography," 270.

63 For example, Dimitri Tselos, "Exotic Influences in Frank Lloyd Wright," *Magazine of Art* 47 (April 1953), 160–69, 184; also by Tselos, "Frank Lloyd Wright and World Architecture," *Journal of the Society of Architectural Historians* 28 (March 1969), 58–72. Among others, Gabriel Weisberg, "Frank Lloyd Wright and Pre-Columbian Art – The Background for His Architecture," *Art Quarterly* 30 (Spring 1967), 40–51.

64 Wright, "Autobiography," 267.

65 Letter from Frank Lloyd Wright to Aline Barnsdall, January 7, 1920, FLWA.

66 Extensive descriptions and details are provided in Smith, *Frank Lloyd Wright: Hollyhock House*, esp. 80–108.

67 Alofsin, *Frank Lloyd Wright: The Lost Years*, 226. Alofsin also lists many of the published sources available to Wright.

68 "The Sunken Maya Race of Yucatan," *The Pan-American Magazine* 36 (November 1923), 201–2. Among earlier articles including detailed illustrations is Herbert J. Spinden, *A Study of Maya Art: Its Subject Matter and Historical Development*, Memoirs of the Peabody Museum of American Archaeology and Ethnology, Harvard University, vol. 4 (Cambridge, Mass.: Peabody Museum, 1913), plate 2.

69 Among the first illustrated articles on Lhasa are J. Deniker, "New Light on Lhasa, the Forbidden City," *Century Magazine* 66 (August 1903), 544–54; "The Unveiling of Lhasa," *Current Literature* 38 (April 1905), 347–52; Shaoching H. Chuan, "The Most Extraordinary City in the World: Notes on Lhasa – The Mecca of the Buddhist Faith," *National Geographic* 23 (October 1912), 959–72; and John Claude White, "The World's Strangest Capital," *National Geographic* 29 (March 1916), 273–95. Wright's photograph of Lhasa is noted in Edgar Tafel, *Apprentice to Genius: Years with Frank Lloyd Wright* (New York: McGraw-Hill, 1979), 165.

70 The illustration was published in Thomas A. Joyce, *Mexican Archaeology* (London: Philip Lee Warner, 1920), p. XXV. 1. In addition to the displays he saw at the expositions of 1893 and 1915, several publications on Pre-Columbian architecture provided impressive photographs and drawings of such large-scale development, including Barnard Shipp, *The Indian and Antiquities of America* (Philadelphia: Sherman and Co., 1897); Thomas A. Joyce, *Mexican Archaeology: An Introduction to the Archaeology of the Mexican and Mayan Civilizations of Pre-Spanish America* (London: Philip Lee Warner, 1914); Sylvanus Griswold Morely, *The Inscriptions at Copan* (Washington D.C.: The

Carnegie Institution, 1920), with a frontispiece astonishingly similar to Louis I. Kahn's visionary renderings of Philadelphia's Market Street East; and T. A. Joyce, "The Archaeological Heritage of Mexico," *Pan-American Magazine* 35 (October 1922), 197–203.

71 Frank Lloyd Wright, *A Testament* (New York: Horizon Press, 1957), 111–12.

72 Edgar L. Hewett, "America's Archaeological Heritage," *Art and Archaeology* 4 (December 1916), 257–66. A similar blurring of distinctions occurs in Paul Radin, *The Story of the American Indian* (New York: Boni and Liveright, 1927).

73 Richard J. Neutra, *Wie baut Amerika?* (Stuttgart: Julius Hoffman, 1927), esp. 59–77.

74 J. P. Harrington, "House-Builders of the Desert," *Art and Archaeology* 4 (December, 1916), 299–306.

75 As reflected in Norman Bel Geddes, *Miracle in the Evening*, ed. W. Kelley (Garden City, N.Y.: Doubleday and Company, 1960), esp. chapters 9 and 10, 98–167.

76 H. De Fries, *Frank Lloyd Wright: Aus dem Lebenswerke eines Architekten* (Berlin: Verlag Ernst Pollak, 1926).

77 He was apparently willing to jeopardize the larger Wendingen publication of his work in order to support De Fries. Letter from Frank Lloyd Wright to H. J. Wijdefeld, January 7, 1925, FLWA.

78 Except where otherwise indicated, information on these commissions is drawn from Sweeney, *Wright in Hollywood.*

79 Frank Lloyd Wright, "The Art and Craft of the Machine" (1901), in Pfeiffer, *Collected Writings* 1, 65–66; and Wright, "Ausgeführte Bauten und Entwürfe," 107.

80 Wright, "In the Cause of Architecture: Second Paper," 127.

81 Wright, "The New Imperial Hotel, Tokio," 180.

82 His characterization of the typical concrete block, and one of several summaries of how he came to conceive the system, appears in Wright, "Autobiography," 276–77.

83 Frank Lloyd Wright, "In the Cause of Architecture IV: Fabrication and Imagination" (1927), in Pfeiffer, *Collected Writings* 1, 242–43.

84 Frank Lloyd Wright, "In the Cause of Architecture I: The Logic of the Plan" (1928), in Pfeiffer, *Collected Writings* 1, 252.

85 Wright, "Autobiography," 277.

86 Ibid., 287.

87 Ibid., 288.

88 Letter from Frank Lloyd Wright to Louis Sullivan, March 3, 1923, FLWA.

89 In addition to the account in Sweeney, *Wright in Hollywood,* the house is also described in Smith, *Frank Lloyd Wright: Hollyhock House,* esp. 168–69. It was Smith who discovered the location of the proposed house; I am grateful to Robert Sweeney for sharing this information with me and for taking me to the site.

90 FLWA 2304.008.

91 Wright, "In the Cause of Architecture: The Logic of the Plan," 253.

92 Letter from Frank Lloyd Wright to Chas. W. Ennis, February 5, 1925; FLWA.

93 John Brinckerhoff Jackson, *Discovering the Vernacular Landscape* (New Haven and London: Yale University Press, 1984), 70.

94 Jackson, 155.

95 Frank Lloyd Wright, "Modern Architecture, Being the Kahn Lectures" (1931), in Pfeiffer, *Collected Writings* 2, 64.

96 Ibid., 76.

97 Wright, "The Disappearing City," *Collected Writings,* 93.

98 Ibid., 72.

99 Ralph Waldo Emerson, "Nature," in *Essays and English Traits,* ed. Charles W. Eliot (New York: P. F. Collier and Son Corporation, 1937), 228. The first edition of this essay had appeared in 1844.

100 Wright recalled that he was "called away to Tahoe" during the construction of La Miniatura; "Autobiography," 288. One of the drawings for the Tahoe project is dated June 29, 1923; FLWA.

101 Information on the history of the area and the ownership of the land comes from Edward B. Scott, *The Saga of Lake Tahoe,* vol. 2, 2nd ed. (Crystal Bay, Lake Tahoe, Nevada: Sierra-Tahoe Publishing Co., 1957), esp. 17, 126–31, 381; and Paul E. Nesbitt, *The History of Emerald Bay, Location of Emerald Bay State Park,* written as a unit inventory (Sacramento: Resource Protection Division, Department of Parks and Recreation, 1989), esp. 2–3.

102 The hotel to have replaced the Tallac was designed by Walter Webber and was to have been erected by Anita M. Baldwin; it is described in "Historic Pile to Live Again" and illustrated as "An Ancient Castle of Flanders Transplanted in the High Sierras" in the *Los Angeles Sunday Times,* November 28, 1915.

103 The chain of title is summarized in Nesbitt, 2.

104 This and following quotes of Jessie Armstrong are taken from an interview, Mrs. Walter Bush with Jessie Armstrong, ms. 70/130 C, Bancroft Library, University of California, Berkeley. I am grateful to Kathryn Smith and Robert Sweeney for bringing the interview to my attention, and for directing me to other sources of information regarding Lake Tahoe.

105 As reported in Sweeney, *Wright in Hollywood*, 105–6.

106 Ibid., 106–7.

107 The *Tahoe* was launched in 1896 and ended service only in 1940; the *Meteor* was launched in 1876 and ended service in the 1930s. During the time that Wright visited, the *Tahoe* left Tahoe City around nine in the morning and circled the lake in a counterclockwise direction; the *Meteor* circled in the opposite direction, and would have left Emerald Bay Camp at mid-afternoon and landed at Tahoe City around five that evening. Information on the lake's steamers and their schedules is taken from Owen F. McKean, *The Railroads and Steamers of Lake Tahoe* (The Western Railroader, not dated), 14, and *A Lake Tahoe Album: Photographs, 1850–1940* (Tahoe, Nevada: Caesars Tahoe, 1980), not paginated.

108 Notes on the perspective of the Shore type cabin, FLWA 2205.003, indicate these materials: "white sand blocks, stained boards, copper hip and ridges." Elsewhere on the drawing, also in Wright's hand, is the note, "block technique," presumably referring back to Doheny. The notes appear to have been added later, as was often the case, and may have been appended while Henry-Russell

Hitchcock was working with Wright on the catalogue of his work, *In the Nature of Materials* (New York: Duell, Sloan and Pearce, 1942).

109 According to texts accompanying illustrations in De Fries. The site plan of the inn in De Fries was prepared for publication from a drawing sent by Wright, presumably the surviving site plan, which carries crop marks and other notes indicating its adaptation. For several drawings published in De Fries, no originals have yet been found.

110 Frank Lloyd Wright, notation to plan and elevation, FLWA 2205.008.

111 The photograph is published in De Fries; the original has not been found.

112 Frank Lloyd Wright, "In the Cause of Architecture V: The New World" (1927), in Pfeiffer, *Collected Writings* I, 245.

113 The club was originally founded in 1887 as the Adirondack Mountain Reserve, renamed the Ausable Lake and Mountain Club in 1892, when its principal buildings began to be erected, and later became known simply as the Ausable Club; Harvey H. Kaiser, *Great Camps of the Adirondacks* (Boston: D. R. Godine, 1982), 51–53. I am grateful to Richard Longstreth for arranging my visit to the club.

114 Robert Chambers Reamer's design is illustrated and discussed in David L. Leavengood, "Old Faithful Inn: Yellowstone Park's Rustic Wonder of 1903," *Interior Design* 58 (February 1987), 306–7. It had been described and illustrated in "A Rustic Yellowstone Park Hostelry," *Western Architect* 3 (October 1904), 4–7.

115 Interview, Mrs. Walter Bush with Jessie Armstrong. Presumably this was

one of the cabin types; she does not identify which.

116 For example, Nesbitt, illustration of Washoe Tipi at Emerald Bay Camp, not numbered.

117 For example, both the conical and long forms are illustrated and identified as "wigwams" in David I. Bushnell, Jr., "Ojibway Habitations and Other Structures," *Annual Report of the Board of Regents of the Smithsonian Institution* (Washington, D.C.: Smithsonian Institution, 1917), 609–18. The "wigwam" began to be differentiated as a permanent structure at about this time; see, for example, T. T. Waterman, "North American Indian Dwellings," *Annual Report of the Board of Regents of the Smithsonian Institution* (Washington, D.C.: Smithsonian Institution, 1924), 461–85.

118 A major visual source of Pre-Columbian architecture, well illustrated with examples of sweeping scale and with individual temples, is Désiré Charnay, *The Ancient Cities of the New World: Being Voyages and Explorations in Mexico and Central America from 1857–1882*, trans. J. Gonino and Helen S. Conant (New York: Harper and Brothers, Franklin Square, 1887).

119 Sources of angular elements in Wright's early work, especially as they manifest themselves in his decorative details, are discussed in Alofsin, *Frank Lloyd Wright: The Lost Years*, esp. 39, 260.

120 Wright, "Autobiography," 111.

121 Ibid., 234.

122 Interview, Mrs. Walter Bush with Jessie Armstrong.

123 Nesbitt, 11; Scott, 131.

124 The history of the Nakoma Country Club commission is documented in Mary Jane Hamilton, "The Nakoma Country Club," *Frank Lloyd Wright and Madison: Eight Decades of Artistic and Social Interaction*, ed. P. Sprague (Madison: Elvehjem Museum of Art, University of Wisconsin–Madison, 1990), 77–82.

125 Perspective and details, Library of Congress drawing 152.37.

126 Letter from Frank Lloyd Wright to the Nakoma Directors [1924], FLWA.

127 FLWA 2405.011.

128 Frank Lloyd Wright, "In the Cause of Architecture," *Architectural Record* 23 (March 1908), 157.

129 Descriptions by early tourists include Charles Francis Saunders, "The Lowest, Hottest, Dryest Spot in America," *Travel* 34 (December 1919), 25–28, 48; and Zane Grey, "Death Valley," *Harper's* 140 (May 1920), 758–70.

130 Described in "Mysterious Death Valley Is Unmasked: Auto Club Maps and Signs Make Once Feared Region of Desolation a Rather Nice Place for a Spring or Fall Vacation," *Touring Topics* 13 (April 1921), 13–15. Among other automobile associations then being formed was the American Automobile Association, established in March 1902; Fink, 31. The lure of automobiles, Indians, and the desert (in New Mexico) was also described by D. H. Lawrence in his essay "Indians and an Englishman," *Dial* 74 (1923), 144–52.

131 Ernest McGaffey, "In the Beginning, God Created Desolation – Death Valley," *Touring Topics* 14 (June 1922), 16–20, 34–42.

132 Zapatka, 96–128.

133 "Desert Road," 819A309, filed under California, Los Angeles, Views, Highways, U.S. Geographic File, Library of Congress.

134 Obituaries, "Allan G. Odell, 90, Burma Shave Executive Linked Beards to Bards," *New York Times*, January 22, 1994, and "Leonard C. Odell, 83, Poet for Burma Shave," *New York Times*, October 8, 1991.

135 Unless otherwise indicated, biographical information on Johnson, his family, and his associates comes from Dorothy Shally and William Bolton, *Death Valley's Fabulous Showplace: Scotty's Castle* (Yosemite, California: Flying Spur Press, 1973), esp. 8–19, and Hank Johnson, *The Man and the Myth: Death Valley Scotty* (Yosemite, California: Flying Spur Press, 1972), esp. 7–8, 22–40.

136 As recorded in letters from Johnson to his mother, October 31, 1905, November 2, 1905, November 21, 1905, and January 15, 1906, Shadelands Ranch Historical Museum, Walnut Creek Historical Society, Walnut Creek, California (hereinafter Shadelands). I am grateful to Elizabeth Isles and Rosemary Mazzetti for their generous assistance in making materials available to me.

137 The history of land acquisition, together with a history of the site, is documented in Susan J. Buchel, *Scotty's Home Was Not His Castle: A Historical Survey of Death Valley Scotty's Lower Vine Ranch* (Field Report, in partial fulfillment of the Master's Degree (University of California, Riverside, March 1985), esp. chain of title notes, 21.

138 Letter from A. M. Johnson to Walter Scott, May 19, 1921, Shadelands.

139 Letter from A. M. Johnson to Walter Scott, July 12, 1921, Shadelands.

140 The date is consistently reported in accounts of Scotty's Castle. Confirming this, an examination of purchase orders shows a marked increase in the purchase of portland cement and other building materials beginning in November 1922 and continuing into early 1924. Death Valley National Monument, Scotty's Castle Museum Collection (hereinafter DVNM), mss. 15, box 3, folder 2, book 8, purchase orders, 1921–31. I am grateful to Marcia Stout and Blair Davenport for their assistance in my research.

141 "Death Valley Scotty Building Home on Desert," July 25, 1923, unidentified newspaper clipping. Johnson is mentioned in a second newspaper clipping, "Scotty Again Gets Publicity," unidentified and not dated. Both clippings are in scrapbook 15919, DVNM.

142 "Scotty Mystery Thick As Ever," October 23, 1923, unidentified newspaper clipping, scrapbook 15919, DVNM.

143 "Scotty Has Mine, Goldfielders Say," *Goldfield Tribune*, 27 December 1923, scrapbook 15919, DVNM.

144 Letter from A. M. Johnson to Walter Scott, January 9, 1922, Shadelands.

145 Sweeney, *Wright in Hollywood*, 250, n. 11.

146 The letter of agreement from Johnson to Wright is dated July 19, 1924, and is in the FLWA. On February 2, 1924, Schindler wrote Neutra that Wright was in Los Angeles until the end of the month and mentions a skyscraper project in Chicago; Sweeney, Chronology, 191.

147 Wright's stay at the Beverly Hills Hotel is documented in Sweeney, Chronology, 191. A. M. Johnson recalled Wright staying there in a letter to Henry-Russell Hitchcock, June 18, 1941. Wright had thought the date was 1922, but as Hitchcock said in a letter to A. M. Johnson, February 6, 1941, Wright's memory was "rather vague as to exact dates." Correspondence between Hitchcock and Johnson, mss. 19, box 7, folder 9, DVNM.

148 Letter from A. M. Johnson to Henry-Russell Hitchcock, June 18, 1941; mss. 19, box 7, folder 9, DVNM. The account corresponds with one by George C. Lyon, who had been a student at Deep Springs College at the time, and remembered the party stopping to visit on their way to Death Valley in the late fall of 1923. Evidence now suggests a slightly later date, as noted below. Mr. Lyon's account was enclosed with his letter to Richard Bernstein, Scotty's Castle, September 24, 1987, DVNM.

149 Wright, "Autobiography," 291.

150 *Rand McNally Official 1923 Auto Trails Map District Number 1916*, Map Division, Library of Congress.

151 In 1995, the college is still active; information comes from "Deep Springs College," a promotional brochure, and from its president, Sherwin W. Howard, whom I interviewed during a visit in January 1994. I am grateful to President Howard for assisting me in research at the college and for taking the time to describe the institution's objectives to me. Although located in California, its mailing address is Dyer, Nevada.

152 Information on Sachse, a confirming account of Wright's visit that places

it in March 1924, and references to correspondence confirming this date, are from Jan Vleck, a 1969 graduate of Deep Springs College who has undertaken research on these questions. I am grateful to Mr. Vleck for sharing his information with me, and to President Howard for putting us in touch.

153 Robert Sweeney and Neil Levine, working with postmarks and period calendars, have determined this date from correspondence in the possession of Sachse's daughter, Heide Moore. Sachse died in 1977. An account by James S. Mansfield, who attended Deep Springs College from 1922 to 1925, also places the visit as being in 1924; I am grateful to Jan Vleck for sending me a copy.

154 I am grateful to Jan Vleck for this information, and for furnishing extracts of letters confirming the above dates.

155 As recorded in Hitchcock, *In the Nature of Materials*, 124.

156 Letter from A. M. Johnson to Henry-Russell Hitchcock, June 18, 1941, DVNM.

157 "Million Dollar Cottage Going Up in Death Valley," December 30, 1924, source not noted, scrapbook 15919, DVNM.

158 Areas of cut and fill required to accommodate Wright's design became apparent in studying the design in relation to topographic surveys.

159 "Touch of Egypt Transported to Scotty's Canyon," *Tonopah Times*, January 7, 1925, scrapbook 15919, DVNM. The article reported that Scotty had sent plans signed by Frank Lloyd Wright, and the description that follows could only have been

made by examining drawings such as those that survive.

160 The element was built as an aviary; its evolving function is suggested on various site plans, for example, FLWA 4015.014, 4015.017, and 4015.018.

161 Letter from A. M. Johnson to Henry-Russell Hitchcock, June 18, 1941, DVNM.

162 As recounted by Martin D. de Dubovay, an artisan who worked on the project that Johnson actually built. Taped interview, 1976, position 5:18, DVNM. Johnson's characterization of Wright's design as sepulchral was confirmed by Mary Liddecoat, who overheard Johnson making a similar remark. Miss Liddecoat was a close friend of the Johnsons in the 1920s and was later named by Johnson president of the Gospel Foundation, which he established. I interviewed Miss Liddecoat on October 24, 1994, and am grateful for her openness.

163 Letter from Matthew R. Thompson II to James B. Thompson, Superintendent, Death Valley National Monument, April 11, 1975, DVNM.

164 Shally and Bolton, *Scotty's Castle*, 11.

165 Stanley W. Paher, *Death Valley's Scotty's Castle: The Story Behind the Scenery* (Death Valley: KC Publications Inc., 1985), 44.

166 Letter from Henry-Russell Hitchcock to A. M. Johnson, February 6, 1941, mss. 19, box 7, folder 9, DVNM.

167 Both elements are illustrated and described in Charles B. Hunt, *Death Valley: Geology, Ecology, Archaeology* (Berkeley, Los Angeles, and London: University of California Press, 1975), esp. 5–6 and 66–87.

168 Detailed biographical information and extensive documentation of the

Gordon Strong commission can be found in Mark E. Reinberger, "Frank Lloyd Wright's Sugarloaf Mountain 'Automobile Objective' Project" (Masters thesis, Cornell University, January 1982). Reinberger presented a shortened version, with additional information, in "The Sugarloaf Mountain Project and Frank Lloyd Wright's Vision of a New World," *Journal of the Society of Architectural Historians* 38:52 (March 1984), 38–52. Unless otherwise noted, references to Reinberger are to his thesis.

169 Reinberger, 5–6.

170 Ibid., 6–7.

171 According to an informational brochure, "Sugarloaf Mountain," distributed at the site by Stronghold Incorporated, 7901 Comus Road, Dickerson, Maryland.

172 U.S. Bureau of Soils, soil map, Frederick County, Maryland (Washington, D.C.), 1919.

173 Anna I. Jonas, *Geologic Map of Frederick County* (Maryland Geological Survey in Cooperation with U.S. Geological Survey, 1938).

174 Reinberger, 9.

175 Letter from Gordon Strong to Frank Lloyd Wright, September 2, 1924, filed with Gordon Strong's papers at Stronghold, Incorporated, 7901 Comus Road, Dickerson, Md., 20842 (hereinafter Stronghold). Stronghold, Incorporated, is a nonprofit corporation organized by Gordon Strong in 1946; it owns and operates the Sugarloaf Mountain property, which is open to the public.

176 Letter of agreement from Gordon Strong to Frank Lloyd Wright, September 22, 1924, Stronghold.

177 For example, De Fries.

178 Zapatka, esp. 96–97.

179 As specified in the letter of agreement cited in n.176, September 22, 1924.

180 Letter from Frank Lloyd Wright to Gordon Strong, not dated, Stronghold.

181 Eric Mendelsohn, *Letters of an Architect*, ed. Oskar Beyer, trans. Geoffrey Strachan (London, New York, and Toronto: Abelard-Schulman, 1967), 71–73. The date of the letter describing his visit to Taliesin is November 5, 1924.

182 Reinberger, 68.

183 Anthony Alofsin, "Frank Lloyd Wright and Modernism," in Riley, *Frank Lloyd Wright, Architect*, 40. Schindler had worked for Wright from 1917 through 1921, and on occasional projects until 1923; Werner M. Moser, from Switzerland, worked for Wright from 1923 to 1928.

184 Frank Lloyd Wright, "In the Cause of Architecture VII: The Meaning of Materials – Concrete" (1928), in Pfeiffer, *Collected Writings* I, 301–4.

185 Letter from Frank Lloyd Wright to Gordon Strong, November 10 [1924], Stronghold.

186 Letter from Gordon Strong to Frank Lloyd Wright, November 14, 1924, Stronghold. In the same letter, Strong refers to his one prior visit to Taliesin, presumably the one during which he and Wright discussed the commission in the summer of 1924.

187 Harold F. Blanchard, "Ramp Design in Public Garages," *Architectural Forum* 35 (November 1921), 169–75. Strong had remembered the source as something called the Ramp Building Corporation of New York, but I have found no evidence that any such organization ever existed.

188 Letter from Frank Lloyd Wright to Gordon Strong [December 1924], Stronghold. Although the letter is undated, it contains holiday greetings, and the portion dealing with the scale debate places it between December 8, 1924 (letter from Gordon Strong to Frank Lloyd Wright, Stronghold) and December 31, 1924 (telegram from Wright to Strong, Stronghold).

189 Telegram from Gordon Strong to Frank Lloyd Wright, not dated; telegram from Wright to Strong, December 31, 1924; both in Stronghold.

190 Telegram from Gordon Strong to Frank Lloyd Wright, January 11, 1925, Stronghold. Other communications over the debated scale include a letter from Strong to Wright, December 3, 1924, and a telegram from Wright to Strong, December 3, 1924; both in Stronghold.

191 Neutra's involvement with the design (illustrated with two additional drawings in Neutra's hand from the Neutra Archive, UCLA Special Collections) is discussed in Thomas S. Hines, *Richard Neutra and the Search for Modern Architecture* (New York and Oxford: Oxford University Press, 1982), 54, figs. 38, 39. It is conceivable that these drawings reflect Neutra's independent development of an early concept; had they been officially sanctioned by Wright, it is unlikely that Neutra would have taken them with him when he left Wright's employ.

192 For an examination of this evidence, see Reinberger, 34, 101–3.

193 FLWA 2505.059.

194 Letter from Gordon Strong to Frank Lloyd Wright, April 6, 1925, Stronghold.

195 Letter from Frank Lloyd Wright to Gordon Strong, April 29, 1925, Stronghold.

196 Reinberger has documented the early history of the planetarium as it relates to Wright's scheme and has speculated on aspects of its iconography; 114–17.

197 Telegram from Gordon Strong to Frank Lloyd Wright, August 25, 1925. Wright had called Strong's office on August 24; memorandum from IMP (presumably Strong's secretary) to Strong, Stronghold.

198 Telegram from Frank Lloyd Wright to Gordon Strong, August 26, 1925, Stronghold. Letters of invitation were sent to Benjamin F. Affleck, 210 South LaSalle Street; Earle Shultz, in the Edison Building; Lewis B. Ermeling, 134 South LaSalle Street; Alfred MacArthur, at the National Life; and Kent O. Mitchell, at the Real Estate Loan Department of the New York Life Insurance Company.

199 Wright, "In the Cause of Architecture VII: The Meaning of Materials – Concrete," 300.

200 Among many publications on Maillart, one of the more recent is David P. Billington, *Robert Maillart and the Art of Reinforced Concrete* (New York, Cambridge, Mass., and London: The Architectural History Foundation and MIT Press, 1989). The Valtschielbach Bridge is illustrated on p. 36.

201 Letter from Frank Lloyd Wright to Gordon Strong, September 8, 1925, Stronghold.

202 Letter from Gordon Strong to Frank Lloyd Wright, September 8, 1925, Stronghold.

203 Letter from Frank Lloyd Wright to Gordon Strong, September 22, 1925, Stronghold.

204 Letter from Gordon Strong to Frank Lloyd Wright, October 14, 1925, Stronghold.

205 Letter from Frank Lloyd Wright to Gordon Strong, October 20, 1925, Stronghold.

206 Ibid.

207 A drawing had been published in Elias Ehrenburg, "Ein Entwurf Tatlins," *Frülicht* 3 (Spring 1923); it was reprinted in *Frülicht: eine Folge für die Verwirklichung des neuen Baugedankens*, Ulrich Conrads, ed. (Berlin: Ullstein, 1963), 172. Other proposals for spiral structures during these years include Hans Poelzig's *Flughaus* (ca. 1918, unbuilt) and Herman Obrist's Monument (ca. 1902, unbuilt). Both are illustrated in Wolfgang Pehnt, *Expressionist Architecture* (New York and Washington, D.C.: Praeger, 1973), 158.

208 As recounted in Bruce Brooks Pfeiffer, *Frank Lloyd Wright Drawings: Masterworks from the Frank Lloyd Wright Archives* (New York: Harry N. Abrams, Inc., 1990), 163. Early publications of the minaret include Ernst Herzfeld, *Samarra: Aufnahmen und Untersuchungen zur Islamischen Archaeologie* (Berlin, 1907), plate 3.

209 Weisberg, "Frank Lloyd Wright and Pre-Columbian Art," 50. The watchtower at Oaxaca was published in Brantz Mayer, "Observations on Mexican History and Archaeology," *Smithsonian Contributions to Knowledge* 9 (Washington, D.C.: Smithsonian Institution, 1857), 26. In this publication, it is noted that the drawing had first been published by the Smithsonian in 1856.

210 For example, as illustrated in Stuart E. Grummon, "Ancient Pyramids of the New World," *Travel Magazine* 43 (June 1924), 27–28; and Edgar L. Hewett, "The Chaco Canyon in 1921," *Art and Archaeology: The Arts Through-

out the Ages* 14 (September 1922), 114–30.

211 These overlooks are, in 1995, open to the public and described in brochures available to visitors. A road to the summit was never constructed. Strong's later additions are described in Reinberger, 21–23.

212 Letter from Gordon Strong to Frank Lloyd Wright, December 3, 1924, Stronghold.

213 Frank Lloyd Wright, "Modern Architecture, Being the Kahn Lectures" (1931), in Pfeiffer, *Collected Writings* II, 63.

214 Letter from Frank Lloyd Wright to Gordon Strong, July 10, 1929; Stronghold.

215 His letter of thanks for returning the drawings, from Frank Lloyd Wright to Gordon Strong, September 26, 1929, Stronghold. The rendered set of prints and cover sheets also remains in Stronghold's possession.

216 Wright, "The Disappearing City," 105.

217 Wright, "Modern Architecture, Being the Kahn Lectures," 76.

218 He praised Jens Jensen in Frank Lloyd Wright, "Chicago Culture" (1918), in Pfeiffer, *Collected Writings* I, 157. He requested financial support from Jensen, letter from Frank Lloyd Wright to Jens Jensen, November 12, 1927, FLWA. Wright's professional connection to landscape architects is summarized in Charles E. Aguar, "Wrightscapes: The Landscape Architecture of Frank Lloyd Wright" (final narrative report, NEA Grant 90-4216-0047 (October 1991). I am grateful to Indira Berndtson for bringing this report to my attention.

219 Letter from Frank Lloyd Wright to Alexander Woollcott, December 7, 1927, FLWA.

220 For an account of the Arizona Biltmore as it related to Wright, see Sweeney, *Wright in Hollywood*, 120–40.

221 For a lively discussion of the Biltmore and Wright's involvement, see Brendan Gill, *Many Masks: A Life of Frank Lloyd Wright* (New York: G. P. Putnam's Sons, 1987), 302–7.

222 Death Valley's Furnace Creek Inn continues, in 1995, to operate as a luxury resort; its history is summarized in a booklet by Ron Miller, "Fifty Years Ago at Furnace Creek Inn," (Los Angeles: Death Valley Forty-niners, 1977).

223 Sweeney, *Wright in Hollywood*, 140–42.

224 A rendering of the hotel and a map showing its location were published in *Arizona Good Roads Association Illustrated Road Maps and Tour Book* (1913; reprinted, Phoenix: Arizona Highways magazine, 1976), 188–89.

225 As made clear by Martin's response, telegram from Darwin D. Martin to Frank Lloyd Wright, April 6, 1928, FLWA.

226 Letter from Frank Lloyd Wright to John Lloyd Wright, not dated, John Lloyd Wright Collection, folder XIII/7, No. 90, Avery Library, Columbia University, New York. I am grateful to Janet Parks and her assistants for making this information available.

227 Letter from Frank Lloyd Wright to Dr. A. J. Chandler, April 30, 1928, FLWA.

228 Edgar Kaufmann, jr., discussed this pattern in his lectures at Columbia University in January 1971 and in his article, "Precedent and Progress in the Work of Frank Lloyd Wright," *Journal of the Society of Architectural Historians* 39 (May 1980), 145–49. Similar themes are explored in Grant Hildebrand, *The Wright Space: Pattern and Meaning in Frank Lloyd Wright's Houses* (Seattle: University of Washington Press, 1991).

229 Letter from Frank Lloyd Wright to Lloyd Wright, June 1, 1928, as quoted in Sweeney, *Wright in Hollywood*, 143–44. Wright later used many of the same terms in describing the design in the special 1938 issue of *Architectural Forum*; see Pfeiffer, *Collected Writings* III, 283.

230 Bruno Taut, *Weg zum Kristallhause im Wildbachtal*, in *Alpine Architektur* (Hagen: Folkswang-Verlag, 1919).

231 Wright, "Autobiography," 329.

232 Ibid., 327.

233 Ibid., 336.

234 Wright described aspects of his planned approach in a letter to Leerdam, the Dutch manufacturer contracted to create the blocks; letter from Frank Lloyd Wright to P. M. Cochius, March 5, 1929, FLWA.

235 Wright, "Autobiography," 336.

236 Frank Lloyd Wright, "Two Lectures on Architecture" (1931), in Pfeiffer, *Collected Writings* II, 100.

237 Wright, "In the Cause of Architecture VII: The Meaning of Materials – Concrete," 297.

238 Wright, "Autobiography," 329.

239 Frank Lloyd Wright, "In the Cause of Architecture III: The Meaning of Materials – Stone" (1928), in Pfeiffer, *Collected Writings* I, 275.

240 Letter (with Christmas greetings) from Frank Lloyd Wright to Alexander Woollcott [December] 1928, FLWA.

241 Letter from Frank Lloyd Wright to Dr. Chandler, December 31, 1928, FLWA.

242 Letter from Frank Lloyd Wright to Philip LaFollette, Bank of Wisconsin, March 4, 1929, FLWA.

243 Donald Leslie Johnson, *Frank Lloyd Wright Versus America: The 1930s* (Cambridge, Mass., and London: MIT Press, 1990), esp. 21–23.

244 Letter from Frank Lloyd Wright to Franz Aust, March 5, 1929, FLWA.

245 Letter from Frank Lloyd Wright to A. Lawrence Kocher, April 10, 1929, FLWA.

246 Letter from Frank Lloyd Wright to Alexander Chandler, July 10, 1929, FLWA. Wright's early trips by automobile are discussed by Bruce Brooks Pfeiffer, in Collected Writings 3, 70.

247 Wright, "The Disappearing City," 109.

248 Wright, "Autobiography," 344–45. For a discussion of automobile trips, see p. 337.

249 Letters from Frank Lloyd Wright to Pen Page, August 6, 1929, and Darwin D. Martin, September 7, 1929, FLWA.

250 In a letter to his former assistant, Werner Moser, Wright mentions "six boys" who are working with him, including two from Germany, one from Prague (presumably Vladimir Karfick), one from Bavaria, and two Americans; one from Japan was also expected; Frank Lloyd Wright to Werner Moser, July 25, 1929. Among former clients with whom he reestablished contact was A. W. Cutten, letter from Frank Lloyd Wright to Arthur W. Cutten, October 7, 1929, among friends, Samuel Hill, the road builder he had met in Japan who was, in 1929, involved with the Aerocrete Company in New York; letter from Frank Lloyd Wright to Samuel Hill, September 28, 1929. All letters, FLWA. Samuel Hill's papers are housed at the Maryhill Museum of Art, Goldendale, Washington 98620.

251 According to Wright, "estimates made by reliable contractors" totaled $483,846.00 for construction of the hotel; with service unit and architect's fee, $576,231.26; with furnishings, $740,000. Letter from Frank Lloyd Wright to Alexander Chandler, November 20, 1929, FLWA.

252 Sweeney, *Wright in Hollywood*, 161. Owen D. Young was chairman of General Electric and was instrumental in helping solve Germany's post–World War I financial problems. His widely hailed plan, which called for considerable private investment, was put into effect in 1930, leading to talk of Young becoming a presidential candidate. See Floyd Norris, "Six Decades Later, Germany Will Pay War Debt," *The New York Times*, (January 6, 1995), D1, D4.

253 Sweeney, *Wright in Hollywood*, 169.

254 Letter from Frank Lloyd Wright to Richard Lloyd Jones, November 18, 1929, FLWA.

255 Letter from Frank Lloyd Wright to Richard Lloyd Jones, September 12, 1930, FLWA.

256 Bruce Goff discussed this with me during the summer of 1974, while I was completing research for my doctoral dissertation on his work. Goff's involvement is summarized in David G. De Long, *Bruce Goff: Toward Absolute Architecture* (New York, Cambridge, Mass., and London: The Architectural History Foundation and MIT Press, 1988), 45.

257 Although Ras El Bar is generally dated 1927, Robert Sweeney has examined correspondence that confirms 1932 as the correct date. I am grateful to Mr. Sweeney for sharing this information.

258 In 1995, a modified version of the design is under construction, as reported in many articles, including Joe Schoenmann, "Terrace OK Is Final," *Capital Times* (October 27, 1994). The design is described in Anthony Puttnam, *Monona Terrace: Feasibility and Predesign Analysis Report* (Taliesin Associated Architects: Spring Green and Madison, Wisconsin, December 12, 1990).

259 I am grateful to Bruce Brooks Pfeiffer for this information.

260 Edgar Kaufmann, jr., "Frank Lloyd Wright: Plasticity, Continuity, and Ornament," *Journal of the Society of Architectural Historians* 37 (March 1978), reprinted, Edgar Kaufmann, jr., *9 Commentaries on Frank Lloyd Wright* (New York, Cambridge, Mass., and London: The Architectural History Foundation and the MIT Press, 1989), 119–127. Kaufmann regarded this as one of his seminal statements, as I learned when we taught a seminar on Frank Lloyd Wright at Columbia University; his opinion remained unchanged several years later, when we worked together on the editing of *9 Commentaries*.

261 Frank Lloyd Wright, "The Japanese Print: An Interpretation" (1912), in Pfeiffer, *Collected Writings* I, 125.

262 Edgar Kaufmann, jr., "'*Form* Became *Feeling*': A New View of Froebel and Wright," *Journal of the Society of Architectural Historians* 39 (May 1980), 145–49. See also Cronon, *The Architecture of Frank Lloyd Wright*, 15–16.

263 "The Japanese Print: An Interpretation," 117. Others believe specific geometric shapes held greater meaning, for example, Alofsin, *Frank Lloyd Wright: The Lost Years*, esp. 5, 122.

264 Frank Lloyd Wright, "The Frozen Fountain" (1932), in Pfeiffer, *Collected Writings* III, 67–68.

265 Frank Lloyd Wright, "The Bad Lands" (1935), in Pfeiffer, *Collected Writings* III, 175–76.

266 For a discussion of natural versus cosmic order, see John Brinckerhoff Jackson, *A Sense of Place, A Sense of Time* (New Haven and London: Yale University Press, 1994), esp. 32, 35–36.

267 "In the Cause of Architecture V: The New World," 247.

268 Among several publications illustrating the Funerary Temple of Queen Hatshepsut is Brig. Gen. P. R. C. Groves and Maj. J. R. McCrindle, "Flying Over Egypt, Sinai, and Palestine," *The National Geographic Magazine* 50 (September 1926), 312–55.

FRANK LLOYD WRIGHT:

Architect of Landscape

ANNE WHISTON SPIRN

Frank Lloyd Wright saw "land as architecture"
and shaped its outward appearance to express his
vision of its inner structure.[1] Writings, drawings, and
built work all testify to Wright's lifelong passion for
nature and landscape. He wrote dozens of essays
on the subject, more than any other architect, living
or dead. He was a keen observer of natural form,
an experienced architect of landscape; hundreds of
drawings display his interest and insight: rhododen-
dron and pine captured in a few pencil strokes,
plans covered with detailed notes on planting and
grading, sections showing deft modifications to terrain. Like the Japanese landscapes he admired, some
of Wright's greatest works were large compositions
of buildings and gardens, roads and waterways, fields
and groves.

Despite the centrality of nature and landscape
to Wright's life and work, there is little written on
his landscape compositions, certainly no comprehensive or definitive treatment, and few seminal
works, with the result that they are frequently mis-
understood.[2] What accounts for the puzzling void
and the persistent misreadings in studies of such
a great architect? The answer lies in the complexity
of the subjects, in the nature of landscape, in the
nature of Wright.

The very qualities of the medium pose a challenge to the description, history, and criticism of
landscape architecture. Landscapes are both given

and built; they are phenomena of nature and prod-
ucts of culture. Landscapes comprise rivers, hills,
trees, buildings, and roads. Scales and boundaries are
fluid; a small garden is a landscape; so is a valley.[3] The
hill garden at Taliesin, with its grassy mound, trees,
walls, and steps, is a landscape; so is the complex of
house, terraces, courtyards, and gardens all built
into and around the hill, as is the larger Jones Valley,
with its buildings, roads, fields, groves, streams, ponds,
and hills. Jones Valley, in turn, is but a small part of
the even larger landscape of the Wisconsin River
Valley, with its rivers, forests, towns, and highways.
Seen thus, landscapes and buildings are continuous,
not contiguous. A landscape resists perception as
an object or even "an expanse of scenery seen by
the eye in one view," a typical dictionary definition.[4]
Landscapes are dynamic and evolving, not static,
their surface the sum of processes – water flow,
plant growth, human dwelling.

Landscape is the material context within
which we live: the habitats we humans share with
other organisms, the places we shape to express
our ideas and values. In modern use, the words
"landscape" and "nature" are often employed inter-
changeably. But nature is an idea, not a place; an
idea, moreover, for which many cultures have no
single name or notion.[5] Many critics have interpreted Wright's statements about nature in light of
the word's modern use, and this has led them to

mistake his reverence for nature as deference to landscape.[6] Wright consistently capitalized "Nature," but never "landscape."

Wright's understanding of nature was grounded in his family's Emersonian philosophy; he was steeped from early childhood in countless quotations, discussions, and sermons drawn from Emerson's writings.[7] Wright's knowledge of landscape came from experience; observing and shaping landscapes were part of everyday life from the time he plowed, planted, hoed, and harvested fields as a boy, to when as a man he terraced hillsides, planted gardens and groves, dammed streams to generate power and make lakes and waterfalls, laid out contours for plowing that traced curving landforms, and selected sites for Sunday picnics. Such philosophy and experiences were a central part of the life he designed for and shared with Taliesin's apprentices from 1932 until his death in 1959.[8]

What Wright *said* and *wrote* about nature and landscape and what he actually *did* were complex and sometimes seem contradictory. Without a clear-eyed comparison to the built, his texts have served mostly to confuse.[9] Were one dealing with another architect, one might attribute his apparent inconsistencies to a superficial appreciation of nature and landscape. This was certainly not the case with Wright. Given his background, one must see Wright's landscapes as deliberate constructions. Apparent contradictions between texts and works are clues to Wright's priorities and intentions, to the evolution of his ideas, or to ways that our own assumptions and perceptions may differ from his. Wright wrote many texts over half a century (1894–1959) for different purposes (self-expression, self-promotion, self-justification, teaching).[10] While numerous themes remained constant throughout his career, certain important ideas and their application to landscape design developed over time.

The key to understanding Wright's approach to landscape (including the grand, unrealized projects of the 1920s) lies in those where he made his home and exerted continuous influence for decades: the Jones Valley of southern Wisconsin and the desert of central Arizona. He was born to the first and chose the second; the two must be seen together, as he experienced them, the one in contrast to, clarifying, the other. Hundreds of photographs spanning nearly sixty years document his

engagement with these landscapes.[11] Dozens of quick sketches and plans covered with scribbled notes are windows into his thinking about these places across the years.[12] These images enable us to assess what he actually *did*, year by year, to follow the dialogue between built landscapes and texts, to identify the principles that guided the work. With these principles in mind, one may better appreciate what Wright intended in projects that were destroyed or unrealized, such as Doheny Ranch, the Lake Tahoe summer colony, the Johnson compound, the Strong automobile objective, and San Marcos in the Desert. And one can see more clearly the significance of his place within a larger tradition of landscape architecture.

"Truth in Beauty": Unifying Jones Valley

Any account of Wright and landscape must begin with the place where his autobiography begins and ends – Jones Valley, near Spring Green, Wisconsin. One cannot overemphasize the significance of this place for Wright. It was his home, school, laboratory, touchstone.[13]

Comparing views of the valley a century or more ago with the same views today, one is struck by the contrast between rough and smooth, by how profiles of landforms have been rounded and ordered.[14] The landscape appears sculpted, and indeed it is. A grove of trees rounds off the angular top of Midway Hill; rows of curving crops accentuate the landform. Gone are a host of buildings and fences that once stood down in the valley along the main road; only buildings designed by Wright himself remain in view along the western slopes. Just as eighteenth-century English landowners embellished their estates – planting groves, damming streams to form lakes, moving whole villages, building landmarks to guide the gaze – Wright transformed Jones Valley into a celebration of the landscape of southwestern Wisconsin and the cultural heritage of his mother and her family. Wright would certainly have agreed with Humphrey Repton's assertion that "to improve the scenery of a country, and to display its native beauties with advantage" is an art; Repton's three principles – "Utility, Proportion, and Unity" – were among Wright's own.[15]

The Lloyd Jones family arrived in the valley in 1856. They found a long valley enclosed by parallel,

147

Frank Lloyd Wright, photographer. *Hillside Home Farm from Enos Jones Farm.* ca. 1900. Note Romeo and Juliet tower, Hillside Home School, and Midway Hill to the right. Collotype, 9 × 3 ¼ in. State Historical Society of Wisconsin, WHi (P2312) 20 lobed ridges of flat-bedded limestone and sand-stone that formed smaller valleys within the larger whole. A stream flowed through the valley and out into the broad floodplain of the Wisconsin River. Despite family folklore, the Lloyd Joneses were not pioneers. Previous settlers had already farmed the bottomlands, and nearby Tower Hill had been a site of lead-shot manufacturing since about 1825.[16] The family planted crops and built a homestead near where the Hillside Home School buildings now stand. From the Home Farm at Hillside, they gradu-ally expanded their holdings. By the time Frank Lloyd Wright spent summers on his Uncle James's farm, in the 1870s and 1880s, his grandparents, uncles, and aunts owned and farmed much of the valley.[17] Wright began to shape the valley through commissions for family members well before he began Taliesin in 1911: from Unity Chapel (1886), to buildings for his aunts' school on the site of the Home Farm (Hillside Home School, 1887; 1902); the Romeo and Juliet windmill (1896); and Tan-y-deri (1907), the house for sister Jane (fig. 147).

From 1911, when his mother purchased just over thirty-one acres for him, Wright quickly extended the scope of his interventions to the land itself: clearing trees and brush, planting gardens and groves, damming the stream, grading roads.[18] He expanded his holdings whenever possible, gradually

consolidating many small farms into one large estate. By the time of his death in 1959, the Taliesin Fellowship controlled about three thousand acres within and beyond the valley.[19] Over the course of half a century, from 1911 to 1959, Wright reshaped the valley to conform to his ideals and those of his family, giving form to their Emersonian philosophy and their motto – "Unity." Wright felt that while his family had stressed the "beauty of truth," they had neglected the "truth of beauty," and he set out to redress that failure.[20] The glory of Taliesin as it ultimately evolved was in the whole landscape of hills and valleys, buildings and roads, fields, gardens, and groves, the disparate elements unified in a sweeping composition. By 1959, his words of 1932 were no longer an exaggeration: "I saw it all, and planted it all."[21]

Wright took an extraordinary series of pho-tographs of the valley around 1900, a decade before he began Taliesin.[22] The photographs pre-sented his aunts' boarding school to prospective students and their families. Several show building interiors, but most depict outdoor play and the surrounding valley. These images, when compared to a succession of photographs taken by others from 1912 to 1959, form a benchmark from which to assess how he changed the landscape.[23] Two of them are especially fine, including one of the pond

below the Hillside Home School where the composition is reminiscent of Japanese prints and Wright's own drawings of this time (fig. 148). The other is particularly important, for it depicts the hill now occupied by Taliesin, with Midway Hill beyond (fig. 149).[24] Wright shot three views of this hill (actually the end of a ridge), all from a vantage not visible from the school or even from his family's lands. All other views are closer to the school or within its view. The perspective and number of these images demonstrate Wright's interest in the site ten years before its purchase; the quality of the photograph reproduced here reveals the affinity he felt for the place. Two other images are useful as context and points from which to assess subsequent change; together they comprise a panorama of the valley from south to north and show several buildings that Wright later tore down or moved (the southwestern portion is illustrated in fig. 150).

In 1900, there were a few trees in the ridgetop pasture and second-growth trees and shrubs on the steep, north- and east-facing slopes where Wright built his house ten years later. A soil survey of 1914 identified the soils on the property: the most fertile land is on the valley floor and lowest slopes (now under cultivation or underwater); the high ground is rough and stony, the weathered rock crumbly, the soil highly erodible.[25] The report recommended cultivating the gently sloping, lower land and warned that most of the remaining land should be used as pasture or, where slopes were steep, kept as woods. Wright ultimately managed the landscape in keeping with these recommendations, particularly as he gained agricultural experience (see figs. 158–161).[26] He built his house on a band of "rough stony land" just below the hilltop – the least fertile soil on his property – and retained the woods on steep slopes below.[27] Wright also knew from experience how cold the exposed ridgetops were in winter, how hot the valley bottom could be in summer, and how cool the breezy upper slopes, especially under the shade of trees. That "no house should ever be *on* any hill... [it] should be *of* the hill" is a principle well known to farmers.[28]

From the edge of this ridge near the end of Jones Valley there were sweeping views of the Wisconsin River, Tower Hill, and distant hills across the broad, level floor of the ancient river's floodplain. There were also more enclosed views within the smaller valley, up to Uncle James's farm and the family chapel, and back to Romeo and Juliet above Hillside.[29] Windows framed these prospects: the living room provided a series of square views panning north-northwest to south-southeast, from Wisconsin River to Unity Chapel; Wright's bedroom/studio looked out toward Hillside, a view of rolling hills punctuated by Romeo and Juliet.[30] As Wright wrote in 1938, "Landscape seen through the openings

149

Frank Lloyd Wright, photographer. *Two Hills Showing Future Site of Taliesin, at Right, with Midway Hill in Background, from Route C near Present Entrance to Taliesin.* ca. 1900. Collotype, 9 ¼ × 2 ½ in. State Historical Society of Wisconsin, WHi (x3) 47172

150

Frank Lloyd Wright, photographer. *Jones Valley, Looking Northwest from near Current Intersection of Routes 23 and T.* ca. 1900. Note Midway Hill at far left, Taliesin Hill at center. Collotype, 9 ¼ × 2 ¾ in. State Historical Society of Wisconsin, WHi (x3) 37026

148

Frank Lloyd Wright, photographer. *View of Skating Pond and Jones Valley, Looking East from Below Hillside Home School Toward Unity Chapel.* ca. 1900. House and barn to left still stand near intersection of Routes 23 and T. Collotype, 9 ½ × 3 ¼ in. State Historical Society of Wisconsin, WHi (x3) 47173

of the building thus placed and proportioned has greater charm than when seen independent of the architecture. Architecture properly studied in relation to the natural features surrounding it is a great clarifier and developer of the beauty of the landscape."[31] Wright shaped landscapes as scenes framed by windows and designed buildings to be seen as part of a landscape. Views of the surrounding landscape from within the house were as artfully composed, as carefully selected as the Japanese paintings and prints on the walls. The clerestory windows in the studio (now the office) frame a view of the hilltop much like a long scroll punctuated by slender, vertical mullions: the outline of the knoll, the tree in the tea circle, and the sky beyond. In the loggia, the correspondence between framed views of the landscape outside and of Japanese landscape paintings hung on the walls inside is deliberate and explicit. In 1914, the windows of the loggia were set in frames whose top and bottom were continuations of those of the Japanese landscape painting on the adjacent wall.[32] In 1925, the windows of the loggia were replaced by a series of long, narrow, glass doors – like a Japanese screen – that frame a view of the hills across the valley: Bryn Mawr, Bryn Canol, and Bryn Bach, all named by his grandparents. Wright fitted inner shutters made from a lacquer screen of teak with gold-colored glass of a rosy cast like the gold backdrop of a Japanese painting.[33] The wood frames blocked the balcony and roof overhang from view when the doors were closed. Art and life, landscape and building, all merge here.

Taliesin – "shining brow" – is an apt name for this place where building, landscape, and life are united.[34] The English word "brow" links landform and human face; it originally referred to eyebrow and only later to landform. The brow of a hill is its "projecting edge…standing over a precipice."[35] At Taliesin, the buildings rest on a notch cut into the hillside and jut out over the steep slopes below to form the brow.[36] Perched terraces and garden "rooms" were a distinctive part of Taliesin from the outset, as was the entrance drive up a long, steep slope.[37] Originally, carriages and cars drove up the entrance road, retaining wall and hill on the left, through a porte-cochère, took a sharp turn into an intimate, walled court between buildings and hill, the drive flanked by flowers, then out another gate

into a square courtyard (fig. 151).[38] When Wright later rerouted the entrance road downslope of the buildings, the basic configuration and character of the inner courts remained the same and persists today; the farmyard was elaborated as a work court and an upper motor court (fig. 152). The tea circle and hill garden also appear in photographs of Taliesin from 1912 and early plans and drawings (fig. 153). The prospects they afford are counterpoints to the refuge provided by the courts. Many features of Taliesin's buildings and gardens resemble photographs, attributed to Wright, of Fiesole, Italy, in 1910 and match his reminiscences: walking up "the hill road" with Mamah Borthwick Cheney into a narrow street bordered by walls, walking in "the high-walled garden that lay alongside the cottage," sitting near a "little fountain."[39] One senses Wright strove to build Mamah's life into the gardens as well as the house; the suite of walled courts, tea circle, and hill garden embody memories of their short, shared life.[40]

Notwithstanding the undeniable connections to Wright's Italian experience, the courts and gardens at Taliesin bear a strong resemblance to the work of Gertrude Jekyll in the vocabulary of flower borders, walls, steps, and pools and the geometry of their structure (see figs. 151, 153). Wright was familiar with Jekyll's work. He read *Home and Garden* in 1900, the year it was published, and said it was a book "that should be in every library," for it exemplified his own approach to landscape design.[41] Jekyll opened *Home and Garden* with a description of her newly built house. The site was near her childhood home, the house built of "sandstone that grows in our hills," its oak beams cut from trees along a nearby lane she remembered admiring when she was young.[42] This text must have resonated deeply in Wright, who was photographing Jones Valley about that time and perhaps thinking already of the home and garden he would build there. Debts to English and Italian gardens and landscapes do not diminish Wright's achievement at Taliesin. His genius lay in assimilating diverse traditions, exploiting them for his own ends, blending them in a fresh expression that was undeniably his own. As he said himself, "The New in art is always formed out of the Old."[43]

The tea circle is a pivotal place that negotiates a graceful transition between the lower courts

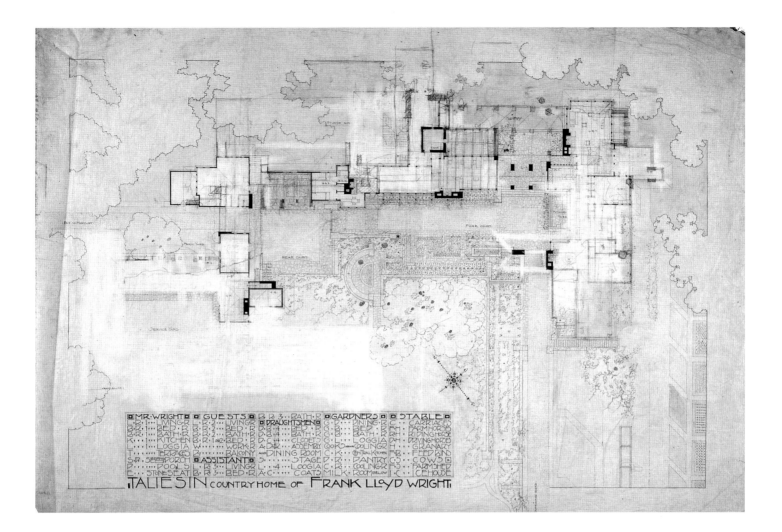

151
Frank Lloyd Wright. *Taliesin, near Spring Green, Wisconsin. Plan.* ca. 1912. Ink on linen, 30 x 43 in. The Frank Lloyd Wright Foundation, 1403.011

152
Frank Lloyd Wright. *Taliesin, near Spring Green, Wisconsin. Plan.* 1925. Ink, pencil, and colored pencil on tracing paper, 35 x 57⅝ in. The Frank Lloyd Wright Foundation, 2501.060

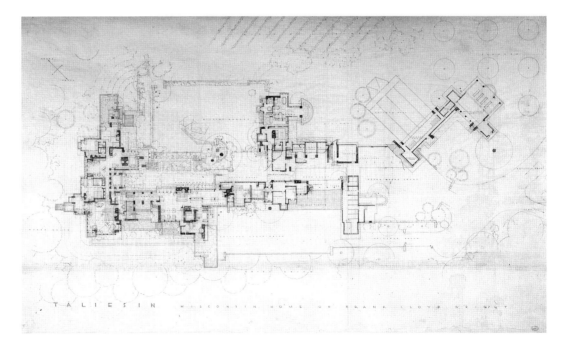

153
Henry Fuermann, photographer. *Hill Garden and Tea Circle, with Fields Beyond.* 1911–12. Black-and-white print, 8 × 10 in. The Frank Lloyd Wright Foundation, 1104.012

and the hill garden. Like that of the courts, the form of the tea circle was established early and has remained relatively constant since 1912. One can see it as an exedra, a semi-circular niche with a bench, and appreciate its relation to similar essays of steps, niches, and benches in Italian and English gardens; perhaps there is also a bit of the Japanese in the turn and turn again movement as one mounts and descends. It was sometimes referred to as the "council ring," suggesting a link to Jens Jensen's council rings, gathering places defined by circles of stones around a campfire.[44] In the tea circle, instead of fire at the center, there was once "a spring or fountain that welled up into a pool at the center of the circle."[45] All of these influences may have come into play, but Wright transformed them into this wonderful place, so shady and breezy on a hot summer's day, a delight to the eye, to the body in movement. Taking tea in the tea circle became a daily ritual at Taliesin from the 1930s if not before: "The four o'clock tea bell brings the Fellowship together for a welcomed respite from the day's work. Cooling sounds of ice rattling in tall glasses fall on ear as we climb the steps to the circular stone bench the 'council ring.'"[46] Wright knew how to enjoy a garden.

Unlike the tea circle and lower courts, the hill garden changed radically over time. It is completely misleading to say, as many critics have, that Wright "preserved" the hill or left it "undisturbed," for he transformed it from rough pasture in a grove of trees into an open, rounded mound. In fact, it is not really a hilltop so much as the lowest end of a long ridgeline (see fig. 150); Wright made it *seem* like the top of a hill by concealing the higher portion of the ridge with a wing of buildings and by directing the gaze southward to where the slope falls away beyond the garden wall. By the late 1930s, the profile of the hill garden was a smooth curve covered with soft, closely clipped grass (fig. 155). Originally, the ridge was flatter on top, its form less perfectly round; this is clearly visible in a photograph of 1912, before the steps were built from tea circle to "hilltop."[47] Another photograph from approximately the same time shows the hill garden as a grove of trees with rough grass underneath – much like the pasture it had been (see fig. 153). Gradually the trees disappeared, all remnants of the stumps were removed, and the long grass was replaced with turf. Wright inserted cut stones into the turf – an

154
View of hill garden. 1934–37. State Historical Society of Wisconsin, Howe Collection, WHi (Howe), TSP7

155
View of hill garden. Late 1930s. State Historical Society of Wisconsin, Howe Collection, WHi (Howe), TSP6

B-605
RESIDENCE FRANK LLOYD WRIGHT TALIESIN SPRING GREEN, WIS.

idealized version of limestone ledges – and rounded and smoothed the landform into a representation, an abstraction of a hilltop (see figs. 154, 155).[48] This was typical of how he rounded off the valley as a whole through a gradual simplification of the given form. Ironically, like much of the rest of the landscape Wright graded and planted, the mounded slope and ledges of the hill garden have often been seen as naturally occurring rather than constructed. Even many of the fellows who arrived after the mid-1940s assumed that the ledges and smooth terrain had just always been there.[49] Like the browhouse, the hill garden embodies a correspondence between human body and landform – a round mound, like a breast or pregnant woman's swelling belly, enclosed by angular walls of stone and surmounted by the tower with dovecote.[50] Given Wright's belief in the symbolism of forms and the association of doves with love and devotion, it seems reasonable to read the circular mound as feminine and the square enclosure as masculine, then to interpret it further as memorial to Mamah and Mother, as representing the fertility of the valley embraced by the lover, son, architect.[51]

The wall surrounding the hill garden sets it off from the surrounding landscape. There was a distinct difference between the two from at least the 1920s; rough meadow of long grasses grew right up to the wall and was juxtaposed to the clipped grass within the enclosure. Abstraction of landscape features and juxtaposition of the wild and the domesticated were strategies Wright frequently employed later; in fact, they became signal characteristics of his landscapes from the 1920s on, including the unbuilt projects of that decade, such as Doheny Ranch and San Marcos in the Desert (see figs. 7, 126).[52] He built the cantilevered terrace outside his bedroom/study just below the hilltop in 1937 (fig. 156), at about the same time he was also designing Fallingwater.[53] Here also, the built is juxtaposed to the wild. The terrace juts out over the wooded slope below, affording views over the lake, across the valley to the chapel and the farm, where he used to stay as a boy, and back beyond Midway across the hill to Romeo and Juliet and Tan-y-deri. This elevated prospect gives one a sense of comfortable control, like lord of the manor, over all one surveys.[54]

156
Terrace outside Wright's study cantilevered over the "wild," wooded landscape below. 1938–51. State Historical Society of Wisconsin, Howe Collection, WHi (Howe) TSP5

Taliesin was planned as "a garden and a farm behind a workshop and a home."[55] Outside the wall on the southwest-facing slope, Wright planted a large orchard and vineyard. These remain today, though the vineyard is much smaller. The S-shaped stone retaining wall on the southeast-facing slope once incorporated cisterns to irrigate the gardens below, laid out in a grid; they are depicted in a photograph and on drawings of about 1912 (fig. 157; see fig. 151). Apparently the gridded gardens were designed to present a colorful pattern, for people reportedly drove by just to look at them.[56] This was a poor location for gardens and for such a layout; the slope was steep and the soil too erodible. The gridded gardens soon disappeared and were replaced by grass and trees; the cisterns remain (although they were no longer operative by the late 1930s). Grapevines and vegetable gardens were planted later in long, straight rows more or less aligned along the contours (see figs. 159, 161). Vegetable and flower gardens were moved finally to a field near Hillside, where crops and flowers were planted in colorful, curving bands like contour lines (fig. 158).[57] By the late 1930s, Wright employed contour plowing for the farm fields. This must have appealed to him as a way to fuse patterns of work and landforms, for he celebrated the way agricultural labor shaped the land: "The entire field is become a linear pattern – a plan of routine. Work."[58] According to Bruce Pfeiffer, Wright had the contoured plow lines recalibrated every few years, and not just for aesthetic reasons: he was adamant about not losing soil.[59] Whenever the ground was regraded, as around the newly built

157
Cisterns and grid of gardens on slopes below Taliesin. After 1914. The Frank Lloyd Wright Foundation, 1403.003

158
Striped gardens of vegetables and flowers along contours near Hillside. 1940s. The Frank Lloyd Wright Foundation, 2501.1340

upper dam in 1947, strips of sod were cut from the pasture and laid out along the graded slopes, and then bare soil in between was seeded with grass.[60] Cornelia Brierly recalls that professors from the University of Wisconsin brought their students to see Wright's contour planting.[61] "He laid it all out, it was beautiful," she said.

The lower hills in the valley are generally rounded and rolling. Where the rock crops out, at Midway, for example, the hills tend to be more ragged. This is quite clear in winter; as the sun moves behind Midway, light comes through the trees and silhouettes their branches, revealing the ground plane as a pyramidal mass. Wright rounded off Midway Hill by permitting trees to grow up on the side facing Taliesin in the 1950s. The result was a convex form, in contrast to the original, straighter slopes, which were eroded and rocky; he left open the rounder form facing Hillside and behind. Just above Midway, the croplines and the road curve with the landform.

Various plans depict the landscape as it existed and as Wright envisioned it might be: "Garden planning at Taliesin is done in the same way as building planning. Using a large map of the farm and a box of colored pencils, the entire garden layout is planted."[62] Successive site plans delineate fields and allocate crops among them; Wright reviewed and revised the plans periodically.[63] An early plan, published in 1913, features a "water garden," orchards, vineyard, reservoir, and the gridded gardens.[64] Notes on this plan show that Wright conceived plantations on a grand scale: "1000 barberry (1/3 dwarf), 1000 hawthornes, 1000 plums (assorted), 100 weeping willows, 500 rosa rugosa, 500 white pines." Wright later used a survey of 1920 as a base for several plans that seem to fall roughly into three time periods: 1920s–30s, 1930s–40s, 1940s–50s (fig. 159).[65] The buildings, roads, and fields relate closely to photographs from the 1920s and early 1930s (figs. 160, 161).[66] The photograph in figure 160 shows the landscape as it must have looked in the 1920s after the entrance road from Route 23 was built; curved fields bounded by fences match the shapes on the plan.[67] The plan also shows the two enormous areas on the hillside behind Taliesin planted in the long, straight lines of the vineyard (shown with crosses) and a single vegetable or fruit – asparagus, onions, raspberries (shown as colored lines). The rows are

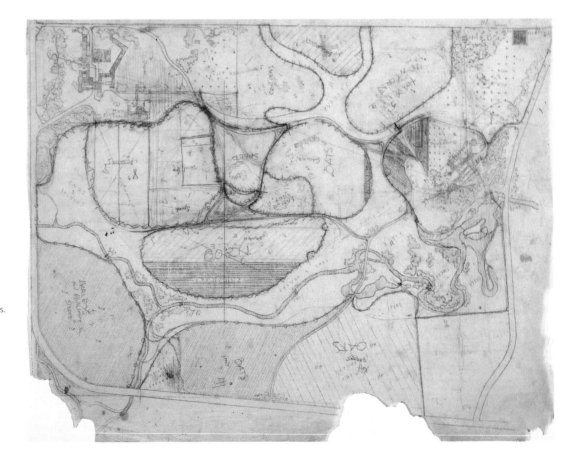

159
Frank Lloyd Wright. *Farm Plan.* 1920s–30s.
Pencil and colored pencil on tracing
paper, 28 ¼ x 35 ⅛ in. The Frank Lloyd
Wright Foundation, 3420.009

160

Taliesin, looking northeast across fields
and pasture to tower, hill garden, and
house in distance. 1922–32. Note correlation of fenced fields and pasture
with those drawn in fig. 159. The Frank
Lloyd Wright Foundation, 2501.1339

161

Aerial photograph of Taliesin with lake
construction under way. ca. 1932.
Note correlation of many roads, fields,
stream, lake with those drawn in
fig. 159. The Frank Lloyd Wright Foundation, file 1169 014–016

visible in aerial photographs, as are the rounded shapes of fields (see fig. 161).[68] With the arrival in 1932 of the first apprentices, Wright had the labor force to work on an expanded scale commensurate with his vision, and later plans are covered with notes on what existed ("quack grass patch covered up with tar paper") and what could be, drawn changes to roads, and written instructions regarding things to do ("take out fence, use this fence elsewhere," "clear away brush leaving only good sized trees," "tear down old school," "zinnias everywhere . . . transplant wild grape vines about stonework and chimneys . . . hollyhocks around walls and fences."[69] A plan from the 1940s–50s shows the shores of the upper lake, an expanded lower lake, and new construction at Midway including the row of triangular pighouses along "Pork Avenue."[70]

Reviewing these plans and photographs, reading Wright's descriptions of farming activities, one cannot help but wonder if there has ever been a farmer quite like Frank Lloyd Wright. In fact, Wright had a role model very close to home. His Uncle Jenkin Lloyd Jones had long pursued a similar approach to farming and landscape design on his summer retreat down the road from Taliesin at Tower Hill. From 1895 to 1915, Jenkin delivered a series of sermons on topics such as plowing, sowing, weeding, reaping, tree planting, reforestation, road making, and barn building, which he collected under the title "The Gospel of the Farm."[71] The language of the sermons bears a marked resemblance to Wright's discussion of the same topics in his autobiography. Jenkin calls the cow "a minister of the beautiful as well as of the useful" and reminds his readers of the "famous" dictum: "Treat your cow as though she were a lady."[72] The pasture shown on Taliesin farm plans, such as the one in figure 159, seems tailored to illustrate Jenkin's sermon: a long broad promenade for horses and cows in curvilinear spaces between fields, winding around the hill along lake and stream, where the animals formed "a glittering decoration of the fields and meadows as they moved."[73]

Wright drew and redrew alternative road alignments on plans and aerial photos.[74] The entrance drive was changed several times to match reconstructions of the house; the one constant was falling water as part of the entry sequence. When the main entrance was changed again from Route C to Route 23 in about 1937, Wright insisted that everyone use it: "We all had to come in that way," recalled John deKoven Hill. Wright insisted that the roadsides be carefully maintained. His attention to the alignment and appearance of the roads reflected his fascination with automobiles and movement and his concerns for revealing landform and shaping a beautiful scene. "Mr. Wright loved to operate the road grader," said Brierly. "It was terribly bumpy, smoothing out the ruts and gravel. Mrs. Wright didn't like him to, but he did anyway" (see photograph on p. 185).[75]

Wright had a fascination and much experience with dams, ponds, and falling water.[76] The dam below Taliesin was always a significant feature and served several functions. It raised "the water in the Valley to within sight of Taliesin,"[77] creating a lake that mirrored the clouds and bounced light from the sky back up to the windows of the house. Water from below the falls was sent "by hydraulic ram, up to a big stone reservoir built into the higher hill, just behind and beyond the hilltop garden, to come down again into the fountains and go on down to the vegetable gardens on the slopes below the house."[78] Into the 1940s, water falling over the dam powered the generator that produced electricity for the Taliesin complex; a generator house once sat alongside the dam.[79] Dam and waterfall were among the first things visitors saw as they turned off the road and proceeded through the gate and up the hill to the house. In 1947, another dam was constructed upstream from the first to form an upper lake below Midway; a road led through the gate on Route 23 and over a bridge below the waterfall over the upper dam.[80] The lakes and dams required constant maintenance and frequent draining, regrading, and rebuilding. The water features evolved from meandering pools in the early water garden to two lakes after the upper dam was built in 1947.[81] Over the years, Wright regraded and reshaped the shorelines and lake bottoms (see the lake under reconstruction in fig. 161).[82] He also built and rebuilt the lower dam. Many versions are depicted in snapshots and postcards: an early dam, low and narrow; later dams, higher and broader; a sheet of water flowing smoothly over a curved lip into the water below; a cascade splashing over stepped rocks; a combination of cascade on one side and sheet flow over the main fall. Wright explored dams for years before the culmination of building/waterfall at Fallingwater in 1936. In his plans for the Strong automobile objective of 1924–25, he included a dam with a smooth sheet of water falling from its lip (strikingly similar to the waterfall in the famous drawing of Fallingwater), even though it would have entailed pumping water to the hilltop site (see fig. 113).

Wright gradually enlarged his estate, which enabled him to further shape the views from his windows and from the roads approaching Taliesin.[83] He bought property whenever he could, then destroyed the existing structures and replanted the land. "He burned a tavern, and people were furious!" Brierly recalled.[84] Wright bought the pig farm on the corner of Routes C and 23, tore down the buildings, and installed a vast field of red petunias in the triangular intersection. He designed a snack bar overlooking the Wisconsin River that could be reached by an overpass ("Taliesin Viaduct") on horseback or on foot. By the early 1950s, the Taliesin property extended all the way down Route 23 along the Wisconsin River to the intersection of Route 14; Wright planted three pine groves, one at each point of the huge triangle at the intersection and considered installing a sign that read "Taliesin Parkway – 3 miles."[85] Wright may have been sentimental about the valley where his family settled, but he held no such feelings for the structures they built. In 1933, he ordered apprentices to tear down the barn of the Hillside Home School and salvage the materials for reuse; he issued the same instructions nearly twenty years later, when he had them dismantle the 1887 Hillside Home School building.[86]

Wright intended that Taliesin be "self-sustaining if not self-sufficient . . . its own light-plant, fuel yard, transportation and water system," providing "shelter, food, clothes, and even entertainment."[87] A principal tenet of the Taliesin Fellowship was learning through doing, and apprentices spent hours each day working on the estate: they grew food, made wine, cooked, cut firewood, built and rebuilt structures and gardens. Kevin Lynch described his experience at Taliesin in 1937: "The new apprentice must learn how to handle a tall bundle of cornstalks, or how to cut a green oak plank, or how to translate a drawing for a building, or how to lay plaster, or even the most efficient method of scrap-

ing oatmeal from a pot. . . . It is the attempt to grasp the new ideal of hard work, of creative activity, of 'learning by doing,' of enthusiastic cooperation in solving common problems, that makes the life of the new apprentice so full and so fascinating here."[88]

The ideal of sustainability was never fully realized there; despite Wright's aversion to cities, Taliesin was always supported by urban activities and populations (for example, fees for lectures and architectural commissions). After the Taliesin Playhouse opened in 1933, the admission charge for films shown on Sunday afternoons provided additional income.[89] As the Fellowship grew, winter posed an additional challenge to sustainability – fuel for all the fireplaces and boilers that heated the residences and studio came from the woods. In 1934, Eugene Masselink wrote that cutting the firewood necessary to heat the buildings and studio all winter threatened to obliterate the woods around Taliesin.[90] Early that summer, Wright announced the next winter would be spent in Arizona. On January 23, 1935, the Wrights and the apprentices – thirty people in all – loaded drafting tables, the partially constructed Broadacre City models, and canned fruit and vegetables on a new red truck and set off across the country to Arizona.[91] Eugene Masselink, who drove Wright's car, captured the experience of that journey and the excited anticipation of arrival in Arizona, Wright's promised land:

Magically we came from the mountains as the sun was nearing the horizon and we rode out upon the Arizona desert. Tall ancient saguaro and graceful waving ocatillo and the vivid green on the floor of the desert and the purple mountains beyond. A garden like none I had ever seen. A desert like something I had never dreamed. The mountains were softened by the distance and the fading light and the desert plants stood out strong in the long low streaks of sunlight. The new forms, the vivid green, the purple shadowed rock masses and the blue sky and the movement of the car winding in and out and around. Suddenly a quick stop. . . and with startling theatrical rapidity all the cars of the caravan caught up with us and there the truck which had proceeded was waiting. The procession was resumed and as we started from home, so we entered the destination of the long journey."[92]

"Pioneer" in Paradise Valley

For one who has spent his or her life in a forest biome, with soft light filtered through humid air and leaves, with spongy ground cloaked in lush green growth, the desert is shocking: bright crystalline light, but above all the clarity and stark simplicity of landscape structure revealed. For Wright, for whom structure was a passion, the desert was a revelation. As he later wrote, "We found Paradise."[93]

Many months of the 1920s – Wright's "wilderness years" as Reyner Banham called them – were spent in the dry landscapes of California's chaparral and Arizona's desert.[94] This was a pivotal period for Wright. His designs from 1911 on for his estate at Taliesin had prepared the ground for the large-scale landscape proposals of the 1920s that prompted his first encounters with the desert: A. M. Johnson's compound near Death Valley, Chandler's San Marcos resort in the Sonoran Desert in Arizona. Though they were never built, Wright later adapted many aspects of these proposals to Taliesin West. In his drawings for San Marcos in the Desert, for example, he placed the buildings and gardens on a prowlike platform looking out over the landscape and let the desert come right up to the base of the retaining wall, juxtaposing the cultivated and the wild much as he later did at Taliesin West and had done already at Taliesin. This approach was strikingly different from the norm of walled-in gardens in Spanish/Moorish style or the irrigated green, grassy lawns and groves of trees of the "pastoral" resort.[95]

Building and living at Ocatilla, the desert camp Wright built near the proposed site of San Marcos in the Desert, were seminal experiences of great personal significance, though the whole episode lasted only a few months, from January to May 1929. In "Freedom," book three of the *Autobiography*, Wright turned from reflection on the past and present to speculation on the future. He described Ocatilla in a spirit of excitement and optimism as a "preliminary study," "the first of an 'Arizona type.'"[96] Banham later discerned in Ocatilla "an air of freshness and new invention usually associated with the beginning of an architect's career," remarkable in a man of sixty, and ranked it as one of the great personal statements in twentieth-century architecture (see figs. 134–136).[97] Banham regarded Ocatilla as a "second beginning" to Wright's career. It is no won-

der he later made Arizona his second home, that he oriented important sight lines at Taliesin West to repeatedly draw the eye to South Mountain (and thus to the site of Ocatilla on its southern slopes). Ocatilla marked the rise and renewal of Wright the phoenix.[98]

Ocatilla is an essential link between Taliesin (or "Taliesin North," as Wright sometimes called it) and the more permanent desert outpost he built later at Taliesin West.[99] The structures of Ocatilla, like those at Taliesin, embraced a hilltop with a "camp fire" – like the tea circle – just below the crown (see fig. 135). The enclosed hilltop – like the hill garden – provided a prospect of the surrounding landscape from within a protected enclave and gave a "measure of privacy" to the quarters downslope.[100] Bedrooms, living room, dining room, office, and studio were small structures, some grouped at right angles to one another like miniature versions of the main wings at Taliesin, all sited more or less along the contours, much like the relation of building to hill at Taliesin (see fig. 136). Unlike the earliest version of Taliesin, however, where a single orthogonal grid organized the layout of buildings, courts, and gardens, *two* grids structured the site plan of Ocatilla. Wright offset the grids from one another by 120 degrees in response to the V-shaped hilltop, an angle he also expressed in the seats embracing the campfire. The individual units were aligned along the lines of these two grids, foreshadowing the strategy he developed further at Taliesin West eight years later.

Up until the 1920s, Wright's landscape compositions were dominated by a single orthogonal grid. This sometimes led to problems on steeply sloping or irregularly shaped terrain, as in the gridded gardens at Taliesin (see figs. 151, 157).[101] Working in complex topography on large landscape compositions in the 1920s, Wright gradually adopted structural strategies more appropriate to sloping, irregular terrain with views in various directions. At the Johnson desert compound (1924), for example, he organized the plan with several axes aligned in response to terrain and views, a strategy he also used in a design for the Nakoma Country Club and employed again four years later at San Marcos in the Desert (see figs. 80, 124).[102] By the time he drew the new site plan for vineyard, gardens, and farm buildings at Taliesin, Wright had aligned them within a new grid oriented roughly perpendicular to the line of the slope, at a forty-five degree angle to the grid of the earlier plan (see fig. 152). At Ocatilla, when Wright *overlaid* two grids in a structural geometry derived from the terrain, he brought to resolution ideas with which he had been working throughout the 1920s and sowed the seeds that would come to fruition in Taliesin West.

In Arizona Wright was a "pioneer." In 1929 at Ocatilla and in the late 1930s at Taliesin West, he reenacted the experience of his mother's family in the 1850s, settling in a landscape that seemed remote, the nearest road a dirt track, the nearest settlement a few miles away.[103] Like Jones Valley in the 1850s, however, the area was already well populated by the 1930s; Paradise Valley was a rapidly growing winter resort frequented by many tourists, including wealthy Chicagoans.[104] Unlike Jones Valley, Paradise Valley did not sustain the Fellowship; they brought canned fruits and vegetables from Wisconsin, relied upon Wright's son David for oranges from his orchard, and some years received weekly train shipments of eggs from Taliesin.[105] Food in nearby Scottsdale was expensive, and Wright complained of having to pay "resort prices," which he could ill afford.[106]

Wright bought property at the foot of the McDowell Mountains on a gentle, south-facing slope with panoramic views over Paradise Valley to distant mountains (fig. 162). The hills behind have heaps of shattered rock at their base, all covered with desert varnish, black and red from many years' exposure to cycles of moisture and evaporation. The ground is hard, with rocks scattered across the surface as if cast there. Two deep washes structure the site. Their steep sides, breadth, and long heaps of loose rocks and gravel are clues to the violent force of waters that come crashing down the stony hillsides after rainstorms. Dozens of small, shallow washes lace the whole area. Wright sited Taliesin West up against a hill between a large wash to the west and a smaller wash to the east. Here, as Wright put it, "we decided to build ourselves into the life of the desert."[107]

Taliesin West is an integrated complex of buildings, courtyards, and gardens aligned, notched, and knit into this landscape: walls, roofs, pergolas, and paths catch sunlight and cast shadows; sight lines point to distant landforms; walls cut into,

162
Taliesin West, Scottsdale, Arizona, and surrounding desert, seen from atop mountain. ca. 1940. State Historical Society of Wisconsin, Howe Collection, WHi (Howe) TSP1

extend above, reach out to the immediate terrain. Segments of the main path and most of the buildings (studio, dining room, kiva, the Wrights' living quarters) are aligned along a straight line that forms the spine of the complex. Wright considered the orientation of this spine carefully; an early drawing shows a different orientation with the present one drawn over it.[108] The spine is aligned so that the walls of the buildings that line it receive both morning sun and afternoon light, and so that ends of the main path point to distant landforms.[109] This spine, moreover, is not an isolated axis but is embedded within two grids, as an orthogonal line in one grid and a diagonal in the other. All the disparate parts of the place are held within the lattice structure formed by these two intersecting grids. Lines of movement through Taliesin West zig and zag along the lines of the two interlocking grids. This structure of spine and grids has accommodated changing

164

Taliesin West, showing pergola and court notched into slope. Early 1940s. State Historical Society of Wisconsin, Howe Collection, WHi (Howe) TSP2

needs and considerable expansion relatively gracefully over the past half century (fig. 163).

Buildings, gardens, paths, and patios are set into the slope in some places, elevated on a platform above the desert in others (fig. 164). This is a landscape meant to be walked through. Approaching and moving through the complex along the spine, you enter at grade, descend a few steps, turn and turn again, ascend, turn down the main path with a wall at shoulder height, your eye just above the level of the retained slope. Go straight and you emerge at grade again; turning right through a loggia, you descend onto a platform elevated above the desert floor. As in a Japanese stroll garden, you turn repeatedly, your eye drawn to the "borrowed" view of landmarks in the distant landscape.[110] At Taliesin West, your eye is directed again and again to South Mountain and the site of Ocatilla on its far side; Wright incorporated landmarks of personal significance as he had in the Jones Valley with Romeo and Juliet, Midway Hill, Bryn Mawr, Bryn Canol, and Bryn Bach. Patterns of life and landscape merge over time as repeated shuttling along Taliesin's paths weaves you into the landscape, immediate and distant.

Wright planned this structure carefully from the outset, then built it gradually. A survey and grading plan of about 1938 with meticulously calculated spot elevations guided the necessary digging and filling and gives a precise picture of how Wright shaped the landscape (fig. 165). An area labeled "DIG" marks an east-west notch cut into the slope for the studio and main path behind; areas marked "FILL" delineate the broad, raised paths at the edge of the prow garden. The sunken area in the middle of the garden was at existing grade; Wright merely enclosed it (see figs. 163, 165). This was a lot of excavation and filling to accomplish with picks and shovels. As Brierly recalled: "All we did the first year was dig!"[111] And Wright said his wife Olgivanna thought "the whole opus looked more like something we had been excavating, not building."[112]

The second year, 1938–39, the apprentices commenced walls and buildings; Hill remembers the construction proceeded swiftly within the framework set the preceding year.[113] They took the materials of the desert and reordered them. Desert rocks – huge boulders, sharp-edged stones, rounded "goose-eggs" from the washes – were set in a rosy matrix

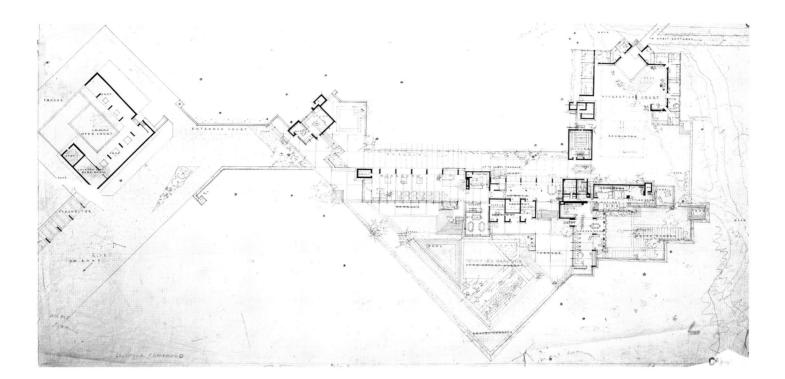

163
Frank Lloyd Wright. *Taliesin West,
Scottsdale, Arizona. Plan.* ca. 1942. Ink
on paper, 22 × 44 in. The Frank Lloyd
Wright Foundation, 3803.135

165
Frank Lloyd Wright. *Taliesin West,
Scottsdale, Arizona. Grading plan.*
ca. 1938. Pencil and colored pencil on
tracing paper, 25 × 29 in. The Frank
Lloyd Wright Foundation, 3803.049

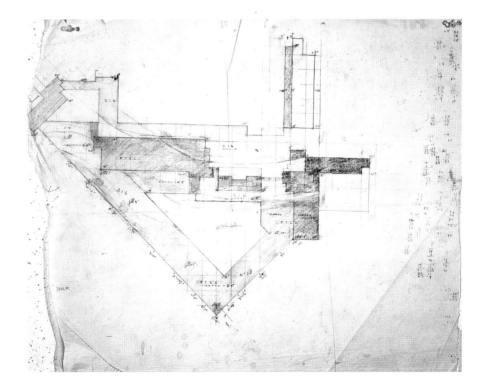

of concrete made from desert sand to form the walls of platform and structures. The rocks float in this matrix, their positioning startling in its dynamism, unrelated to the positioning one would expect in a wall, prompting one to wonder about the processes of their formation. As Wright said, "Here in Arizona, one is much closer to the cataclysm." It is just this sense of cataclysm that the walls convey (see fig. 166).

By 1942, the prow garden was built.[114] The plants of the garden were those of the surrounding desert, massed as single species and reordered in planters and beds of angular shapes. Yucca filled a large bed next to the pool in the sunken part of the prow garden, and prickly pear another planter (fig. 166). Staghorns lined the path at the base of the pergola and retaining wall behind the studio, and a mass of prickly pear next to the petroglyph near Wright's office marked another "dot" along the line of that axis. The cacti were transplanted from the desert; photographs show Wright directing apprentices moving a huge saguaro.[115]

The prow garden is the counterpart of both hill garden and cantilevered terrace at Taliesin (built the same year as the initial construction of Taliesin West). Desert and garden meet at the wall and the view is elevated, as in hilltop garden and terrace; here, desert wilderness once surrounded the garden, not fertile fields. The garden is an oasis open to the desert, jutting out into it (see fig. 162). The wall does not enclose the oasis but marks a boundary, inviting comparison between the domesticated and the wild, the human-built garden and what Wright called "a grand garden the like of which in sheer beauty of reach, space and pattern does not exist . . . in the world."[116]

Taliesin: One Book, Two Chapters

In inhabiting the two places [Wisconsin and Arizona], you learn. You have the open book of nature. On the one page you have efflorescence, richness, ease, what comes of great . . . well I suppose actually it's a form of decay. Perhaps this vegetation that grows all over so abundantly is a form of mold that comes upon the more accurate elements — the stone foundation of things. But when you get out here, you're back to the foundation.[117]

166
Taliesin West, prow garden, looking from sunken garden to terrace, garden room, and cove. Early 1940s. Note how massed desert plants and walls of desert masonry "capture" the hill beyond — covered with similar rocks and plants — as borrowed scenery. State Historical Society of Wisconsin, Howe Collection, WHi (Howe) TSP3

From 1938, Wright divided his life between Wisconsin and Arizona, journeying twice each year by automobile back and forth across the American landscape, his schedule driven by seasonal heat and cold, the cycle of spring planting and fall harvest. The juxtaposition of the two landscapes clarified each and kept his perceptions fresh. Perhaps his tendency to romanticize both was encouraged by periods of absence and the fact that he spent the most pleasant seasons in each, did not contend with the harsh Wisconsin winter or torrid Arizona summer. Progressively, the two Taliesins, in the relationship between buildings and landscape, came to resemble summer cottage and winter camp rather than year-round dwellings.

Wright returned to both each year full of ideas for change, seizing afresh the task of reshaping buildings and gardens: "It was pandemonium for two weeks – tearing out walls, rebuilding," recalled Bruce Pfeiffer.[118] The built landscapes of the two Taliesins are similar yet different; structured by similar principles, but taking different shape, each in dialogue with the other and with its own landscape (see figs. 152, 163). Despite all the changes over the years, buildings and gardens at Taliesin are rooted in the first half of Wright's career, fixed by foundations that survived successive fires and demolitions, while Taliesin West represents a new chapter in his work. Bruce Pfeiffer remembers when the stone marker inscribed with the words "Taliesin West" was set up near the entrance. Wright pointed to the name "Taliesin" molded into the wall of the parking area opposite – "That's the book," he said, then pointed to the new marker – "And that's the chapter."[119]

By identifying Taliesin as a book and the places he came to call Taliesin North and Taliesin West as chapters, Wright underscored the role of Taliesin as text with purposeful plot and the two places as essays elaborating similar themes. Together, the Taliesins embody in built form Wright's ideas on nature and landscape. They are villas, as Ackerman has defined the type, distinguished from farms or ranches by "the intense, programmatic investment of ideological goals…rooted in the contrast of country and city, in that the virtues and delights of the one are presented as the antitheses of the vices and excesses of the other."[120] The Taliesins present in tangible form Wright's ideas of a world made better by design. They are the built versions of his utopian texts, *Disappearing City*, *When Democracy Builds*, and *The Living City*.[121] As villas, the Taliesins belong to a tradition thousands of years old where dwelling is simultaneously functional, pleasurable, and ideological, where landscape is embellished to express ideas of nature and humanity.

Nature, Landscape, and Wright's Principles of Landscape Design

Wright revered nature, not landscape, and his use of the two words was distinctly different. When Wright spoke of nature, he spoke of principles, of authority for architectural form, and his words were abstract. He rarely mentioned "landscape"; when he did describe a landscape, his language was vivid but focused upon recurrent features or patterns rather than idiosyncratic variables. The *peculiarities* of a local landscape held no interest for him; he wrote, for example, of *the* prairie, as an abstract ideal, not *a* prairie. He interpreted the prairie as a horizontal plain, emphasizing its flatness (most prairie landscapes have a rolling topography), and designed most of his "prairie style" houses for sites that were originally forested or in the transition zone between forest and prairie.

Wright used "nature" in several senses – as essential quality, material reality, and divine force – and often moved from one sense of the word to another without transition.[122] In his early writings, he emphasized the first two senses; in later years the metaphysical emerged more explicitly. He wrote in 1912 that by "Nature," he did not mean "that outward aspect that strikes the eye as a visual image of a scene or strikes the ground glass of a camera, but that inner harmony which penetrates the outward form…and is its determining character; that quality in the thing…that is its significance and its Life for us – what Plato called…the 'eternal idea of the thing.'"[123]

Later in life, Wright described why he capitalized the word "nature": "Nature should be spelled with a capital 'N,' not because Nature is God but because all that we can learn of God we will learn from the body of God, which we call Nature."[124] This remark is pure Emerson, who had written similar words more than 150 years earlier: "the noblest ministry of nature is to stand as the apparition of God."[125] To Wright nature held the key to "the *right* ordering of human life"; nature was an ideal, "an original source of inspiration" from which to craft art and civilization.[126] He saw the artist – himself, for example – as nature's prophet and art as a moral force whose task was to reveal how society might create institutions that were "harmonious" with universal principles. "Ideas exist for us alone by virtue of form."[127] The artist's work was thus "the revelation" of the "life-principle which shall make our social living beautiful because organically true."[128] These ideas were well developed by 1900 and fully worked out by 1912, when Wright first constructed Taliesin.[129]

In "The Japanese Print: An Interpretation" (1912), Wright employed Japanese art as a vehicle through which to express his own philosophy of nature, art, and architecture; it is an essential text for understanding his intentions in landscape architecture. The essay distills and expands upon earlier texts and lays the foundation for his future writing on the subject. At the heart of the essay is Wright's idea of "conventionalization," the process whereby one draws out the inner nature of the material world (a process Wright equated with civilization): "Real civilization means for us a right conventionalizing of our original state of Nature. Just such conventionalizing as the true artist *imposes* on natural forms."[130]

To Wright, landscape was often an imperfect, outward manifestation of nature; the task of the architect was to bring the outer in closer conformity with the inner ideal, its *nature*, or essential characteristics. This accounts for seeming inconsistencies between texts and acts: his veneration of nature, on the one hand, and his imposition of architectural form upon landscape, on the other. This distinction is not so obvious to most modern readers, for "nature" and "landscape" are commonly equated.[131] Wright had contempt for what he called "some sentimental feeling about animals and grass and trees and out-of-doors generally," as opposed to reverence for nature as an internal ideal, the very "'nature' of God."[132]

Here lies the fundamental difference between Wright and landscape architect Jens Jensen. The two friends agreed that nature should be the authority for design, but they disagreed on the proper interpretation of that authority and "argued incessantly

about the nature of nature."[133] Jensen's naturalistic designs for parks and gardens *imitated* the outward appearance of nature as reflected in the regional landscape. Wright believed that a "true artist" must "impose" an idealized geometry derived from a landscape's inner nature upon the given or "natural forms."[134] Wright's critique of Western art can be read as a critique of naturalistic landscape design: "Where the art of Japan is a poetic symbol, much of ours is attempted realism, that succeeds only in being rather pitifully literal."[135] To Wright the outward appearances of natural features were important only for the hints they provided to their "inner nature" as expressed in their underlying structure. This structure is what he sought to clarify in his landscapes and buildings.

"Structure is the very basis of what I call reality," wrote Wright in 1937, the year before construction began on Taliesin West.[136] Twenty-five years earlier, in "The Japanese Print," he had asserted that structure was "at the very beginning of any real knowledge of design. And at the beginning of structure lies always and everywhere geometry."[137] By structure, he meant the way that elements are united into "a larger unity – a vital whole."[138] Though his definition of structure remained fundamentally the same, it evolved between 1912 and 1937, the years in which he published the two texts and was engaged with the original Taliesin and Taliesin West. In 1912, he stressed that structure was "pure form, as arranged or fashioned and grouped to 'build' the Idea" and geometry (Euclidian) was "the grammar of the form," "its architectural principle."[139] At Taliesin from 1911 to 1914, Wright grouped the squares, rectangles, and circles of buildings, terraces, and gardens in a highly sophisticated play of blocks within a single orthogonal grid. By 1937, when he declared, "Nature could not have static structure first if she would," he was emphasizing the "organic," dynamic quality of structure: its origin in ideal conception, then unfolding, a product of creative process, shaping and shaped by function.[140] This describes the structure of Taliesin West, a complex lattice that holds within it varied forms and has accommodated much change over the years. The two Taliesins represent a profound shift in structural strategy. Here, as in so many other respects, Wright has one foot in the past, the other in the future.

There is often an unresolved tension in his works and texts between static "eternal" geometry and dynamic "organic" structure.

Apart from his native terrain, the landscapes that moved Wright most powerfully were those whose underlying structure was expressed clearly in the shape of their surface, as in deserts.[141] Given the importance to Wright of landscape structure as embodied by landforms and plants, his work *had* to respond when he moved from the gently rounded deciduous trees and layered landforms of Wisconsin's Driftless Area to the spiky desert plants and angular landforms of the arid Southwest. How apt that the hill garden is a rounded mound enclosed by a square of layered limestone walls, the prow garden a triangle elevated by walls of rocks tumbled in mortar like talus at the base of desert mountains.

Wright took care to distinguish between outer and inner form – shape and structure – but the irony is that he himself often fell into the trap of imitating outer shape and ignoring inner structure. Jensen chided Wright for designing flat roofs, which echoed the horizontality of the prairie's ground plane but were poorly adapted to the region's heavy snowfall. Taliesin West was built into the land and out of it, the geometry of its plan inspired by the angles of the surrounding terrain, but when floods swept down off the nearby slopes, they sometimes washed right through the buildings. When Wright responded to the surface form of a landscape rather than to the processes that shaped its underlying structure, he ran into trouble.

Abstraction, as opposed to imitation, is an important device for Wright, a means of fusing the real and the ideal.[142] Abstraction is a process of simplifying landscape features, stripping away details that do not contribute to the intended meaning, and emphasizing significant detail. Through abstraction, or "conventionalization" as he had called it in early texts, Wright sought to express the unity of inner essence and outward appearance, as in the perfectly rounded form of the knoll in the hill garden and the steps/ledges cut to appear as if they were layered bedrock revealed, but their edges straighter than one would find in "nature" (see fig. 154). "Abstraction is stark form," said Wright in 1937, "in abstraction it is the structure or pattern of the thing that comes clear, stripped of all realistic effects, divested of any realism whatsoever."[143] Wright often juxtaposed the ideal and the real, abstracted landscape form and given form, the cultivated and the wild: cantilevered terrace over "wild" slopes below; raised garden on prow and the desert; hilltop garden enclosed by wall and the freely growing grass beyond (see figs. 156, 162, 166).[144] Experiencing all these contrasts together heightens the appreciation of each. Juxtaposed in the mind's eye, as they were in Wright's life, the Taliesins sharpen the perception of their two landscapes; hill garden and prow garden are equivalents, each an abstraction, a re-presentation of the region.

For Wright, abstraction also meant a progressive geometrization of outward form, since he believed that natural features were underlain by "an essential geometry." He wrote, for example, of how a "Japanese artist grasps form always by reaching underneath for its essential geometry. . . . By the grasp of geometric form and sense of its symbol-value, he has the secret of getting to the hidden core of reality."[145] Wright stressed this principle of abstraction in his teaching; as apprentice John Lautner reported in 1934, "We are learning to see the essence of the abstract here at Taliesin."[146] At Taliesin West, Wright abstracted the formal structure of the landscape, the angles of mountain peaks and talus at the base of nearby hills, and applied that triangular geometry to the form of house and garden and the structure of the whole (see figs. 163, 166).

Geometry, for Wright, was "an aesthetic skeleton" that held symbolic meaning: "certain geometric forms have come to symbolize for us and potently to suggest certain human ideas, moods, and sentiments – as for instance: the circle, infinity; the triangle, structural unity; the spire, aspiration; the spiral, organic progress; the square, integrity."[147] Through "subtle differentiations of these elemental geometric forms," and "a sense of [their] symbol-value," form could be made to *signify*.[148] Wright employed this idea in both buildings and gardens. Gardens, however, are different from buildings in one respect: they embody both real *and* idealized nature. Landscape features may be representations of the world, but they are also the world itself, physical reality and idea together, the *source* of metaphor and metaphor. A tree can be a tree and The Tree, a path both path and The Path. The round mound may be an abstraction of a hill, but it is also a hill, not merely a representation. The fusion of the real and the ideal in Wright's landscapes contributes to their aesthetic and symbolic power.

Buildings were central and integral to Wright, and they were his primary means of integrating varied landscape features into a unified composition. One cannot imagine Wright as the designer of a place like Stourhead where the main event, the park in the valley, is a separate world from the house.[149] Wright's landscapes are also inconceivable without the structures that order the landscape even as they respond to it. The terraces and gardens of Taliesin emanate outward from the dwelling; the reverse is also true: landscape suggested the form of the buildings, the size and placement of windows. It is often impossible to say where building ends and landscape begins. This point was brought home to me while I was working on the present essay. To describe Wright's approach to landscape design as distinct from his buildings proved impossible. Again and again, I found myself inside the buildings looking out to distant views of hills, lakes, trees, and buildings, following the plane of interior floor to exterior terrace, then outside, tracing the line of walls and roofs as they slid into terrain in a fusion of building and earth. Wright's work is part of a larger tradition of architecture that embraces the idea of landscape and building as continuous, where building interiors are like landscapes, where the real and the ideal are always in dynamic tension.[150]

The same principles guided Wright's design of buildings and landscapes; both were architecture.[151] Plants were materials that should be "massed and grouped," each according to its "true nature — that is, as it naturally grows best to show its full beauty as a lilac, a syringa, an elm, an oak, or a maple. . . . The formality necessary to harmonize these growing things with man's surroundings is sought and found in the architectural nature of the plan, the division, the enclosure, the arrangement."[152] Wright applied these principles to landscape design throughout his career, from the high walled enclosure of the gardens in his prairie-style houses, to the lower wall enclosing the hill garden at Taliesin, to the wall raised above the desert at Taliesin West; all are organized by the geometry of the plan through divi-

sion, enclosure, and arrangement. At the Taliesins, places where he worked over a long period and exerted the most control, buildings and landscapes gradually merged. One finds oneself, as Wright was with Japanese architecture, stumped to determine "where the garden leaves off and the garden begins, . . . too delighted with the problem to attempt to solve it."[153]

It was these very qualities of structure, abstraction, symbolic form, and correspondence of buildings and landscape, of interior and exterior space that attracted Wright to Japanese landscape art.[154] At both Taliesins he employed principles of Japanese garden design of different times and traditions: simplification and condensation, miniaturization or embodiment of the large in the small, correspondence between parts and whole, "shakkei" or borrowed scenery, and what Mitsuo Inoue has called "movement-oriented architectural space."[155] Just as the small garden of stones and raked gravel at Ryoanji can be read as a microcosm of Japan, the hill garden at Taliesin can stand for the landscape of southwestern Wisconsin. Wright also used the hill garden as borrowed scenery when he captured the long, horizontal view of the hilltop with clerestory windows running the length of the room. In Japan, shakkei entails far more than incorporating a view, it means "capturing a landscape alive," and there is a whole tradition of gardens composed around borrowed scenery.[156] Wright "captured" scenery with windows, eaves, tree trunks, and sky. At Taliesin West, for example, he captured the landscape of Paradise Valley by holding it between sky above and open, elevated platform below. South Mountain is a prominent element in this borrowed landscape, its significance emphasized by being captured in different ways — at the bend in the path, framed by the loggia, repeatedly hidden and disclosed as one moves through the stroll garden that is Taliesin West. The Japanese tradition of movement space, as defined by Inoue, is episodic, entailing successive spaces or views, revealed a bit at a time, and irregular in structure compared to "geometric space."[157] The stroll garden, with its twisting, turning path, views concealed, then revealed, imparts a sense of flux and mutability. At Taliesin West, Wright fused geometric and movement space; the zigs and zags are not irregular but structured by the lines of two orthogonal grids. Static "eternal" geometry and dynamic "organic" structure are held in deliberate tension.

Wright understood landscape as dynamic, as subject to constant change, and growth was among the primary "life principles" of his "organic" architecture.[158] His own homes at Taliesin in Wisconsin and Arizona are brilliant essays on landscape design that can accommodate growth and change. As Brierly observed, "Mr. Wright never cared about things lasting. He was satisfied just to see them take shape."[159] The buildings and their landscapes were built and rebuilt, shaped and reshaped in successive paroxisms of creative destruction. Their very essence was change, their current form the result of addition and subtraction, accretion and erosion, growth and decay.[160]

Wright's Landscape Legacy

Wright left a rich legacy of landscapes – written, drawn, and built – whose scope and significance have barely been realized.[161] Most extraordinary are the two places he shaped and inhabited during much of his lifetime – the Taliesins. Though altered radically since his death in 1959, hundreds of photographs from 1900 to 1959 enable us to think ourselves back in time, to experience successive stages of these places, to appreciate the scale of Wright's achievements. The importance of the two landscapes is amplified by their embodiment of principles of design worked out in texts, drawings, and constructions over half a century, each medium illuminating, clarifying, and extending the others for us today as they must have done for Wright himself. It is one thing to read, "We decided to build ourselves into the life of the desert," and quite another to examine the plan of cut and fill, to see photographs of people digging and moving rocks and plants, to experience the reality of the place itself, how its very structure is knit into the desert. The Taliesins were Wright's landscape laboratories for ongoing experiments in form, feeling, and meaning; they are ideas in the original sense of the word: "visible representations of a conception; realized ideals."[162] All this would be more than sufficient to set them among the most important landscape compositions of the twentieth century. Their significance, however, is deeper still.

Steeped in the picturesque while advancing the modern, the Taliesins are important links between past and future, chapters in a much larger book on nature and landscape, essays on how to celebrate our human selves as part of nature. The Taliesins belong to a vision of architecture and landscape architecture as social arts whose task is to perfect a union of human and non-human nature. Wright shared roots in Transcendental philosophy and scientific agriculture with Frederick Law Olmsted (1822–1903), his predecessor in this tradition.[163] Jens Jensen (1860–1951) and Lewis Mumford (1895–1990) were peers and friends. Among Wright's successors are Kevin Lynch (1918–1984) and Lawrence Halprin (b. 1916), whose visit to Taliesin in 1941 inspired him to become a landscape architect.[164] Wright's contribution to this tradition was extraordinary. He believed that architecture – of buildings and landscapes – could become "natural" if designed according to principles derived from nature. The aim of his art was "truly no less than the creation of man as a perfect 'flower of Nature.'"[165]

Notes

I have written this essay mainly from primary sources – from the landscapes themselves, from photographs, maps, and drawings spanning more than one hundred years, from Wright's texts, from conversations with people who witnessed him shaping landscapes first hand. Without the generous assistance of colleagues, archivists, and members of the Taliesin Fellowship, it would have been difficult to assemble and interpret the material. William Cronon's landmark essay on Wright, "Inconstant Unity," formed an invaluable foundation for my work that was extended by subsequent conversations. Jack Holzhueter of the State Historical Society of Wisconsin gave me an orientation to the place of Wright's family in Wisconsin history and introduced me to essential nineteenth- and early twentieth-century material, which I might otherwise have overlooked. I am grateful to David Benjamin and Andy Kraushaar of the Visual and Sound Archives for their help in making this material accessible, and to an anonymous collector for showing me the full set of Wright's photographs for the Hillside Home School. Bruce Brooks Pfeiffer shared many memories and observations and brought key drawings to my attention; without them some of my observations would still be surmise. Conversations with Cornelia Brierly, John deKoven Hill, and Mary Frances Nemtin also provided insights that sharpened my interpretations of the physical traces and photographic and written evidence left by Wright on landscape. I am indebted to Penny Fowler for arrangements, introductions, and discussions, and to the Taliesin Fellow-

ship for granting me free access to Taliesin North and West. Sam Spirn's sharp eyes on site at Taliesin and his work in the archives were invaluable. Sylvia Palms and Emily Stern searched out texts in the library. Many people read earlier versions of this essay and made valuable suggestions: Cornelia Brierly, Bill Cronon, David De Long, Penny Fowler, Kenneth Helphand, John deKoven Hill, Jack Holzhueter, Nicholas Olsberg, Bruce Pfeiffer, Paul Spirn, and Bob Sweeney. I would like to thank the Canadian Centre for Architecture and the Library of Congress, without whose support for travel to archives and landscapes writing this essay would have been impossible, and Christine Dufresne for her deft management of the publication process. Finally, I am grateful to David De Long for his insights into the unbuilt projects and for extended conversations.

1   Wright made numerous references in this vein, for example: "The land is the simplest form of architecture." Baker Brownell and Frank Lloyd Wright, *Architecture and Modern Life* (New York: Harper and Brothers, 1937), 17.

2   Among the most seminal essays on Wright's landscape compositions are: William Cronon, "Inconstant Unity: The Passion of Frank Lloyd Wright," in *Frank Lloyd Wright, Architect*, ed. Terence Riley (New York: The Museum of Modern Art, 1994) and Walter Creese, *The Crowning of the American Landscape* (Princeton: Princeton University Press, 1985), 241–78. Other scholars have made important observations about the Taliesin landscapes, though their primary focus was on the buildings: James Ackerman, *The Villa*

(Princeton: Princeton University Press, 1990); Neil Levine, "The Story of Taliesin: Wright's First Natural House," in *Taliesin 1911–1914*, ed. Narciso G. Menocal (Carbondale: Southern Illinois University Press, 1992); and Reyner Banham, "The Wilderness Years of Frank Lloyd Wright," *Journal of the Royal Institute of British Architects* (December 1969), 512–19.

3   I know of no definition of landscape adequate to our modern multi-faceted understanding of the phenomenon, and this is too large a task to tackle here. Serious writing on landscape design has been a neglected arena and has been mainly the domain of landscape architects, geographers, and scholars of garden history. See my essays "Reclaiming Territory: Four Books on Landscape," *Progressive Architecture* (February 1993), 103, 117, and "Seeing/Making the Landscape Whole," *Progressive Architecture* (August 1991), 92–94.

4   *Webster's New International Dictionary of the English Language*, 2nd ed. (Springfield: Merriam, 1955).

5   See "Ideas of Nature," Raymond Williams, in *Problems in Materialism and Culture* (London: Verso, 1980).

6   In "Inconstant Unity," Cronon sketches the philosophical background of "nature" as Wright perceived it. I will not repeat that discussion here.

7   See Cronon, 9–14.

8   There are many similarities between the program of the Taliesin Fellowship and that of the school founded by his Aunt Nell and Aunt Jane (opened in 1887, closed in 1917), which Wright's sons John and Lloyd attended. Mary Ellen Chase, a teacher at Hillside Home School, called it "a school, a home, and a

farm all in one." Mary Ellen Chase, *A Goodly Fellowship* (New York: Macmillan, 1939), 94. There were many distinguished visitors, including Wright's Uncle Jenkin, the Chicago minister. Like the Taliesin apprentices later, students worked in the gardens, stables, and barnyards, decorated the chapel each week with flowers and greens and joined teachers in contributing to the weekly services. See also Florence Fifer Bohrer, "The Unitarian Hillside Home School," *Wisconsin Magazine of History* 38 (Spring 1955), 151–55.

9   One could cite many examples. Gwendolyn Wright's description of Fallingwater as responding "perfectly to the natural landscape, nestling comfortably into the particular contours" of its site is a case in point. Gwendolyn Wright, "Frank Lloyd Wright and the Domestic Landscape," in Riley, *Frank Lloyd Wright, Architect*, 80. While certain aspects of Fallingwater may have been inspired by specific features of the site (such as horizontal terraces by rocky ledges), the house itself is boldly imposed upon hillside and stream rather than comfortably nestled. Wright's frequent statement that architecture should begin by responding to the "ground" did not mean that he would hesitate to restructure it radically in order to bring out what he conceived to be its inner essence or to express certain "cosmic laws." He also often applied a design he had developed for one location to another, quite different, site.

10 His writings on Taliesin are cases in point. "The Japanese Print" was published while he was in the throes of designing and building Taliesin for the first time; while it ostensibly is not about this particular project, it never-

theless represents a working out in words of the very ideas he sought to express in the buildings/landscape of Taliesin. The reflections on Taliesin in *An Autobiography* of 1932 and 1943 were written from memory and from a desire to promote his work and justify himself (in regard to his aunts and their school, for example, of which there are accounts that conflict with his). His description of the Wisconsin landscape in "Desert Architecture" was spoken within the context of teaching apprentices to "read" landscape. Frank Lloyd Wright, "The Japanese Print: An Interpretation" (1912), in *Frank Lloyd Wright: Collected Writings*, vol. I., 1894–1930, ed. Bruce Brooks Pfeiffer (New York: Rizzoli in association with The Frank Lloyd Wright Foundation, 1992); "An Autobiography" (1932 and 1943), in *Frank Lloyd Wright: Collected Writings*, vol. II, 1930–1932, ed. Bruce Brooks Pfeiffer (New York: Rizzoli in association with The Frank Lloyd Wright Foundation, 1992), and vol. IV, 1939–1949, ed. Bruce Brooks Pfeiffer (New York: Rizzoli in association with The Frank Lloyd Wright Foundation, 1994); "Desert Architecture" (November 28, 1954), in *Frank Lloyd Wright: His Living Voice*, ed. Bruce Brooks Pfeiffer (Fresno: California State University Press, 1987).

11 Photographs by Wright and others in the iconographic collections of the State Historical Society of Wisconsin (hereinafter SHSW) and the archives of The Frank Lloyd Wright Foundation provide a remarkable record. At the SHSW alone, there are several collections: Woods (descendents of Wright's Uncle Enos Lloyd Jones), Hillside Home School, and John H. Howe.

My method in studying the Taliesins was to assemble copies of these photographs and to work with them on site in Wisconsin and Arizona to determine the place from which each was taken in order to compare the landscape then and now and to establish a chronology among them. The photographs also served as foci of individual conversations with Taliesin fellows Cornelia Brierly, John deKoven Hill, Mary Frances Nemtin, and Bruce Brooks Pfeiffer, who have been members of the Taliesin Fellowship since 1934, 1938, 1946, and 1949, respectively. These conversations, which were held in winter 1995, were extremely important in fixing dates for many of the photographs and for interpreting their significance. Written descriptions by members of the Taliesin Fellowship were also very helpful: books by former apprentices Edgar Tafel, Edgar Kaufmann, jr., and Curtis Besinger, and an unpublished manuscript by Brierly sketch a description of life in the Taliesin Fellowship. Columns written by apprentices and Wright himself were published in Wisconsin newspapers under the title "At Taliesin"; over one hundred of them are reprinted in *"At Taliesin,"* ed. Randolph C. Henning (Carbondale, Ill.: Southern Illinois University Press, 1992). The columns have a freshness that comes from the fact that they describe events happening in the present, rather than reflections on the distant past.

12 The drawings are in The Frank Lloyd Wright Archives (hereinafter FLWA), The Frank Lloyd Wright Foundation, Scottsdale, Arizona. The vast majority of them have never been published, yet they provide more insight into Wright's thinking-in-action than the polished drawings frequently pub-

lished and exhibited. In *The Reflective Practitioner* (New York: Basic Books, 1983), Donald Schon identifies "reflection-in-action" as the very heart of professional artistry. As depictions of Wright's "reflection-in-action," these drawings are invaluable to scholars and students and deserve to be made more accessible through publication.

13 Jones Valley must not be confused with the Driftless Area as a whole or with that special region fifty miles to the northeast, the Wisconsin Dells. In "Wright and Landscape: A Mythical Interpretation," Thomas Beebe confuses landscapes that are geologically and botanically distinct and miles apart; the photographs by H. H. Bennett that illustrate the essay are all from the Wisconsin Dells, a landscape so different from Jones Valley as to give a completely misleading impression, particularly for those readers who have never visited Taliesin. See *The Nature of Frank Lloyd Wright*, eds. Carol R. Bolon, Robert S. Nelson, and Linda Seidel (Chicago: University of Chicago, 1988).

14 See photographs from the Woods Collection at the SHSW.

15 Humphrey Repton, *The Art of Landscape Gardening* (including *Sketches and Hints on Landscape Gardening* and *Theory and Practice of Landscape Gardening*), ed. John Nolen (Boston: Houghton Mifflin, 1907), 3, 69. This edition was the first volume of "a series of classics in landscape architecture undertaken at the suggestion and with the cooperation of the American Society of Landscape Architects." Repton (1752–1818) originally published the two works in 1795 and 1803, respectively. Romantic idealism and the picturesque have common roots. For

a description of the picturesque style and ideas it represented, see Christopher Hussey, *The Picturesque: Studies in a Point of View* (London: Frank Cass, 1983); John Dixon Hunt and Peter Willis, *The Genius of the Place: The English Landscape Garden 1620–1820* (Cambridge, Mass.: MIT Press, 1988). I agree with Ackerman when he observed of Taliesin "that in the design as a whole Wright managed to fulfill the aims of the picturesque designers and architects of Downing's time better than any of them had done." Ackerman, 265.

16 Jack Holzhueter, personal communication. This is a zone where prairie and forest meet and mingle. The tops of surrounding hills were bare in nineteenth-century photographs. It is not clear whether they were covered originally by prairie or whether the Lloyd Jones family or earlier settlers had cleared the trees, probably for firewood, construction materials, and for lead smelting and shot manufacture. Since the hilltop soils are relatively infertile, they would hardly have been worth the effort to clear for crops.

17 The Lloyd Jones family was large, with five sons (Thomas, John, Jenkin, James, and Enos) and four daughters (Ellen, Jane, Mary, and Anna), most of whom eventually settled nearby, except Jenkin, who became minister of Unity Church in Chicago. According to Wright's sister Maginel, the family referred to the valley as The Valley of the Clan. See Maginel Wright Barney, *The Valley of the God-Almighty Joneses* (Spring Green, Wis.: Unity Chapel Publications, 1986), 18. For other accounts of the valley in the nineteenth and early twentieth centuries, see Chase, *A Goodly Fellowship*; Creese; and Wright, "Autobiography."

18 See description of circumstances surrounding the purchase and reproduction of warranty deed dated April 10, 1911, reprinted in Anthony Alofsin, "Taliesin I: A Catalogue of Drawings and Photographs," in Menocal, 99.

19 A plan labeled "Taliesin Farms" indicates properties controlled by the fellowship; the total area is listed as "Approx. 3000 acres." The FLWA 3420.003.

20 "The family did not so well know the truth of BEAUTY." Wright, "Autobiography," 113.

21 Ibid., 226.

22 Wright took this series of more than two dozen photographs for his aunts' school (possibly in return for tuition for his children who attended the school). To my knowledge, only four from the series have been published before – two of Romeo and Juliet, one of the valley, and another of adults and children playing golf. This book reproduces an additional three never published before. The photographs were taken at different times of the year; several are winter landscapes with snow on the ground. I have established the location of each in the field. They were printed as collotypes mostly in an oblong format and presented in a paper wallet, dated 1900, with a description printed in red and black letters: "HILLSIDE HOME SCHOOL/A collection of views in and about the/home the school the surrounding/country and characteristic bits of class/work HILLSIDE WISCONSIN NINETEEN HUNDRED." A separate sheet describes the purpose: "This collection of views is intended to become a contemporary record of the Hillside Home School work and will enlarge with the growth of the

school. In this way it is hoped to convey to those who may never have visited it a clearer idea of the atmosphere of the work than could be obtained otherwise." Many of these images are now in the collection of the SHSW (Woods Collection), but a full set, including the original paper wallet, exists in a private collection. I am greatly indebted to Jack Holzhueter for bringing these to my attention and to the owners for permitting me to see them. I have no evidence that Wright took *all* of these photographs; clearly, however, he did undertake to print and present them. The design of the typeface on the wallet, layout of the text, and combination of red and black ink resemble other printed matter Wright produced around that time. These photographs were taken during the same period that Wright photographed weeds and his son John. Wright's career as a photographer was short-lived. After the early 1900s, he exploited photography as a tool rather than an expressive medium. He engaged photographers such as Henry Fuermann and Pedro Guerrero to photograph his work and used aerial photographs to study Taliesin's landscape. A study of Wright's use of photography is outside the scope of this essay, but it is badly needed, and there is ample material.

23 Early photographs of Taliesin taken by Henry Fuermann ca. 1912 are reproduced in Alofsin, "Taliesin I: A Catalogue of Drawings and Photographs," in Menocal. Photographs were also taken during construction (see Clifford Evans Collection, Marriot Library, University of Utah, Salt Lake City). Edgar Tafel took a series of photographs of Taliesin in June 1959 (just two months after Wright's death), which he published in Edgar Tafel, *Apprentice to Genius: Years with Frank Lloyd Wright* (New York: Dover, 1985), 214–15. Hundreds of other photographs from 1912–59 are in the the John H. Howe Collection, SHSW, and in the FLWA.

24 I was able to verify this identification in October 1994; once the leaves are off the trees, one can trace the characteristic shape of Midway, and to the left of Midway, the slope of the distant hill on the far side of Route 23.

25 A. R. Whitson et al., "Soil Survey of Iowa County, Wisconsin," *Wisconsin Geological and Natural History Survey Bulletin* 30 (Soil Series 4), 1914.

26 While I have been unable to determine whether Wright ever had a copy of the soil survey, it is quite possible, even likely, that he did. The map included with the report is dated 1910 but shows a structure on the site of Taliesin; its scale is one inch to the mile, with contour intervals of twenty feet. According to the report, the "first recorded attempt at farming [in Iowa County] was in 1829." Nineteenth-century farmers found the soils lost productivity with continued cropping and turned increasingly to dairying by the 1880s; by 1914, Iowa County was "distinctly a dairy county." Whitson, "Soil Survey of Iowa County, Wisconsin," 46–47.

27 In his autobiography, Wright described how difficult it was to tell where the house began and the ground left off, but nowhere could I find any signs of foundation meeting bedrock. Houses built by Cornish miners at Mineral Point (twenty miles south of Jones Valley) such as the Polperro House of 1843 (now preserved as part of Pendarvis Historic Site), however, fit Wright's description perfectly. He must certainly have seen these and may very well have been inspired by the way the foundations of the house merge with the rock, all of the same stone. There are both limestone and sandstone in Jones Valley; Hillside School buildings, the foundation of Romeo and Juliet and Taliesin are all built of the tawny native stone.

28 Wright, "Autobiography," 224. These words, however, must be taken with a grain of salt; Wright did build atop the hill here (the tower and dining room) and elsewhere.

29 One still has the views within the valley, though the river is now hidden by trees when they are leafed out.

30 A photograph of the living room by Hedrich-Blessing shows the Rieder pig farm, big as life, smack in the middle of the picture framed by the window second from the right along the east-facing wall (reproduced in Pfeiffer, *Collected Writings* III, 165). The view described from the study is depicted in a photograph in the Howe Collection, SHSW.

31 Wright, *Architectural Forum*, 68 (January 1938), 3; quoted in Creese, 262.

32 See photograph reproduced in Pfeiffer, *Collected Writings* II, 243 (FLWA 1403.0033).

33 I am indebted to Penny Fowler for pointing out how the narrow French doors of the loggia resemble Japanese screens, for bringing the photograph of the loggia (reproduced in *House Beautiful* 98 [November 1955], 234) to my attention and for telling me about the gold glass, and to John deKoven Hill for details about the shutters.

34 See Levine for a discussion of the allusion to Taliesin, the Welsh bard. See also Scott Gartner, "The Shining Brow: Frank Lloyd Wright and the Welsh Bardic Tradition," in Menocal.

35 *Oxford English Dictionary.* The meaning of brow evolved from earlier
meanings related to the human face,
to eyebrow, then lower part of the
forehead jutting out over the eyes,
then the whole forehead.

36 Whatever exposed rock there may
once have been is no longer in evidence; one wonders what happened
to all that fill. When one compares
Taliesin hill before and after, it
becomes clear that Wright built *up*
the hill. How massive the Taliesin
complex is, seen from this perspective!

37 Alofsin has catalogued and discussed
early views and drawings of Taliesin.
See Alofsin, "Taliesin I: A Catalogue
of Drawings and Photographs," in
Menocal.

38 See succession of plans and early
photographs for how the drive and
courts evolved from 1911 to 1913
in Alofsin. As he has cautioned, one
must take care not to mistake these
early plans for documents of what
was built. Wright prepared many
drawings for publication to represent
his ambitions for Taliesin. Photographs
are therefore extremely important
in verifying what was indeed constructed and when.

39 See Wright, "Autobiography," 220–21
for text and 222–23 for photographs
of Fiesole attributed to Wright.
Ackerman and Levine have both
remarked upon the resemblance of
Taliesin to Tuscan villas such as those
of Fiesole, where Wright lived with
Mamah Borthwick Cheney immediately before their return to the
United States, but did not link these
observations to Wright's text. See
Ackerman, 263; Levine. Cheney was
the wife of a client with whom
Wright lived in Europe and built
Taliesin; she was murdered at Taliesin
in 1914.

40 Wright declared this intention: "A
dream in realization ended? No,
woven a golden thread in the human
pattern of the precious fabric that is
Life: her Life built into the house of
houses. So far as may be known –
forever!" Wright, "Autobiography," 221.

41 Gertrude Jekyll, *Home and Garden:
Notes and Thoughts, Practical and
Critical, of a Worker in Both* (London:
Longmans Green, 1900). Frank Lloyd
Wright, "Concerning Landscape
Architecture," in Pfeiffer, *Collected
Writings* I, 56. This was an unpub-
lished written address of 1900.

42 Jekyll, 14, 4–5. The text of *Home and
Garden* describes a home and landscape that resembled Taliesin in many
other respects.

43 Letter from Frank Lloyd Wright to
Lewis Mumford, January 7, 1929,
Special Collections, Mumford
Papers, folder 5477, University of
Pennsylvania Library, Philadelphia.

44 Jensen designed council rings for
parks and gardens as gathering
places in which people would talk,
tell stories, perform. He saw the
council ring as a symbol of democracy, where all people were equal,
and of "the brotherhood of all living
things." See Ronald Engel, *Sacred
Sands* (Middletown, Conn.: Wesleyan
University Press, 1983), 200–1. A
council ring was part of Jensen's
design for the grounds of the
Sherman M. Booth house (1910–11).

45 Wright, "Autobiography," 226.

46 Henning, 68. The column was published on August 8, 1934.

47 This photograph by Fuermann, originally published in *Architectural Record*
23 (January 1913), has been reproduced many times since.

48 When Cornelia Brierly arrived in
1934, there were shrubs on the hill,
but no trees in the grass outside

the tea circle. The stepped ledges
were there, but more were added
later. John deKoven Hill arrived in
1938, and the shrubs in the hill garden were gone. Brierly and Hill,
personal communications.

49 Mary Frances Nemtin, personal communication. Whereas the early ledges
were installed in the side of the
mound well before the 1930s, John
deKoven Hill recalled placing the
large rock where the jar now sits.

50 These associations are not far-
fetched. Wright's Uncle Jenkin referred
to Tower Hill's "bosom," "breast," and
"splendid fecundity" in a sermon
titled "The Reforestation of Tower
Hill"; see Thomas E. Graham, ed. *The
Agricultural Social Gospel: The Gospel
of the Farm by Jenkin Lloyd Jones*
(Lewiston, N.Y.: Edwin Mellen, 1986).
See also Hans Biedermann, *Dictionary
of Symbolism* (New York: Meridian,
1992), 100–2. The dovecote was ren-
ovated around 1932 into a bedroom
for John Howe.

51 Wright described the symbolism of
forms in "The Japanese Print," 117.
The hill garden, however, is merely a
representation of fertility, for hilltops
are not fertile here, the valley bottoms are. The rounded form of the
hilltop has evoked strong associations. Ackerman, for instance, has
written that the hill resembled a
"burial mound" (262); Levine reminds
us of the connection between the
hill garden and Mamah's death (21)
and of Wright's description of how
he "cut the garden down and filled
to overflowing with the flowers a
strong plain box of fresh, white pine,"
how he and his son John laid her
body "down to rest among the
flowers. The flowers that had grown
and bloomed for her." Wright,
"Autobiography," 239.

52 See the essay by David De Long in this volume for an elaboration of these ideas in relation to the projects of the 1920s.

53 The terrace was built before Hill arrived in 1938; he remembered it as new at that time, and that Wright's birthday had been celebrated on the terrace the year before. Hill, personal communication.

54 Grant Hildebrand has described Wright's employment of prospect and refuge in his buildings. Wright also used these devices in his landscape compositions. Grant Hildebrand, *The Wright Space: Pattern and Meaning in Frank Lloyd Wright's Houses* (Seattle: University of Washington Press, 1991).

55 Wright, "Autobiography," 226.

56 William Weston told this to Hill, who related the story to me. "The gardens were very important to Mr. Wright," said Hill, "he always had a series of remarkable gardeners." Hill, personal communication.

57 Thus Wright applied the technique of contour plowing (aligning the furrows along the slope to prevent erosion) to the kitchen garden. Hill was in charge of these gardens. The vegetable gardens were moved to Hillside a few years after he arrived at Taliesin in 1938. Hill, personal communication.

58 Wright, "Autobiography," 183. Terence Riley has explored this idea in "The Landscapes of Frank Lloyd Wright: A Pattern of Work" in Riley, *Frank Lloyd Wright, Architect*, 96–107.

59 Pfeiffer, personal communication.

60 This technique can be seen in numerous photographs in the Howe Collection, SHSW, and in FLWA. See FLWA 4509.0001, for example. Hill noted that they had a machine for cutting sod: "We were always cutting sod to lay along the roadsides where they had washed out." Hill, personal communication.

61 Franz Aust, a professor of landscape architecture at the University of Wisconsin, regularly brought his students to Taliesin, and a group of students under the direction of F. T. Matthias did a topographic survey for Wright in 1934. See FLWA, Farmland File 3420.010.

62 Henning, 198. From a column published on March 15, 1934. I am grateful to Randolph Henning for sending me this and other columns that were not published in "At Taliesin."

63 See FLWA, Farmland File. I am grateful to Bruce Pfeiffer for bringing these plans, one of which is reproduced here, to my attention.

64 The plan was drawn by someone else, but Wright made scribbled notes on this copy. FLWA, Farmland File 3420.003.

65 The plans appear to have been drawn upon over and over again at different times, but it is possible to establish approximate dates based on whether or not certain features are shown or missing. Taken together, they span Wright's entire tenure at Taliesin. The survey of November 8, 1920, at a scale of one inch equals one hundred feet, indicates the area of his property (about 182 acres) and the value of the house ($115,000).

66 The octagonal barn, which was torn down in 1933, is shown on the plan as still standing; the vegetable gardens are still located just downslope of the hill garden; and the old access road to Tan-y-deri is shown along the western property line (Wright later considered changing the location of this road, but this wasn't done until after his death). The entrance road from Route 23 built in 1922 is shown.

67 Note the dovecote in the tower on the hill, which means the photograph was taken before 1933.

68 FLWA, Farmland File 3420.009. The difference in orientation of the lines of crops in the two areas of fruits and vegetables is to accommodate change in direction of the slope.

69 FLWA, Farmland File 3420.006.

70 FLWA, Farmland File 3420.005.

71 The sermons were published in *Unity*, a church-related newspaper, and *Hoard's Dairyman*, a farm journal owned by W. D. Hoard, a governor of Wisconsin. Many of them are collected in Graham. I am indebted to Jack Holzhueter for bringing them to my attention.

72 "Barn Building" (1908), in Graham, 189.

73 Wright, "Autobiography," 226.

74 See plans and photographs from the Farmland File. Wright also drew directly on photographs in developing his site plans for Lake Tahoe and the Johnson Compound. See De Long and figs. 77, 78.

75 Brierly, personal communication. Mrs. Wright had good reason for disapproving of the road grader. In 1936, Wright's secretary, Eugene Masselink, wrote to Lewis Mumford: "Mr. Wright would write himself but he has suffered a painful accident – being tossed from the road grader while making a new road – couple of ribs broken – neck wrenched – leg twisted – but is around again now and will no doubt write to you himself – soon." Letter from Eugene Masselink to Lewis Mumford, July 1, 1936, Special Collections, Mumford Papers, folder 5478, University of Pennsylvania Library, Philadelphia.

76 Wright recounted his fascination with running water and his favorite

77 recreation as a boy – "building dams of sticks and stones" across a stream. Wright, "Autobiography," 117. He had at least several prints from Hokusai's Waterfall series in his personal collection; three were included in *Frank Lloyd Wright, The Japanese Print* (New York: Horizon, 1967).

77 Wright, "Autobiography," 226.

78 Ibid.

79 Wright's generator "house" was a miniature prairie-style house, not a shack; undoubtedly this was something of a joke. One photograph depicts the generator house, sitting on the dam over a cascading waterfall, as it looked when newly built (FLWA 2501.005); many others show it in varying stages of disrepair). Every evening, someone had to climb out onto the dam to turn a wheel that diverted water from the reservoir to the hydroelectric generator. Hill, personal communication. Brierly and Hill both tell stories of how sometimes the lights would gradually dim or the projector would go out in the middle of a film, and one of the apprentices would have to go down and clear a turtle that had gotten stuck in the generator.

80 These are depicted in a photograph, FLWA 4509.0001.

81 These can be seen in a succession of photographs. The upper dam was removed after Wright's death.

82 The changes in Wright's thinking about the shape of the lakes can be seen in numerous sketch plans in the Farmland File.

83 He planted a grove of pines miles away from the house near the intersection of Routes C and 14 and designed a sign for "Taliesin Parkway." FLWA 5610.003. I am grateful to Bruce Pfeiffer for showing me these drawings.

84 Brierly, personal communication.

85 Drawing of sign (not by Wright) is in FLWA, 5610.003. The pines still stand in the triangular property across Route 23 from the motel.

86 Edgar Tafel, *Apprentice to Genius* (New York: Dover, 1985), 111. The process of tearing down the school building was described in an illustrated article by Jeanne Lamoureux, "Taliesin… Rural Workshop for Master Builders," *Harvester World* (August 1950), 2–7. The caption to one photograph reads: "Conducting a symphony of destruction, Mr. Wright, in the left foreground, directs the apprentices as they tear down the old to make way for the new." I am indebted to Bruce Pfeiffer for bringing this article to my attention.

87 Wright, "Autobiography," 227.

88 Kevin Lynch, "At Taliesin" column printed in the *Madison Capital Times*, fall 1937, quoted in Tridib Banerjee and Michael Southworth, *City Sense and City Design: Writings and Projects of Kevin Lynch* (Cambridge, Mass.: MIT Press, 1990), 17. Lynch was nineteen when he wrote this column. He later became a revered teacher and seminal theorist of urban design and planning, who acknowledged Frank Lloyd Wright and Lewis Mumford as his two mentors.

89 These were advertised in the weekly columns published in Madison newspapers. See Henning.

90 Eugene Masselink, "The Arizona Trek," in "At Taliesin," February 10, 1935, Henning, 106–7. Though there were many reasons for the move to Arizona, preservation of the woods was what Masselink chose to focus upon.

91 There were seven cars in addition to the truck. In 1935 and again in 1936, the group stayed at La Hacienda in Chandler. In 1935, they built most of the Broadacre City model in the courtyard of La Hacienda in time to load it onto the truck on April 1 to transport it back east for exhibition, first in New York City, then in Madison, Pittsburgh (Edgar Kaufmann paid the costs for its construction), and Washington, D.C. See relevant columns reprinted in Henning. The fellowship returned to Arizona in 1938 to begin construction of Taliesin West; very few "At Taliesin" columns were written after that.

92 Henning, 109–10.

93 Frank Lloyd Wright, "Living in the Desert: Part One – We Found Paradise," *Arizona Highways* (October 1940), 12–15.

94 Banham.

95 It is easier to celebrate the desert in winter than summer. San Marcos in the Desert was intended as a winter resort, and Taliesin West was not built originally as a year-round dwelling. Wright lived there from late fall to early spring; he was among the first flock of Scottsdale "snowbirds."

96 "Why in any changing period of our relation to the soil are transient buildings not best? Yes, transitory box-boards, batten, and canvas, in Arizona – for a preliminary study? Why not? These slight means may catch and reflect divinity of idea quite as well as the great sahuaro." Wright, "Autobiography," 331–32.

97 Banham, 517.

98 De Long cites a letter from Wright to his son John where he refers to himself thus: "Phoenix seems to be the name for me too." See De Long, 102.

99 Other important links were the unbuilt designs for the Johnson Desert Compound and San Marcos in the Desert. See De Long. Ocatilla also can be spelled ocotillo or ocatillo. The accepted spelling for the plant the camp was named for,

Fouquieria splendens, is ocotillo; Wright, however, referred to the camp as "Ocatilla" in early drawings and in texts such as the autobiography, so that is the spelling used here.

100 Wright, "Autobiography," 331.

101 This is not meant to imply that a grid plan is inappropriate to sloping sites. There are many examples of towns on steep slopes where the grid plan works very well, from ancient towns like Priene on. See my essay "Deep Structure: On Process, Form, and Design in the Urban Landscape," in *City and Nature*, Thomas Møller Kristensen et al., eds. (Odense, Denmark: Odense University Press, 1993).

102 See De Long.

103 That dirt track is now Shea Boulevard; Scottsdale was the closest settlement. Brierly, personal communication. For background text and photographs, see Patricia Seitters Myers, *Scottsdale: Jewel in the Desert* (Windsor Publications, 1988).

104 See *Arizona Good Roads Association, Arizona: Illustrated Road maps and Tour Book* (1913), reprinted by Arizona Highways magazine; Bradford Luckingham, *Phoenix: The History of a Sunbelt Metropolis* (Tucson: University of Arizona, 1989).

105 Wright asked Kenneth Lockhardt, Frances Nemtin, and John deKoven Hill to remain at Taliesin during the winter of 1950–51 to mind the farm and send the eggs. Nemtin and Hill, personal communications. See also Besinger, 220–21. The current orchard of orange and grapefruit trees was planned by Wright but planted after his death.

106 Brierly, personal communication.

107 Wright, "Living in the Desert," 12.

108 FLWA 3803.048.

109 Black Mountain was visible through an arch at the eastern end of the main path until Mrs. Wright obliterated the view by expanding her bedroom after her husband's death.

110 For a description of the principle of borrowed scenery ("shakkei"), see Teiji Itoh, *Space and Illusion in the Japanese Garden* (New York: Weatherhill, 1980). For a description of the stroll garden, its relation to interior architectural space, and the concept of "movement-oriented architectural space," see Mitsuo Inoue, *Space in Japanese Architecture* (New York: Weatherhill, 1985). The problem with borrowed scenery is lack of control over the view. Wright was distressed when powerlines were built across his view, but he was unable to stop the construction.

111 Brierly, personal communication.

112 Wright, "Autobiography," in Pfeiffer, *Collected Writings* IV, 170.

113 Hill, personal communication. This was Hill's first year in the Fellowship.

114 See photographs in Henry-Russell Hitchcock, *In the Nature of Materials: The Buildings of Frank Lloyd Wright 1887–1941* (New York: Da Capo Press, 1975, reprint of 1st ed. of 1942 by special management with Hawthorne Books).

115 The "desert" surrounding Taliesin has changed radically as the density of settlement has increased. Seeds have blown in from lawns and gardens of nearby subdivisions. Runoff from roads, parking lots, and irrigated gardens and effluent from sewage treatment have altered the character of plants growing there; there are fewer cacti, more woody shrubs, denser growth than just ten years ago. The tough desert plants of the prow garden are gone, replaced by subtropical ornamentals that require irrigation; these have also replaced much of the original desert plantings within the rest of the complex. I once thought these substitutions occurred after Wright's death, for they destroy the clarity of juxtaposed geometries that once existed between gardens and desert, but am told it was Wright himself who first introduced these foreign plants. Brierly and Hill, personal communications.

116 Frank Lloyd Wright, "To Arizona," *Arizona Highways* 16 (May 1940), 8.

117 Frank Lloyd Wright, "Desert Architecture," 177.

118 Apparently he worked these out in his head, then built directly. According to Pfeiffer, there are no drawings that document these successive changes.

119 Pfeiffer, personal communication. The other two chapters, says Pfeiffer, are Taliesin North and Taliesin East (Wright's apartment in the Plaza Hotel in New York).

120 Ackerman, 286, 12. See also Raymond Williams, *The Country and the City* (New York: Oxford University Press, 1973).

121 Many people have remarked on the similarity between Taliesin and Broadacre City. As Kenneth Helphand and Cynthia Girling have observed: "Grounded as it is in the Midwestern landscape and its pattern of house, field, woodlot, and road, beneath the Broadacre plan it is not hard to discern an idealized and modernized Wisconsin landscape." Kenneth Helphand and Cynthia Girling, *Yard, Street, Park* (New York: John Wiley, 1994), 73.

122 Raymond Williams has called "nature" the most complex word in the English language. He defines three meanings of "nature": the essential or given character of something, "the material world itself, taken as including or not including human

beings," and "the inherent force which directs either the world or human beings or both." Raymond Williams, *Keywords*, rev. ed. (Oxford: Oxford University Press, 1983), 219–24. See also Williams, "Ideas of Nature."

123 Wright, "The Japanese Print," 118. Wright had sold his camera and darkroom equipment by the time he wrote these words. It is clear from this statement why photography ultimately held no fascination for him; it is an art of interpreting outward appearance. While one could argue that Wright did capture in some of his photographs an essential quality or "idea of the thing," to describe rather than to shape was clearly not sufficient for him.

124 Wright, commencement speech at Sarah Lawrence College, New York, in June 1958, attended by Brendan Gill and quoted in his *Many Masks* (New York: Ballantine Books, 1987), 22. Another version of the statement, almost identical, is transcribed from a tape of August 4, 1957, in Pfeiffer, *Frank Lloyd Wright: His Living Voice*, 88. Wright spoke with Mike Wallace in 1957 on the television program "The Mike Wallace Interview." "I've always considered myself deeply religious," said Wright. "Do you go to any specific church?" asked Wallace. Wright replied, "My church [pause], I put a capital 'N' on Nature and go there. I spell Nature with an 'N.' You spell God with a 'G,' don't you? I spell nature with an 'N' – capital." See also Anne Whiston Spirn, "The Authority of Nature: Conflict and Confusion in Landscape Architecture," in *Nature and Ideology*, ed. Joachim Wolschke-Bulmahn (Washington, D.C.: Dumbarton Oaks, forthcoming 1996).

125 R. W. Emerson, *Nature* (Boston: James Munroe, 1836), 77.

126 Wright, "The Japanese Print," 124–25 (emphasis added).

127 Ibid., 119.

128 Ibid., 125.

129 Wright had expressed some of these ideas in his earliest texts, "The Architect and the Machine" (1894) and "Architect, Architecture, and the Client" (1896); he developed them in "A Philosophy of Fine Art" (1900); and he expressed them most fully in "The Japanese Print: An Interpretation" (1912). These four essays permit one to follow the evolution of Wright's ideas on nature and architecture from the time he opened his own practice through the original construction of Taliesin. All four were originally lectures. The first was given the year after he opened his practice, "read to the University Guild, Evanston, Illinois," and the second to the same group two years later. The third was written to be delivered to the Architectural League of the Art Institute of Chicago. The fourth was based on a lecture he gave at the Art Institute and later revised and published as a book. The essays are reprinted in Pfeiffer, *Collected Writings* I.

130 Pfeiffer, *Collected Writings* I, 119, 124 (emphasis added.)

131 Particularly landscapes where the human influence is difficult to discern or is deliberately concealed. See William Cronon, "The Trouble with Wilderness," in *Uncommon Ground: Toward Reinventing Nature*, ed. William Cronon (New York: W. W. Norton, 1995).

132 Wright, "Autobiography," 163.

133 Tafel, 152. Jensen and Wright had offices in the same building in Chicago and had collaborated on numerous

projects, including the Sherman M. Booth house of 1910–11. Though they remained lifelong friends, they stopped working together soon after that. Jensen was a popular visitor to the Fellowship at both Taliesins. See Henning, *"At Taliesin."* He was inspired by Wright's example to found a school, which he called "The Clearing," in Door County, Wisconsin. Like the Taliesin Fellowship, The Clearing survived the death of its founder and is still in operation. See Mertha Fulkerson and Ada Corson, *The Story of The Clearing* (Chicago: Coach House Press, 1972).

134 Wright, "The Japanese Print," 124.

135 Ibid., 120.

136 Brownell and Wright, 277. The last chapter of this book, a dialogue between Wright and Brownell, contains an extended reflection on the meaning of structure.

137 Wright, "The Japanese Print," 117.

138 Ibid., 117.

139 Ibid.

140 Brownell and Wright, 278–81. Wright uses the big, blue Ming tea jar in the garden at Taliesin to illustrate his idea of structure as fusing "ideal" of function and purpose, process of formation, form and use.

141 See Frank Lloyd Wright, "To Arizona" and "The Bad Lands," in Pfeiffer, *Collected Writings* IV, 33–36, and I, 175–78). I disagree with Cronon's point that "Wright had little use for nature in the raw," that he was drawn to domesticated landscapes and turned inward in other settings. Cronon, 19. On the contrary, Taliesin West turned most emphatically outward to the "raw" desert.

142 "To me abstraction . . . is to make clear in some pattern the spirit of the thing." Brownell and Wright, 275.

143 Ibid.

144 Today we might add the juxtaposition of Euclidean and fractal geometry, but this is our concern, not Wright's.

145 Wright, "The Japanese Print," 118.

146 Henning, "At Taliesin," 97.

147 Wright, "The Japanese Print," 117.

148 Ibid., 118.

149 Stourhead is an eighteenth-century English landscape garden at the head of the river Stour in Wiltshire.

150 See, for example, the traditional architecture of Japan, the work of Alvar Aalto, Adèle Naudé Santos, and Australian architects Glenn Murcutt and Richard Le Plastrier.

151 Wright spells out what he sees as the architectural basis of landscape design as early as 1900; see Wright, "Concerning Landscape Architecture," in Pfeiffer, *Collected Writings* I, 54–57. Here he cites Jekyll's *Home and Garden* as a book that "should be in every library."

152 Ibid., 55, 56.

153 Wright, "Autobiography," 246.

154 Though Wright's relationship to Japanese art and architecture has been well documented, his affinity to Japanese landscape architecture has not received much attention. For his role as a collector of Japanese prints, see Julia Meech-Pekarik, "Frank Lloyd Wright's Other Passion," in Bolon et al. For his exposure to Japanese architecture (with an emphasis on buildings), see Kevin Nute, *Frank Lloyd Wright and Japan* (New York: Van Nostrand Reinhold, 1993). The relationship of Wright's gardens and landscapes (including buildings) to those of Japan is a subject that warrants far more study, for there are clearly many parallels. See Margo Stipe, "Wright's First Trip to Japan," *Frank Lloyd Wright Quarterly* 6 (Spring 1995), 21–23, for a list of gardens Wright visited in 1905.

155 Inoue, 137–71. It is not within the scope of this essay to elaborate upon the history of Japanese landscape architecture and the design principles related to its various traditions. Those interested in reading further should refer to the texts of Inoue and Itoh already cited and to Itoh, *The Japanese Garden: An Approach to Nature* (New Haven: Yale University Press, 1972).

156 Itoh, *Space and Illusion in the Japanese Garden*, 15. A famous example of shakkei landscape is the garden of Shugaku-in in Kyoto, which Wright visited and admired.

157 Inoue, 146.

158 Wright's focus was mainly on organic processes and his references were mainly to trees and large plants — oak, pine, ocatillo, saguaro. He tends to neglect inorganic processes (erosion and water and air flow, for example); perhaps this lack of interest relative to inorganic processes contributed to the leaky roofs, occasional floods (as at La Miniatura and Taliesin West), and thermal discomfort that plagued some of his buildings.

159 Brierly, personal comunication.

160 Wright changed the Taliesins year by year throughout his later life. This poses a major problem to those who would preserve their landscapes and buildings (even were one to ignore the fact that the sites have been home and workshop to the Taliesin Fellowship for decades since Wright's death). How does one decide which version to "preserve"?

161 When the second edition of Christopher Tunnard's book on modern gardens (the standard book on the subject) was published in 1948, Taliesin West was among the few examples by Americans featured: the book described numerous gardens by Tunnard (a professor of landscape architecture at Harvard who was born and educated in England), a single garden by California landscape architect Thomas Church, and Taliesin West by Wright. Christopher Tunnard, *Gardens in the Modern Landscape* (London: The Architecture Press, 1948). One would think that Wright's work at Taliesin West would have been liberating for American landscape architects, and indeed I believe there was an influence, yet I have found no documentation or studies of this. Instead, there has been much reference in recent literature to the influence on American landscape architecture of European designers, such as André and Paul Vera and Gabriel Guevrekian, and to the Brazilian Roberto Burle Marx, all of whom were represented in both the first and second editions of Tunnard's book. Wright's influence on American landscape architecture is a subject that warrants much more study.

162 *Webster's New International Dictionary of the English Language*. "Idea" stems from the Greek word meaning "to see."

163 See my essay "Constructing Nature: The Legacy of Frederick Law Olmsted," in Cronon, *Uncommon Ground*.

164 Halprin, personal communication. Lynch said of Wright, "He made me see the world for the first time." Banerjee and Southworth, 18.

165 Letter from Frank Lloyd Wright to Lewis Mumford, January 7, 1929, Special Collections, Mumford Papers, folder 5477, University of Pennsylvania Library, Philadelphia.

SYMBOL AND CATALYST:

The Automobile in Architectural Representation Before 1930

C. FORD PEATROSS

For many early twentieth-century Americans, including Frank Lloyd Wright, the automobile offered a new and thrilling way to experience the landscape and its wonders, both natural and fabricated, and the boundaries that it eliminated were more important than any it imposed. Wright was at the forefront, if not the center, of the development of strategies, forms, and building types intended to accommodate the automobile. In the process, he created and introduced conventions for their representation whose power and brilliance have only begun to have their effect. His own passion for motoring constantly reanimated this dialogue.

The following portfolio of drawings places these developments in the context of the architectural representation of the automobile through 1930, both at home and abroad, so that we may observe the ways in which Wright's work stood apart and was influential. It portrays the progression of the automobile from the role of passive icon to that of a dynamic force in the design of buildings, roadways, and the larger built environment; in the graphic conventions required to represent them; and, ultimately, in the creation of new building forms that emerged to accommodate the automobile, serve its needs, and exploit its possibilities. The influence of the work, both built and graphic, of the architects and draftsmen whose sensibilities were especially attuned to the spirit and potential of the automobile age has been profound.

Frank Lloyd Wright's affinity for and representation of the automobile resulted in a body of work that was substantially different in form and nature from almost all that is represented in this portfolio. Yet with the exception of drawings by Rudolph Schindler, Richard Neutra, and Lloyd Wright, it had little influence before 1930. The critic Lewis Mumford, writing in the 1925 Wendingen edition of Frank Lloyd Wright's work, provided an astute analysis of both the dilemma of Wright's vision and its promise for the future, and assessed Wright's place in smoothing the way in the ever-uneasy relationship between man and machine:

Frank Lloyd Wright's work, as I see it, is an attempt to apply the logic of the machine to humane building. His architectural conceptions are far removed from the conservative architects who will not carry modern processes to their inevitable conclusions; they are equally removed from the notions advocated by architects like Le Corbusier who are not essentially concerned with humane building, and would be quite pleased to remodel our whole environment in accordance with the narrow physical processes that are served in the factory. . . . I trust that the modernism of Mr. Frank Lloyd Wright places him among the new poets and artists, whereas the modernism of l'Esprit Nouveau is but a continuation of an acerbic puritan philosophy that has degraded life and art throughout the whole period of the industrial transition. . . .

There is a parallel between Mr. Frank Lloyd Wright's work and that of some of our modern poets in America; such a man, for example, is Carl Sandburg, Mr. Wright's fellow townsman in Chicago. Both of them have faced our age, have absorbed the broken rhythm of the machine, feel the jagged geometry of our new adventures in space; they have something to express in plastic or literary form that an earlier age was not aware of.

167

James Knox Taylor, supervising architect; Henry C. Wilkinson, delineator. *U.S. Court House and Post Office, Altoona, Pennsylvania. Perspective view and plans.* 1900. Graphite, ink, and gouache on paper, 18 ½ x 24 in. National Archives and Records Administration, Cartographic and Architectural Archives Division, Record Group 121

In the earliest representations we see the automobile placed with increasing frequency and number in the foreground of presentation drawings, usually perspectives, intended to show a project to the client or a popular audience. In drawings for the Office of the Supervising Architect of the Treasury Department made at the turn of the century, a government draftsman managed to give unexpected liveliness and energy to a view of the United States Court House and Post Office planned for Altoona, Pennsylvania, by placing a small automobile in the foreground. In so doing he implied that irrespective of its architectural form, that of a Renaissance palazzo, his building was thoroughly up-to-date.

168
Henri-Edmond Rudaux, artist. *Mercedes Daimler-Motoren-Gesellschaft, Stuttgart-Untertürkheim*. Color lithograph, 44 × 30 in. Graphische Sammlung der Staatsgalerie, Stuttgart

At about the same time, the automobile began to appear in popular illustration and advertising. The background of this poster depicts the Mercedes factory in Stuttgart. However, the architectural perspective takes second place to the images in the foreground, a speeding motorcar and an ascending Zeppelin (introduced in 1900). Both were powered by internal combustion engines and were prime symbols of the technological progress with which Mercedes wished to be popularly identified.

169

Edgar Chambless, architect. *Roadtown. Aerial perspective.* ca. 1910. Page 447 from *Architects' and Builder's Magazine,* old series, vol. 42, no. 11 (August 1910). Fisher Fine Arts Library, University of Pennsylvania, Philadelphia

The culmination of the development of the American streetcar suburb and the evolving principles for the segregation of the direction, levels, and modes of transportation are boldly expressed in Edgar Chambless's scheme for Roadtown. In it, the suburban landscape is defined by a continuous lateral mega-structure that links various forms and levels of transportation (primarily light rail) with commercial buildings on a civic scale.

American transportation terminals of the same period incorporated multi-level systems segregating rail, truck, automobile, and pedestrian transport. The three below-grade levels of McKim, Mead, and White's Pennsylvania Station in New York (1902–11) were equipped with ramps that were designated on the original plans as "carriageways" but served more automobiles than horse-drawn vehicles by the time of the station's completion. Grand Central Terminal in New York (part of the larger Terminal City project), designed by Warren and Wetmore (with Reed and Stem) and opened in 1913, featured exte-

rior ramps and elevated drives channeling traffic from bustling Park Avenue in full acknowledgment of the ascendancy of the automobile. Cutaway perspectives of the terminal's sophisticated system of levels were a source of great pride and were widely published.

THE OHIO RECREATION TOWER CO.
C.H. KNIGHT INVENTOR
606 COLUMBIA BLDG. CLEVELAND OHIO.

170
C. H. Knight, inventor. *The Ohio Recreation Tower Co., Cleveland, Ohio. Perspective.* ca. 1911. The Library of Congress, Washington, D.C., Prints and Photographs Division, G38482, August 28, 1911

Inventor C. H. Knight's 1911 scheme for a multi-story, spiral "recreation tower" in Cleveland, Ohio, focused on the streetcar as a means of transportation and a source of enjoyment, and transformed the mode of transportation into the destination itself. Streetcars would carry patrons up and down the spiraling ramps, providing 360-degree views of the city. At the top a pavilion probably contained a ballroom and dining facilities in addition to viewing platforms, capping this vertical version of an oceanside amusement pier. It is also notable that while the motorcars by which some of the tower's patrons were intended to arrive were few in number, they are prominent in the foreground of the rendering.

171

Antonio Sant'Elia, architect. *La Città Nuova, Airport and Railroad Station with Cable Cars and Elevators on Three Street Levels. Aerial Perspective.* 1914. Black ink and black pencil on paper, 8 ½ × 11 in. Musei Civici, Pinacoteca, Como, Italy

The structures associated with automobile travel were required to meet demanding criteria concerning the freedom, path, speed, ease, and safety of human movement. These in some ways unprecedented functional and spatial imperatives presented new challenges to the conceptualization and figuration of architectural and landscape designs. This is one of the most memorable of a group of perspective drawings that have exerted a dominating influence on urban architectural representation since their first display and publication in the catalogue of the *Nuove Tendenze* exhibition in Milan in 1914. The Città Nuova, the work of the twenty-six-year-old Italian Futurist architect Antonio Sant'Elia, represented Milan in the year 2000. This vision was governed by a complex network of transport services with as many as seven levels. In the catalogue preface Sant'Elia wrote: "The street . . . will no longer lie like a doormat at the level of the thresholds, but will plunge stories deep into the earth, gathering up the traffic of the metropolis connected for necessary transfers to metal catwalks and high-speed conveyor belts." The architectural vocabulary of the Futurists rejected historical precedent and materials in favor of unornamented structures of reinforced concrete and steel; it was enlivened by the dynamism of machines of every type and attuned to the special conditions of modern living.

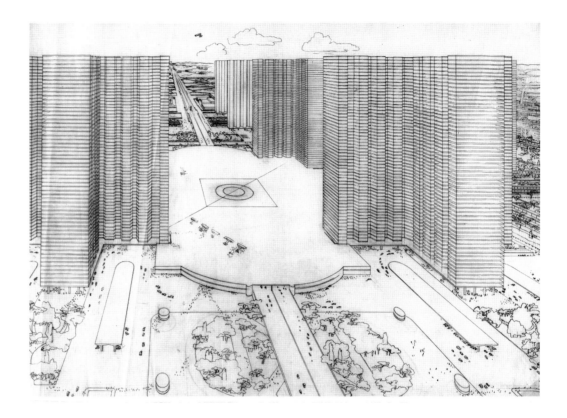

Le Corbusier, architect. *Contemporary City of Three Million Inhabitants, Central Station Flanked by Four Skyscrapers. Aerial perspective.* 1922. Gelatin print on Canson paper, 24 × 30 ¾ in. Fondation Le Corbusier, FLC 3850—plan Voisin

After the Futurists, no architect embraced the automobile more thoroughly than Le Corbusier, and its representation in both his writings and his works, urban and domestic, was of even greater influence. He celebrated the automobile in his *Vers une Architecture* (1923) and *L'Urbanisme* (1925), and it played a governing role in his projects for a Contemporary City of Three Million Inhabitants, exhibited in the Salon d'Automne of 1922, and the Voisin Plan for Paris, a diorama of which was in the *Exposition Internationale des Arts Décoratifs* in Paris in 1925.

In Le Corbusier's work the road became the dynamic raison d'être for structures of all scales and uses. In *L'Urbanisme,* he advocated "speedways," great elevated arterial roads to separate faster from slower traffic, which would be superimposed and segregated from suburban grids of roads and pedestrian traffic: "A modern city lives by the straight line, inevitably; for the construction of buildings, sewers and tunnels, highways, pavements. The circulation of traffic demands the straight line; it is the proper thing for the heart of a city. The curve is ruinous, difficult, and dangerous; it is a paralyzing thing." To further allow the unimpeded

flow of this lifeblood of the urban organism, the entire complex is raised on his signature *pilotis*: "From the fact that the street is no longer a track for cattle, *but a machine for traffic, an apparatus for its circulation,* a new organ, a construction in itself and of the utmost importance, a sort of extended workshop, we shall conclude that it must have more than one story, and that it would be possible, merely by the exercise of common sense, for towns built on piles to materialize."

173

Richard Neutra and Rudolph Schindler,
architects; Richard Neutra, draftsman.
*League of Nations Building Competition
Entry. Aerial perspective.* 1926. Graphite,
ink, and pastel on paper, 12 ¾ × 10 ⅛ in.
Schindler Archive, Architectural Draw-
ing Collection, University Art Museum,
University of California, Santa Barbara

In 1926, Richard Neutra and
Rudolph Schindler submitted an
entry to the League of Nations
design competition. To accommodate arriving and departing automobiles and their interpenetration
of the architectural fabric, the
architects carefully directed vehicles along an L-shaped trajectory
that passed through a covered
gateway and led to a motor court.
Wright's buildings and his conventions for representing them in
drawings deeply influenced Neutra
and Schindler; both had worked
on projects in his office and were
later to influence many other
architects in the same way. In 1926,

Neutra could write that his new
employer, architect Rudolph Meier,
"suddenly. . . discovered that my
designs have a similarity to those of
Wright (I wish they had). In reality
they are tame compromises." With
the notable exception of Neutra's
Rush City Reformed, which owed
more to the urban visions delineated by Le Corbusier and Ludwig
Hilbersheimer, Meier's observation
was correct.

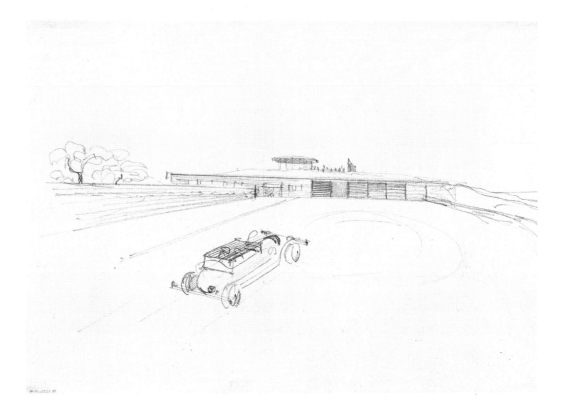

174
Office of Ludwig Mies van der Rohe.
Krefeld Golf Club. Perspective. 1930. Pencil on tracing paper, 8 ¼ × 11 ½ in. The Mies van der Rohe Archive, 19.18, The Museum of Modern Art, New York, Gift of the architect

The circulation and accommodation of the automobile were principal and unusual determinants for Ludwig Mies van der Rohe in his unsuccessful entry in a 1930 competition for the design of a golf club in Krefeld, Germany. Arrival is signaled by a low, elegant pavilion made up of individual garages for the motorcars of club members, and a circular dance pavilion crowns the hill behind. In a series of perspective sketches, Mies explored a wide variety of solutions, from open and enclosed garage bays to an extended carport supported by steel columns like those in his Barcelona Pavilion.

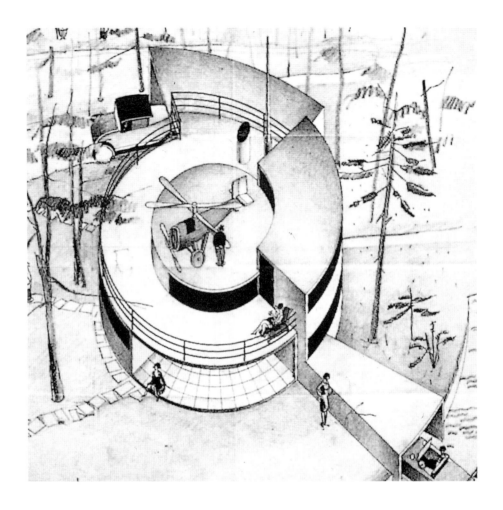

175

Arne Jacobsen, architect, with
Flemming Lassen. *Fremtidens Hus.
Aerial perspective.* 1929. Graphite,
ink, and watercolor on paper,
21 ⅓ x 17 ⅔ in. Samlingen af Arkitek-
turtegninger, Kunstakademiets
Bibliotek, Copenhagen

In his delightful, brightly colored
perspective for the Fremtidens
Hus (House of the Future) of 1929,
Danish architect Arne Jacobsen
allowed for entry on three different levels, by motorcar, motorboat,
and helicopter (the roof is a landing
pad). The house is thus a small-
scale transportation terminal and
its circular form is partially determined by the turning radius of the
automobile. The curving trajectory of the automobile is different
from the rectilinear one that we
have seen in most of the representations up to this point. Jacobsen
designed the house in collaboration
with Flemming Lassen; it won first
prize in a competition, which led to
its construction at a building exhibition in Copenhagen.

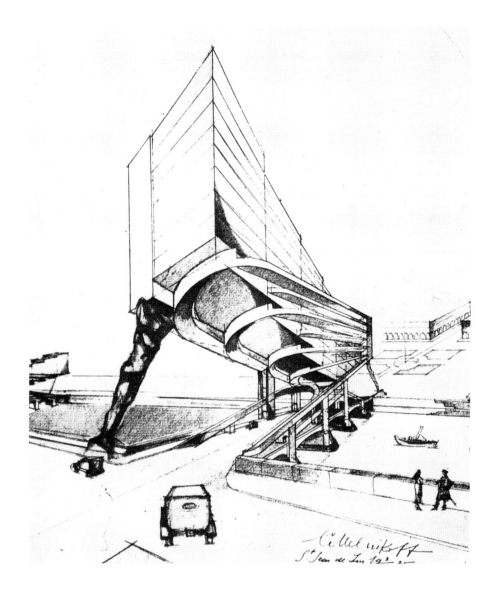

176

Konstantin Melnikov, architect. *Parking Garage over the Seine, Paris, 2nd Variant. Perspective.* 1925. Fig. 91 in S. Frederick Starr, *Melnikov, Solo Architect in a Mass Society* (Princeton University Press, 1981), p. 105. Canadian Centre for Architecture, Montréal

In urban settings, storage of the automobile presented even greater challenges and demanded entirely new forms. The Soviet architect Konstantin Melnikov devised a scheme for a parking garage to be placed over the river Seine in Paris that broke almost every convention in terms of its site, its form, and its method of representation. The perspective illustrated here was for a variant scheme, and the leaning atlantid propping up one corner was intended as a humorous response to critics who had questioned the stability of his first scheme. Significantly, both schemes took joy in exposing the structure's curving ramps, accepting, exploiting, and even reveling in the dictates of the automobile's climbing ability but limited turning radius. That it owes a debt to Le Corbusier's aesthetic of exposure is not surprising, since for Melnikov one of the most memorable parts of his first visit to Paris was being driven around in the great French architect's luxurious motorcar.

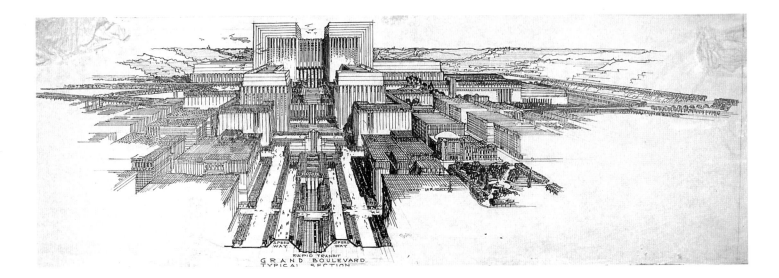

Lloyd Wright, architect. *Civic Center,
Los Angeles. Perspective.* 1925. Graphite
and ink on paper, 9 ¼ × 27 in. The
Mitchell Wolfson, Jr., Collection, The
Wolfsonian, Miami Beach, Florida,
and Genoa, Italy

The roadways or arteries required
to speed traffic through urban
centers remained a principal orga-
nizing element in architectural
representations of the automobile
until the close of the 1920s. The
urban vision that began with
Sant'Elia and Le Corbusier continued to dominate and to influence
the work of a wide range of architects and draftsmen, including
Frank Lloyd Wright's eldest son,
Lloyd Wright. His perspective
rendering for a new Civic Center
for Los Angeles bears the unmis-
takable imprint of Sant'Elia's Città
Nuova in its general form and its
representation of the layering of
transportation systems. The draw-

ing is strongly differentiated from
the Futurist aesthetic by its
incorporation of landscaping in its
terraces, rooftops, and transportation arteries. While Sant'Elia's
drawings may have been brought
to Lloyd Wright's attention by
Rudolph Schindler, Norman Bel
Geddes, or other architects and
designers working in Los Angeles
during this period, the planting
elements reflect many influences.
Among these are his father's work,
his tour of Italian gardens, a brief
stint with Olmsted and Olmsted,
and his own recent work in landscape architecture.

178

Norman Bel Geddes, architect. *Toledo Scale Company, Precision Laboratory Group, Factory Development. Bird's-eye view.* 1929. The Library of Congress, Washington, D.C., Prints and Photographs Division, G4247, August 23, 1930

More than any other built form during the 1920s, the highway emerged as a conspicuous and pervasive element that changed the face and character of the American landscape and provided the focus for many new building types. Planned for an eighty-acre site located on the Dixie Highway between Toledo, Ohio, and Detroit, Michigan, Norman Bel Geddes's widely published 1929 project for an industrial laboratory complex for the Toledo Scale Company was among the first to provide a substantially different, more dispersed, and suburban formula for arterial development. His industrial park sustained and

defined by a system of roadways, seen here in dramatic bird's-eye view, presented a model solution, one that has survived into the 1990s with little modification.

Frank Lloyd Wright on a road grader
at Taliesin, ca. 1930

FRANK LLOYD WRIGHT CHRONOLOGY, 1922–1932

Robert L. Sweeney

This chronology bridges the period in Frank Lloyd Wright's career between his return from Japan in August 1922, after work on the Imperial Hotel, and the founding of the Taliesin Fellowship ten years later, in October 1932. It is excerpted from a much larger work-in-progress, a highly detailed account of Wright's life and work. Most of the information comes from primary sources: correspondence, drawings, manuscripts, public records, and contemporary publications; newspaper accounts frequently are valuable but are used cautiously.

The first column lists significant events in Wright's life and work. The middle column treats the five projects featured in the exhibition and catalogue in detail; the sometimes fragmentary story of their development emerges if the column is read vertically. The third column lists Wright's other work of the period. As nearly as possible, dates for architectural projects coincide with completion of working or presentation drawings. Those designs that were executed are printed in boldface type. Several projects for which there are no known drawings or clarifying information are included; in these cases, the source of information is given. Although the fires at Taliesin in 1925 and 1927 are acknowledged, the subsequent rebuilding processes have not been sorted out and are therefore not mentioned.

1922

AUGUST		Wright's final return from Japan after work on the Imperial Hotel. Arrives in Seattle August 1; at Taliesin by August 20		
				Theater for Harold McCormick (mentioned in Wright to Darwin Martin, September 1, 1922)
OCTOBER	5	Wright to Lloyd Wright: is seriously considering the idea of working on the West Coast; has no work at all; Paul Mueller arriving November 1, may have some ideas; suggests collaboration with Lloyd		
NOVEMBER		"A Building That Is Wrong" (Imperial Hotel), by Louis Christian Mullgardt, published in *The Architect and Engineer*		
	13	Wright and Catherine Wright divorced		
DECEMBER	14	Wright to Mrs. Charles P. Lowes: will be in Los Angeles shortly after the holidays; mentions that Lloyd Wright will be associated with him in practice		
			22	Lowes house, scheme 2, Eagle Rock

1923

JANUARY	7	Writes "In the Cause of Architecture, 'He Who Gets Slapped'" (response to Mullgardt's article; *see* November 1922); published in part in *Japan Advertiser*, February 7, 1923		
FEBRUARY		Wright living and working in Los Angeles. Rents house at 1284 Harper Avenue, Sherman (now West Hollywood), for a studio. Working with him are Lloyd Wright, Kameki Tsuchiura, and, briefly, R. M. Schindler		
	5	Wright to Sullivan: "Have pitched in here to <u>locate</u>"		
	9	Wright's mother, Anna Lloyd Wright, dies, Waldheim Park Sanatorium, Oconomowoc, Wisconsin		

	Wright writes "In the Cause of Architecture: The Third Dimension" (unpublished statement on the work he is about to undertake in Los Angeles)			House over a ravine[1]
	12	Anna Lloyd Wright buried, Unity Chapel Cemetery, Hillside, Wisconsin		Block house 2-story[2] Study for block house in textile block construction[3]
MARCH				**Moore house reconstruction, Oak Park** Barnsdall house, Summitridge Drive (near Summitridge Place), Beverly Hills (first mentioned March 3; notice published that Barnsdall purchased twenty-four-acre site May 18; litigation, Wright vs. Barnsdall, filed February 28, 1924; dismissed June 19, 1952) **Millard house, La Miniatura, Pasadena** (plans approved March 15, 1923; construction begins March 1923; building permit issued July 10; completion notice filed March 29, 1924)
			Doheny Ranch, north of intersection of Doheny and Hillcrest Roads, Beverly Hills	
MAY				Commercial building: concrete, copper, glass (see National Life Insurance Building, October 1925)
JUNE			Lake Tahoe summer colony, Emerald Bay, Lake Tahoe, California	
JULY		12	Wright to Lloyd Wright: mentions Lake Tahoe and Doheny projects	
AUGUST				Community Playhouse, Little Dipper, Olive Hill, Los Angeles (building permit issued November 7; construction begins after November 7;

stops November 22; revised
design completed by Schindler;
ruins partially demolished by
City of Los Angeles employees
after January 17, 1994, earthquake (see February 28 and
May 7, 1924). Litigation, Wright
vs. Barnsdall, filed February 28,
1924; dismissed, June 19, 1952;
litigation, A. C. Parlee vs. Barnsdall,
filed May 7, 1924; settled, July 9,
1925.

Storer house, Los Angeles
(building permit issued
November 7; construction begins
late 1923; completion notice
filed October 27, 1924)

SEPTEMBER	1	Imperial Hotel opens; Kanto earthquake		
	8	Writes "Why the Skyscraper?" (published as *Experimenting with Human Lives* by Ralph Fletcher Seymour, Chicago, 1923)		
		Moves office to 1600 Edgemont Street (Residence B, Olive Hill), Los Angeles		
OCTOBER				Dorothy Martin Foster house, Buffalo
		Returns to Midwest. States that he expects to have studios in Chicago, Hollywood, and Tokyo (interview with William T. Evjue, *Madison Capital Times,* October 18, 1923)		
			Mentions that he is working on two large-scale projects in California – the laying out of what is then known as Holly-wood Hill (Doheny Ranch?) and a big summer resort scheme in Lake Tahoe "to cost millions" (interview with William T. Evjue, *Madison Capital Times,* October 18, 1923)	
NOVEMBER	19	Marries Miriam Noel		
DECEMBER				Barnsdall memorial, Olive Hill, Los Angeles (litigation, Wright vs.

Barnsdall, filed February 28, 1924; dismissed June 19, 1952)

Nakoma Country Club, Madison[4]

Nakoma Memorial Gateway, Madison[5]

	5	Frank P. Deering to Eugene E. Prussing: inquiry about Wright's purchase of Emerald Bay property, Lake Tahoe	
	7	Prussing to Deering: Wright expected in Los Angeles December 9; will discuss Emerald Bay property on return	
	17	Prussing to Wright: inquiry about interest in Emerald Bay	

1924

JANUARY			Freeman house, scheme 1, Los Angeles (see February 1924)
FEBRUARY			**Freeman house, scheme 2, Los Angeles** (plans approved February 1924; building permit issued April 8; work begins in April; completion notice filed March 23, 1925)
			Ennis house, Los Angeles (plans approved February 25, 1924; work begins in March; building permits issued May 1; chauffeur's apartment/garage completed December 1924; house completed August 1925)
	2	Schindler to Richard Neutra: Wright in Los Angeles until end of month, staying at Beverly Hills Hotel; mentions skyscraper project in Chicago (National Life Insurance Building?)	
MARCH		1–2	Wright visits Death Valley Ranch with A. M. Johnson; stops at Deep Springs College en route
		16	Johnson to Wright: concerning Johnson compound, Death Valley
APRIL	14	Louis Sullivan dies, Chicago	
	16	Wright attends Sullivan's funeral; meets Neutra there	

MAY			
		6	Wire, Wright to Lloyd Wright: "Negotiating with Armstrongs owners Emeraldday [sic]...Letter from Jessie Armstrong yesterday suggesting cooperation" [Lake Tahoe summer colony]
JULY	12		
			Richard and Dione Neutra at Taliesin for weekend. Werner and Sylva Moser and Kameki and Nobu Tsuchiura are in residence with Wright
AUGUST			
			Wright asks Neutra to work with him at Taliesin
SEPTEMBER			
			Wright to Neutra: offers work at Taliesin
		2	Gordon Strong to Wright: mentions Sugarloaf, Maryland, project (automobile objective)
		15	Wright to Lloyd Wright: mentions commission for automobile objective in Maryland; indicates that he has not received Tahoe drawings
		22	Strong to Wright: requirements for Sugarloaf Mountain project; includes contract for Wright's signature
			Wright to Strong (undated): returns signed contract
		27	Wright visits Sugarloaf Mountain with Strong and Alfred MacArthur
OCTOBER			
			Richard and Dione Neutra arrive at Taliesin; stay until early February 1925
NOVEMBER			
			Neutra to mother-in-law: mentions project for Johnson compound, Death Valley
			Johnson compound, Death Valley
	3–4		Eric Mendelsohn visits Wright at Taliesin
		14	Strong to Wright: refers to data produced by Ramp Building

Corporation, New York, which "covers practically every detail of garage construction." Discussion of grade of ramp construction; comments that "evidently, straight runs are immensely more economical than curved runs"

		21	Wire, Strong to Wright: discussion of inaccurate contour survey of Sugarloaf Mountain
	30		Wright meets Olgivanna Lazovich at ballet performance in Chicago

DECEMBER		3	Wire, Wright to Strong: inquiry about inaccurate survey	
			Wire, Strong to Wright: explanation of inaccurate survey	
			Wright to Strong (undated): response to Strong's December 3 wire; refers to curving ramps	
		8	Strong to Wright: discussion of Sugarloaf Mountain survey	
		10	Newspaper article describing Johnson compound, source unknown	
				Gladney house, scheme 1, Fort Worth[6] (first mentioned December 20; Lloyd Wright apparently involved; see December 1925)
			Preliminary scheme, automobile objective, Sugarloaf Mountain, Maryland	

1925

JANUARY		11	Wire, Strong to Wright: discussion of Sugarloaf Mountain survey	

FEBRUARY	Olgivanna Lazovich begins living with Wright at Taliesin			

APRIL				Phi Gamma Delta fraternity house, University of Wisconsin, 16 Langdon Street, Madison (preliminary plans approved April 4, 1925; modifications requested October 17, 1925;

Month					
					construction estimates over budget, Wright agrees to redraw plans June 12, 1926; revised plans discussed September 25, 1926; Wright's scheme abandoned October 16, 1926; building finally completed by Law, Law & Potter)
			6	Strong to Wright: inquiry about progress on Sugarloaf Mountain project	
	8	Lazovich divorced from Vlademar Hinzenberg; Lazovich assumes mother's maiden name, Milanoff; given custody of daughter Svetlana Hinzenberg			
	20	Second fire at Taliesin. Living room, bedrooms, kitchen, and dining room destroyed			Republic Building display windows, Chicago (for Gordon Strong; first mentioned December 31, 1924; Strong sends Wright drawing of existing Republic Building facade January 6, 1925)
			29	Wright to Strong: mentions plans for Sugarloaf Mountain	
JULY	10	Wright files for divorce from Miriam Noel			
AUGUST				Automobile objective, Sugarloaf Mountain	
			29	Wright presents plans for automobile objective at Republic Building, Chicago	
SEPTEMBER			8	Strong to Wright: has no definite conclusion about scheme for automobile objective	
OCTOBER					National Life Insurance Building, Chicago (first mentioned February 2, 1924; Johnson discusses project with Wright at Taliesin July 12, 1924; Johnson sends Wright contract for architectural services July 19, 1924; Wright describes structure to Dutch architect H. Th. Wijdeveld October 30, 1925)

		14	Strong to Wright: response to plans for automobile objective		
		20	Wright to Strong: reply to Strong's response to design for automobile objective		

DECEMBER					Gladney house, scheme 2, Fort Worth[7]
	1	Iovanna Wright born to Wright and Olgivanna Milanoff, Chicago			

1926

JANUARY					Skyscraper Regulation

FEBRUARY					Commercial Arts Festival (Steel Cathedral) (first mentioned in correspondence with William Norman Guthrie; apparently envisioned as illustration for Guthrie's book, *The Modern Cathedral*; mentioned again August 1927, October 26, 1927, and January 13, 1930)

APRIL					Martin house, Derby, New York (two alternative preliminary schemes; see May 13, 1926)

MAY				13	**Martin house, Derby, New York** (revisions continue through August; construction begins September; essentially completed November 1927)

AUGUST	31	Wright in hiding in Wildhurst, Minnesota; also there are Olgivanna Milanoff, Svetlana Hinzenberg, Iovanna Wright, a stenographer, and a maid			

OCTOBER	21	Wright arrested on Mann Act charges, Wildhurst			
	22	Released from jail			

1927

JANUARY	6–7	Auction of Wright's Japanese prints, Anderson Galleries, New York			

FEBRUARY	22	Third fire at Taliesin			

APRIL	7	Wright made member of Académie Royale des Beaux-Arts d'Anvers	
AUGUST	6	Wright, Inc., registered with Wisconsin Secretary of State	
	25	Wright and Noel divorced	
SEPTEMBER			Five designs for flat concrete roofs for City of Frankfurt am Main, Germany (mentioned in Wright to Martin, September 13, 1927)
			Gas station (various schemes not distinguished; first discussed September 30, 1927; Wright indicates that he has design October 3, 1927; prototype for Texaco completed in August 1930; model of a gas station exhibited at Art Institute of Chicago in September–October 1930; discussion of project continues through January 1932)

1928

JANUARY			Sun, Moon and Stars, design for Walter V. Davidson (first mentioned March 11, 1927: the design is to be used for a package label for Davidson Markets)
	13	Wright vacates Taliesin on order of Bank of Wisconsin	
		Wright and family move to Phoenix to work with Albert Chase McArthur on design of Arizona Biltmore Hotel (see April 1928)	
FEBRUARY		Preliminary discussion with Alexander J. Chandler re: San Marcos in the Desert	
APRIL			**Arizona Biltmore Hotel, Phoenix** (McArthur requests details for textile block construction from Wright January 2, 1928; Wright signs agreement with McArthur brothers January 25; hotel opens February 23, 1929)

		5	Wright awarded contract to design San Marcos in the Desert	
		19	Wright to Lloyd Wright: engineers working on survey for San Marcos in the Desert	
		30	Wright to Chandler: working on plans for San Marcos in the Desert; mentions camping near site	
				Martin Blue Sky Mausoleum, Forest Lawn, Buffalo (first mentioned January 3, 1927; Martin sends Wright dimensions of cemetery lot September 6, 1927; project exhibited at Art Institute of Chicago in September–October 1930)
MAY			Wright leaves Phoenix	
JUNE		1	Wright to Lloyd Wright: describes San Marcos in the Desert as "an architectural theme based on the triangle"	
JULY			Wright to Martin: mentions that sketches for San Marcos in the Desert are nearly ready	
				School for the Rosenwald Foundation, Hampton College, Hampton, Virginia (first mentioned April 6, 1928; Wright describes project to Martin in July; Wright meets with acting principal of Hampton College fall 1929; reports subsequently to Martin that the project as designed is not satisfactory)
	30		Taliesin sold to Bank of Wisconsin for $25,000	
AUGUST	25		Wright marries Milanoff, Rancho Santa Fe, California	
SEPTEMBER		25	Chandler to Wright: acknowledges receipt of preliminary studies for San Marcos in the Desert. Agreement between Chandler Improvement Company and Frank Lloyd Wright, Architect, Incorporated	
OCTOBER			Proposal for Hillside Home School of the Allied Arts, to be sponsored by University of Wisconsin	

NOVEMBER	P. M. Cochius visits Taliesin; commission to design glassware for Leerdam Glasfabriek, Holland (see May 1929)			
				Hillside Home School for the Allied Arts, Spring Green (first mentioned October1928; project collapses December 1929; see December 10, 1928, and October 1931)
DECEMBER				Jones house, Tulsa (preliminary scheme; first mentioned November 19, 1928; Jones sends Wright requirements for house November 26, 1928; see April 1929)
	10	Wright writes "The Hillside Home School of Allied Arts: Why We Want This School" (see October 1931)		
			18	Wright to Chandler: engineers working on plans for San Marcos in the Desert	Thirty textile block houses, Milwaukee (first mentioned to Chandler December 18, 1928; mentioned again to Lloyd Wright, late December)

1929

JANUARY	Wright and family return to Arizona		
			Ocatilla, Chandler, Arizona (first mentioned April 30, 1928; idea revived January 11, 1929; constructed January–February 1929; Wright and family leave May 24, 1929; camp partially demolished by fire June 2, 1929)
			Chandler block house, Chandler (first mentioned January 14, 1929; reincarnated as Conventional House [see October 1931])
MARCH	Lloyd Wright visits Ocatilla		
	Alice Millard visits Ocatilla		Alice Millard house 2, Pasadena (first mentioned April 6, 1928; discussion continues through September 11, 1931)
APRIL			Jones house, scheme 1, Tulsa (Jones's preliminary response April 15, 1929; Jones offers numerous suggestions for revisions and questions diagonal grid June 4, 1929; see September 1929)

			Camp cabins, Chandler (demolished)
		San Marcos in the Desert, Chandler	
MAY			Cudney house, Chandler Young house, Chandler (first mentioned May 9, 1929) **Vase for Leerdam Glasfabriek**[8]
	9	Wright to Martin: plans for San Marcos in the Desert have been given to contractors for estimates	
	24	Wright and family leave Chandler	
JULY			**Cover designs for *World Unity* magazine** (first mentioned July 10, 1929; Wright sends designs July 16, 1929; revised designs August 26, 1929; Wright expresses unhappiness with cover April 22, 1930) San Marcos Water Gardens, between Cleveland Street and Commonwealth Avenue, Chandler (first mentioned July 10, 1929)
	10	Wright to Strong: discussion of automobile objective; asks that drawings be returned; mentions related project in France	
	29	Wright meets with Chandler in Chicago	
AUGUST	20	Strong to Wright: returns drawings for Sugarloaf Mountain automobile objective	
			Martin gardener's cottage, Derby
SEPTEMBER			Polo stables, Chandler (first mentioned July 10, 1929) **Jones house, scheme 2, Tulsa** (plans completed summer 1929; revisions continue through December; construction begins summer 1930; model displayed at Art Institute of Chicago September–October 1930; house essentially completed August 1931)

	26	Wright to Strong: discussion of revised drawings for automobile objective	
			St. Mark's Tower, St. Mark's in-the-Bouwerie, New York (first mentioned October 19, 1927; sketches mentioned March 4, 1929; Wright requests plot plan August 26, 1929; plans presented October 9(?), 1929; model displayed at Art Institute of Chicago September–October 1930)
OCTOBER	11	Wright speaks at luncheon of American Union of Decorative Artists and Craftsmen, New York	
	29	Stock market crash	
DECEMBER			Page designs for *World Unity* (first mentioned December 26, 1929; revisions requested January 13, 1930; Wright expresses dissatisfaction with revisions January 25, 1930)

1930

JANUARY	3	Miriam Noel dies, Minneapolis	
	7	Strong to Wright: discussion of automobile objective	
	8	Beginning of patent infringement controversy with William E. Nelson regarding concrete block construction system implemented by Wright in California houses and Arizona Biltmore Hotel. Correspondence continues through June 1932, but no record of the final outcome has been located	
	25	Wright mentions new drawings for San Marcos in the Desert	
FEBRUARY			Millard gallery extension, Pasadena (first mentioned April 26, 1929; Wright sends plans to Millard February 17, 1930; discussion continues through December 16, 1931)
MARCH			Noble apartment house, Los Angeles (first mentioned

September 14, 1929; plans sent
March 11, 1930; final mention
December 10, 1931)

MAY	6–14	Delivers Kahn Lectures at Princeton University (see May 1931)
	28	Attends dinner for opening exhibition of his work at Architectural League, New York. Exhibition runs from May 29 to June 12, then travels to Chicago, Madison, Salem, and Milwaukee

AUGUST	Gas station prototype for Texaco
	Grouped Apartment Towers, Lake Shore Drive at Pearson Street, Chicago (based on St. Mark's Tower, New York; first mentioned June 1930)

OCTOBER	1–2	Delivers two lectures, "In the Realm of Ideas" and "To the Young Man in Architecture," at Art Institute of Chicago (see July 1931)

DECEMBER	Delivers two lectures at Denver Art Museum

1931

FEBRUARY	26	Delivers lecture, "Why a World's Fair?"

MARCH	7	Delivers lecture at University of Oregon, Eugene
	12	Delivers lecture at University of Washington, Seattle

MAY		*Modern Architecture, Being the Kahn Lectures for 1930* published by Princeton University Press
	9–31	Exhibition of Wright's work at Stedelijk Museum, Amsterdam. Travels to Berlin, Stuttgart, and Brussels

JULY	*Two Lectures on Architecture* published by Art Institute of Chicago

			Millard garage addition, La Miniatura, Pasadena (first mentioned May 3, 1928; discussion continues through July 9, 1931; construction completed 1931)
	13	Delivers lecture at International Conference on Interior Decoration, Grand Rapids	
AUGUST			New Theatre
SEPTEMBER	21	Leaves for Rio de Janeiro to serve as North American judge of competition entries for a Christopher Columbus Memorial Lighthouse	
OCTOBER		*The Hillside Home School of the Allied Arts: Why We Want This School* published	
			House on the Mesa (model exhibited in *Modern Architecture* at The Museum of Modern Art, New York; Wright's manuscript describing project dated April 25, 1930)
			Conventional House
1932			
JANUARY			Broadacre City (model constructed largely at La Hacienda, Chandler, in 1935)
			Cinema and shops (with John Lloyd Wright), Washington Street, Michigan City, Indiana
FEBRUARY			Capital Journal office building, Salem, Oregon (first mentioned March 18, 1931; client sends Wright boundaries of site and dimensions of building June 19, 1931; Wright sends plans February 15, 1932; final mention July 1, 1933)
	February 10–March 23	Exhibition, *Modern Architecture*, The Museum of Modern Art, New York, includes examples of Wright's early work, Millard house, and House on the Mesa.	
MARCH	30	*An Autobiography* published by Longmans, Green and Co., New York (discussion begins November 1930)	

Willey house, scheme 1, Bedford
Avenue at Prospect Park,
Minneapolis (first mentioned
June 27, 1932; Willey requests
revisions September 28)

OCTOBER   Wright founds Taliesin Fellowship

Notes

1   This project is customarily assigned a date of 1921; however, there is no evidence that Wright began his concrete block experiments of the twenties before early 1923.

2   See comment in n. 1.

3   See comment in n. 1.

4   The date for the Nakoma Country Club is that established by Mary Jane Hamilton. See Mary Jane Hamilton, "The Nakoma Country Club," in *Frank Lloyd Wright and Madison: Eight Decades of Artistic and Social Interaction,* ed. Paul E. Sprague (Madison: Elvehjem Museum of Art, University of Wisconsin, Madison, 1990), 77–82.

5   The date for the Nakoma Memorial Gateway is that proposed by Mary Jane Hamilton. See "The Nakoma Memorial Gateway," in Sprague, 83–88.

6   Dates for the Gladney projects are those supplied by the Frank Lloyd Wright Foundation; however, they have not been verified. Edna (Mrs. Samuel William) Gladney (1886–1961) was distantly related to Wright. She was prominent in Fort Worth as the director of the Texas Children's Home and Aid Society. A motion picture based on her life, *Blossoms in the Dust,* starring Greer Garson and Walter Pidgeon, was released by Metro-Goldwyn-Mayer in 1941. The society was renamed in Mrs. Gladney's honor in 1950 and functions today to create families through adoption. Sam Gladney (1878?–1935) was listed as manager of the Gladney Grain Company in Fort Worth city directories of the mid-twenties. Edna Gladney's papers are in the possession of her niece, Edna Chester. I interviewed Mrs. Chester in Fort Worth on May 12, 1994; a subsequent search of the papers turned up nothing prior to the 1930s.

7   See comment in n. 6.

8   This vase is now in the collection of the Frank Lloyd Wright Foundation. One other example is known: it is housed in the Nationalen Glasmuseums in Leerdam, Holland. J. Troeder, N. V. Vereenigde Glasfabrieken, to Robert L. Sweeney, November 8, 1976.

Index

Vikingsholm, Emerald Bay, Lake Tahoe, 65

villas, 155

W

Ward, F. H., *32*

Warren and Wetmore

Grand Central Terminal, New York, *169*

Washoe tribe, 64

Wasmuth portfolio, 31

water systems, 28, 32, 36, 74, 142, 148–49

Webber, Walter, 18

Weg zum Kristallhause im Wildbachtal (Taut), 106, *128*

When Democracy Builds (Wright), 155

Whitman, Walt, 10

wigwams, 52, 64, 66

Wiley house, 116

Wilkinson, Henry C.

U.S. Court House and Post Office, Altoona, Pennsylvania, *167*

Wolf Lake Amusement Park, near Chicago, *23*, 30, 117

Wood house, Decatur, Illinois, 32

Woollcott, Alexander, 100, 111

World's Columbian Exposition (1893), Chicago, 33, 38

Wright, Anna Lloyd (mother), 10–11, 136, 137, 144

Wright, David (son), 151

Wright, Frank Lloyd

in Chicago, 32, 40, 41, 100

childhood, 10–11, 65, 136, 137

chronology, 185–200

desert dwelling for, 79–80, *88–89*, 112

in Europe, 16, 31, 38–39, 140

in Japan, 16, 33–35, 36

in Los Angeles, 16–30, 38–39, 46

marriages of, 100, 111, 148, 152

as photographer, 137–38, *147–50*

at Taliesin, 33, 38, 39, 111, 136–49, 154, 155, 185

at Taliesin West, 150–54, 155

Wright, Jane (sister), 137

Wright, John (son), 102

Wright, Lloyd (son), 36, 49, 104, 171

Civic Center, Los Angeles, *177*

Wright, Maginel (sister), 11

Frank Lloyd Wright Archive, 19–20, 49, 70

Y

Yamamura house, Ashiya, Japan, 35

Yokohama Bay, Japan, 34

Owen D. Young house. *See* San Marcos in the Desert

Z

Zeppelin dirigible, *168*